POVERTY AND NE

Poverty and Neoliberalism

Persistence and Reproduction in the Global South

Ray Bush

Pluto Press
London • Ann Arbor, MI

First published 2007 by Pluto Press
345 Archway Road, London N6 5AA
and 839 Greene Street, Ann Arbor, MI 48106

www.plutobooks.com

Copyright © Ray Bush 2007

The right of Ray Bush to be identified as the author of this work has
been asserted by him in accordance with the Copyright, Designs and
Patents Act 1988.

British Library Cataloguing in Publication Data
A catalogue record for this book is available from the British Library

Hardback
ISBN-13 978 0 7453 1961 2
ISBN-10 0 7453 1961 0

Paperback
ISBN-13 978 0 7453 1960 5
ISBN-10 0 7453 1960 2

Library of Congress Cataloging in Publication Data applied for

10 9 8 7 6 5 4 3 2 1

Designed and produced for Pluto Press by
Curran Publishing Services, Norwich, England
Printed and bound in the European Union by
Antony Rowe Ltd, Chippenham and Eastbourne, England

Dedicated to Mette, Emile and Leo

Contents

Figures and maps

Figures

Maps

Tables

Abbreviations

ACP	African, Caribbean and Pacific Group of States
AHDR	Arab Human Development Report
APRP	Agricultural Policy and Reform Program
CA	communal area
CAADP	Comprehensive Africa Agriculture Development Programme
CFA	Commission for Africa
DFI	direct foreign investment
DfID	Department for International Development (UK)
EGP	Egyptian pound
EITI	Extractive Industries Transparency Initiative
FAO	Food and Agriculture Organisation of the UN
FDI	foreign direct investment
G8	group of leading industrial capitalist countries plus Russia: United States, UK, Japan, Germany, France, Italy, Canada
GDP	gross domestic product
GoE	government of Egypt
GoZ	government of Zimbabwe
HIES	Household Income and Expenditure Survey (Egypt)
HIPC	heavily indebted poor country
IFAD	International Fund for Agricultural Development
IFIs	international financial institutions
ILO	International Labour Organization
LSCF	large-scale commercial farmer
MAPP	Multi-Country Agricultural Productivity Programme
MDG	Millennium Development Goals
MENA	Middle East and North Africa
MNC	multinational corporation
NEPAD	New Economic Partnership for African Development
OAU	Organization of African Unity
ODA	Official Development Assistance
OECD	Organisation of Economic Co-operation and Development
POLIS	School of Politics and International Studies, University of Leeds
PASS	Poverty Assessment Study Survey
PPP	purchasing power parity
PRSP	poverty reduction strategy paper
SPA	structural adjustment programme
SPLA/M	Sudan People's Liberation Army/Movement

SSA	sub-Saharan Africa
UDI	unilateral declaration of independence
UN	United Nations
UNDP	United Nations Development Programme
UNHCR	United Nations Humanitarian Committee for Refugees
UNICEF	United Nations Children's Fund
USAID	United States Agency For International Development
WFP	World Food Programme
ZNLWVA	Zimbabwe National Liberation War Veterans Association

Preface

This book examines the ways in which poverty in the Global South is created and reproduced. More than a billion people, one in five, live on less than US$1 a day. Poverty is often linked by policy makers to the poor lacking access to the world's resources, land, minerals and food. In contrast this book examines the difficulties the poor have in *controlling* resources and in shaping their use to the promotion of greater equity and social justice. I also show how the uneven spread of commoditization that characterizes the world economy ensures the production and reproduction of poverty. Adherence to neoliberal ideology and practice by international agencies sustains a hegemony that is manifest in the actions of policy makers from the biggest financial organizations to the smallest non-governmental agency.

It is commonplace for 'civilization' to be equated with Western capitalism, and the drive to universalize that ideology has intensified with wars on 'terror' and the idea of progress that is inextricably linked to contemporary capitalism. The poor in the twenty-first century are now seen as guilty of creating violence and unrest in dissent from seeing capitalism as their saviour. Yet if capitalism and industrialism are indeed an answer to global poverty, it is little in evidence. Capitalism as an economic and social system is unable to explain the persistence of global poverty when it fails to redress inequality in the Global South. And among the resources that are seldom explored but are clearly systemic to the ways in which poverty is created and sustained are labour, labour power and labour migrancy.

Labour power is simply the most fundamental element of all wealth creation, and control over it has always been a central component of capitalism and its international system, as we shall see. Capitalism creates destitution by throwing people away when they no longer benefit the structures and processes around them. The failure of capitalism to universally spread the capital-wage-labour relationship, and in fact to benefit from non- or only partial proletarianization, remains a key feature of contemporary capitalism and central to how and why poverty in the Global South takes the form that it does. Policy makers however are unable to understand this. They have no recognition of the historical patterns of poverty creation and reproduction and can do nothing more to explain it than express moral outrage or proclaim its inevitability.

This book explores the persistence of global poverty by exploring the way in which control, use and access to the world's resources are intrinsically part of why so many in the world are poor. I investigate why much donor and international agency policy for poverty alleviation centres on the importance of resource-led growth and why that mantra continues to promote policies of poverty creation rather than its alleviation. I focus on the resources of labour, land, minerals and food. The analysis will situate the ways in which access to these resources and control over them by dominant economic actors has helped shape power and politics in the Global South. Never wholly powerless before the influence of international capital, Southern states have had opportunities and often relative strength to barter improved market positions with multinational companies, international financial institutions and Northern states. Yet those opportunities have seldom led to the promotion of sustainable and equitable development.

Southern state opportunities to benefit from access to resources have been constrained by lack of control of value added and technology and 'know how' retained by multinational companies (MNCs). Southern states have often been constrained by elite power and a reluctance to advance economic policy that would control foreign firms, distribute wealth locally to improve the living conditions of the poor and advance welfare for the majority of citizens.

Yet as I indicate it would be a gross simplification and wrong-headed to suggest that poor governance and corruption in Southern states either caused poverty or in themselves prevent its erosion. I show throughout this book that the preoccupation among donors with governance is frankly a red herring.

People in the Global South are poor because of the ways in which the economies in which they live have been incorporated into the world economy. Thus poverty is not about being left behind but about being actively excluded from an unjust and unequal system of wealth creation. The world's poor have been unevenly incorporated into the world economy in a fragmented manner that creates winners and losers. Broadly speaking, the winners are in the Northern economies, where there are also many losers; and the losers are in the Global South, where there are also many winners who benefit from expulsion of the poor during primitive accumulation of capital.

I trace how the framing of poverty within neoliberal ideology has shaped the ways in which the room for manoeuvre in the Global South has been set outside the boundaries of nation states. Yet I also show how states in Africa, the Middle East and elsewhere are guilty of buying into neoliberal orthodoxies and, even if that has been done reluctantly by governments fearful of losing control over national spoils, it has ensured the persistence of an unequal world.

The Global Millennium Development Goals will not be met. Yet among the hand-wringing and explanations offered for why basic rights necessary to ensure fundamental living conditions will continue to be unmet, there is little focus on the persistent structural obstacles to poverty amelioration. All policy remains focused on tinkering with improving trade, offering higher levels of debt relief or greater quantities of aid. None of these palliatives alone or together will lead to a sustained reduction of poverty in Africa or elsewhere.

The way in which countries in the Global South are included in the world economy is a product of historical struggles, which still continue and have benefited the dominant capitalist economies more than the ex-colonies. It is that incorporation which has largely created the levels of poverty in Africa and the Middle East, and there is nothing in contemporary policy recommendations which will change the asymmetry of that incorporation. There is also little understanding of the ways in which politics and power are constructed in the Global South and how the power of office holders undermines struggles for poverty reduction and redistribution of resources, money and wealth. One reason for this persistent error among policy makers is that 'Africa', the 'Middle East', 'Latin America' and so on are spoken about as if they were homogenous and all their countries unquestionably similar despite the multitude of countries, cultures, languages, and economic and political systems that exist among them. The desire of aid agencies and bilateral donors operating in the Global South to instil order from perceived chaos and peace from crisis and war has led to a uniform delivery of assistance that is often unhelpful and aggravates rather than ameliorates the difficulties it is intended to resolve.

I explore in detail the ways in which neoliberalism has dominated the international debates about poverty. I illustrate this by examining the Commission for Africa (CFA). I show how it failed to offer any radical policy initiative to redress persistent crises in Africa. Many of its recommendations refer directly to the issue of resources, their management and the opportunities they provide for development and poverty amelioration. Yet the CFA and other policy suggestions that I detail fail to break the mould of neoliberalism. They offer only a strategy of further uneven incorporation of poor states into the world economy and raise the false hope that 'globalization can work for the poor'. That mantra is set against the repeated realities of rather seeing the poor working for globalization and benefiting little from it. The contemporary period is marked by an aggressive pattern of commoditization. The persistent reproduction of patterns of primitive accumulation is a mechanism used by dominant economic actors to access the world's resources. This politics of dispossession underpins violence and disorder, destruction and transformation of indigenous means of production and reproduction.

I detail the carnage visited upon the Global South by the consequences of continued uneven incorporation into the world economy and
the failure of Southern politicians to protect their citizens from the harm
and squalor that contemporary capitalism reaps. I show this by exploring capitalism's search for profit and order in its dealings with labour
across frontiers, in the fierce debate and practice regarding land reform,
and what has been called 'a curse of resources' relating to the persistent
impoverishment of economies where there is a long track record of
mineral extraction. I also show how famine and food insecurity is the
product of the commoditization of food. Capitalism's biggest indictment
is that it is an economic and social system that generates famine while it
exports vast quantities of food for people who can afford to buy it. It also
destroys food to keep market prices, and profits, high.

Finally, I indicate how people's resistance to capitalism does have
an impact in restraining some of its worst excesses, and that while capitalism will continue to generate poverty and starvation there is always
evidence that it will not be an enduring mode of production, only a
transition to a more humane and just international political economy.

I thank *Global Dialogue* for permission to reproduce part of an
article that appeared in Volume 6(3-4), Summer/Autumn 2004;
Historical Materialism for part of an article that appeared in Volume
12(4), 2004; and *Development and Change* for part of an article that
appeared in Volume 35(4), 2004. I am also very happy to record a
personal debt of thanks to many people who have shared the ideas
contained in this book. They include MA students over many years at
the University of Leeds in the School of Politics and International
Studies. I am grateful to POLIS for research leave that enabled me to
write and I am especially grateful to colleagues there who work in
development studies. Thanks to Tess Hornsby-Smith and Susan Para-
green for important administrative support.

I benefited from research assistance from Henrietta Abane,
Michael Medley, who also helped enormously with the maps, and
Ahmed Gamal El Din. Thanks especially to Rita Abrahamsen who read
and commented on Chapter 2, Zülküf Aydin who read and
commented on Chapter 6, and Brad Evans for comments on Chapter 7.
Mette Wiggen also read and commented on several chapters and
helped clarify my arguments. I am, as always, indebted to Sarah
Bracking, who looked at several chapters and who often shared with
me her exceptional insights, not only on poverty issues. Thanks also to
Tim Mitchell for responding to requests for help. I enjoy and learn
much from reading his work and also that of Patrick Bond. I continue
to benefit greatly from conversations with Morris Szeftel and Lionel
Cliffe, both now retired from Leeds but luminaries whose analysis of
the crazy world can bring cheer, especially while watching the cricket.

I owe a huge debt of thanks to Mark Duffield, on whom I try out ideas and with whom I enjoy greatly the struggle to understand why policy makers continue to make the mess that they do. I am of course alone responsible for the contents of what follows.

Finally, I have enjoyed research leave, time to think (mostly) away from academic duties and writing at home, greeting Emile and Leo after school even though they might remark: 'You don't seem to have done very much all day.' The book is dedicated to them but most especially to Mette. There was a dark period when it was feared she might not see this book to publication, but such a view was only expressed by those who were unaware of her resourcefulness and courage.

Ray Bush

1 Framing poverty and neoliberalism: the Middle East and North Africa

Framing poverty

This chapter examines the definition of poverty, and locates a critique of neoliberal bias in the claims that the region of the Middle East and North Africa (MENA) has historically low levels of poverty and relatively good levels of income distribution. I argue that the dominant trend in the literature on poverty in the Global South in general, and in MENA in particular, has a neoclassical bias. Among other things, that bias fails to understand that poverty does not emerge because of exclusion, but because of poor people's 'differential incorporation' into economic and political processes. It also raises the question: if MENA has indeed had relatively low levels of poverty and good income distribution, does this complicate the issue of autocracy and the Western drive to remove political 'backwardness' in the region? In particular, the characterization of autocracy and the West's attempt to promote political liberalization is likely to have adverse impacts on the social contract that autocratic rulers have enforced regarding the delivery of basic services.

There has recently been an increased interest in poverty and income distribution in the Global South in general and the MENA region in particular. I examine here much of that literature, identifying a number of similarities within it. A common theme links much of the material, not only in what it says but particularly in what it omits: namely that, despite the mushrooming of interest in poverty and income distribution, we continue to know very little about some key areas, notably the processes and dynamics of political and economic power that generate poverty and inequality, and skew income distribution towards the rich.

Policy-oriented literature seldom offers an understanding of poverty and its possible relationship with political mobilization. That gap is clearly problematic at a time when the United States and its coalition partners promote a military war against the perceived 'axis of evil' with no attempt to address causes of conflict and notably accelerated poverty in MENA. Although Western politicians and the policy literature ignore the link between poverty and conflict, some academic commentators have explored the relationship between poverty and political mobilization (Le Saout and Rollinde 1999; Roberts 2002; Beinin 2001; Bayat 2003; El-Ghonemy 1998).

I want to extend the definition of poverty to include power relations. This chapter also questions statistics on poverty in MENA produced by the international financial institutions (IFIs), and raises the issue of the possible impact that economic reforms may have on reducing the character of the social contract that many states have had with their workers and farmers.

The data and material on poverty and income distribution are voluminous, but are almost entirely driven or conceptualized from within a neoclassical framework. Even where the conservatism of that economic framework appears to be dissipated, as in the perspectives on the characterization of poverty that talk about 'human development' (UNDP), a 'rights-based approach' (UNICEF), the 'livelihoods approach' (DfID), 'social exclusion' (the EU and ILO), and 'human security' (UN) (see Maxwell 2001: 143), the language still seems to be overwhelmingly framed within the binary oppositions of the 'global' and the 'local'. It also stresses the benefit that the liberalization of markets will bring for the poor. There is a view that the 'exclusion' of the poor needs to be reduced (Lipton 1997), but in making this point the crucial issue of how poverty is created and reproduced is lost. In other words, there is a failure to understand that poverty does not emerge because of exclusion but as a result of poor people's 'differential incorporation' into economic and political processes (Bracking and Harrison 2003).

Now more than ever, with US and coalition aggression in Iraq and repeated claims that economic liberalization in the region as a whole will lead *ipso facto* to greater democracy, we need to explore what the possible consequences will be for poverty in MENA. I use the term 'poverty' to refer to 'a deprivation of human capability of essential opportunities and choices needed for the well being of an individual, household or community' (UNDP 2002c: 94).

Poverty clearly does not only mean a lack of income, falling below a poverty line necessary for the purchase of a minimum basket of commodities for basic nutrition, or for the purchasing power parity at which local currency is standardized in 1985 dollars as enough for a person to buy minimum commodities to sustain life (often set at $1 or $2 a day). These two measures dominate the literature on poverty in the Global South, and I return later to dissatisfaction with them and with the quantitative bias in research that underestimates the importance of qualitative data collection, among other things.[1]

I argue that poverty does not occur because of a failure to be integrated into the national, local or international economy, or because of the vulnerability that may accrue through non-incorporation. The mantra of globalization as the panacea for developing countries is expressed repeatedly by the IFIs and donors (World Bank 1995; DFiD 2000, 2006) and I critique this position here and in Chapter 2. I argue that the poor are poor precisely *because* of their incorporation into the reality of the contemporary capitalist economies.

Adverse differential incorporation results in labour regimes that are hugely exploitative, at their worst leading to the recreation of child labour recruitment or a return to 'indentured labour', as in parts of Egypt since Law 96 of 1992, which dramatically removed the protection for land tenants afforded them since Nasser's revolution. Differential incorporation has also led to a decline in employment as privatization creates redundancy, and as job opportunities, in the age of 'globalization', fail to meet demand and labour force growth.

At a macroeconomic level the differential incorporation of MENA fails to address the structural contradictions of high dependency on rent, petroleum, Suez Canal remittances in the case of Egypt, and real estate and worker remittances elsewhere in MENA. The rent economies of MENA reflect the region's dependency on the world economy; they are the product of uneven incorporation as well as the reluctance and failure of MENA regimes to extricate themselves from rentier politics and all that this means: 'Dutch disease', crude project-driven growth, enhanced vulnerability to trade fluctuations, and persistently high military expenditures, including the sale of oil for Western weapons and, with the new security monologue from the Pentagon, a heightened sense of securitization that feeds back into this process and renews it.

No institution, organization or political regime openly condones poverty. Anti-poverty strategies are proclaimed across the world as necessary and important. Some of the narratives of poverty may differ but the strategy to ameliorate it seems to be universal. There is a similarity even in the myriad of superficially contrasting strategy formulations designed to reduce poverty. As Maxwell, among others, has recently observed, these strategies for reducing poverty generally include the raising and spending of money, the provision of incentive or regulatory national economic frameworks, and the reform (downsizing) of public sectors. The latter usually means taking government out of service provision and advocating increased participation (Maxwell 2001: 143), although just what kind of participation, by whom and with what kind of say, usually remains unspecified. These prescriptions for poverty reduction almost without fail include the need for more education, employment, healthcare and protection of the environment (Soudi 2001, among others). Yet little is said about how these prescriptions might be sequenced or funded, and there is still a general preoccupation with money-centred agendas. Poverty and income are seen as issues of 'vulnerability', the new catchword of the IFIs.

In the shopping list of policy reforms intended to improve income distribution and reduce poverty, very little is said about the people who are poor, how they are identified, how they express their grievances at being poor and how, under whatever circumstances in which poverty is to be reduced, the essential driver of such a strategy must be the women and men who are poor. They, moreover, must be seen as agents of social change rather than just victims of exclusion (Jordan 1996).

While superficially there seems to have been progress in relation to how poverty has been viewed in the literature, and especially within the World Bank, moving from the need for labour-intensive growth (World Bank 1990) to the importance of understanding issues of opportunity, empowerment and security (World Bank 2000), this new language is mostly concerned with the efficiency of markets, economic liberalization and the importance of social and human capital, where education and the knowledge economy are intended to provide the umbrella under which the forces of globalization operate. The literature, as we will see, has effectively served to buttress the architecture for global capitalism that was in place by the start of the twenty-first century. This comprised, in Cammack's words:

> the essential elements of a global capitalist system – the authority of capital over labour, goods and investment, the receptiveness of governments to the needs of capital, the presence of domestic and global regulatory orders capable of reinforcing the disciplines essential to capitalist reproduction.
>
> (Cammack 2002: 159)

Moreover, justification for the character of twenty-first century capitalism was spread with an ideology that dismissed any alternatives. Globalization is now seen to be the only game in town: MENA and other regions of the world had better learn the rules and start playing by them – or else.

There is now, therefore, a challenge to the old modernity that was at the core of development studies in the 1960s and 1970s, namely that domestic and international policies that worked against market forces were 'essential to bring about development' (Cammack 2002: 159). In MENA, the consequences of government policies since the 1970s have been to jettison the centrality of state-led policies and import substitution industrialization (Beinin 2001: 142). Economic nationalism has remained as a rhetorical whimper. Populist social policies have diminished, but the promise of growth that was to accompany economic liberalization has not been fulfilled and the desired incorporation into the world economy has failed to boost investment. Even a cursory look at the presence of direct foreign investment (DFI) in MENA indicates that the region has been bypassed by global capitalism. For advocates of globalization, increasing DFI levels are the quintessential feature, viewed as essential to reduce levels of global poverty. Yet the share of the Arab world in total net flow of DFI from 1975–2000 was barely 1 per cent, and the bulk of that went to Egypt (Morocco and Tunisia received more in the late 1990s, but levels were still very low).

While there is now much attention to issues of poverty and income distribution in MENA, these almost universally operate within a framework of neoclassical bias. This is the assumption that markets can be accessed equally between people and the state, and workers and consumers; that markets are neutral arenas to facilitate the efficient allocation of resources and that the state can, at best, help facilitate the smooth running of markets, but must not regulate them. Globalization is an accepted, albeit seldom-defined, feature of the contemporary period; attempts to 'opt out' of global trade are seen as restricting poverty reduction, growth and opportunities for downward income distribution. The poor, a category seldom differentiated, are mostly treated as passive consumers of policy or recipients of donor assistance, and as Bracking and Harrison (2003: 2) note, 'their prior exclusion from "normal" production and markets remains unproblematised'.

The dominance of neoliberal frameworks in characterizing poverty and income distribution in MENA has ensured that commentators on poverty, vulnerability and income distribution have failed to examine (or chosen to ignore) the prior subordination or exclusion of workers and peasants from markets, production and certainly from international economic relationships. The dominant paradigm for examining political and economic transformation after the 1970s was the 'Washington consensus'. There has been much hand-wringing by the IFIs that the policies that culminated in lost development decades across the Global South in the 1980s – namely policies of economic stabilization, structural adjustment and cutbacks in government expenditure – have been superseded by policies proclaiming the importance of the knowledge economy, human capital development and recognition of the importance of limited state intervention in the economy. Yet beyond the claims and counter-claims made by the defenders and critics of the region's economic development, it seems clear that in the heyday of state-led development MENA witnessed rates of economic growth between 1962 and 1977 that were certainly as good as those in the 1980s (Beinin 2001: 147–8).

Another consequence of the neoliberal orthodoxy is the way in which peasants and workers have become invisible in the literature of the politics and society of MENA. As Beinin again has noted:

> Along with a new conception of the economy, the Washington Consensus tends to eliminate workers and peasants as social categories altogether, since their very presence recalls the social compact of the era of authoritarian-populism, which the current regimes can not fulfil.
>
> (Beinin 2001: 148)[2]

The neoclassical bias of the poverty debates in MENA is captured very clearly in the way in which the much publicized and influential *Arab Human Development Report* (AHDR)(UNDP 2002a) was assembled and the way it discussed inequality. It avoided 'crucial issues of money and power' and this ultimately undermined the quality and rigour of the report's own aims and objectives (Le Vine 2002: 2).

There is a further element to the critique of contemporary debates in MENA (and elsewhere): the discussion on poverty and vulnerability fails to explore the relationship between winners and losers in the processes of development. It is possible here to learn from livelihoods literature. As Colin Murray has noted:

> Poverty ... must be understood in a structural or a relational sense if we are to comprehend the diverse trajectories of the poor and the not so poor, in order to 'situate' them in a particular political, economic, social and institutional context but also to approach the very difficult question of how to achieve a reduction of poverty.
>
> (quoted in Francis and Murray 2002: 486)

I return to elements of this critique below, but first let us briefly summarize the evidence and commentaries on poverty and income distribution using the case of countries in the MENA region of the world.

Poverty and income distribution in MENA

The evidence: speaking for itself?

Fred Halliday warned in a note on the Middle East at the turn of the millennium:

> We should long ago have resisted the temptation to see the region as a single integrated political or socio-economic whole, and we

should certainly resist any notion that tries to explain the region's politics and history by timeless cultural features, a Middle Eastern 'essence' or an 'Islamic mindset'.

(Halliday 1999; cf. Bromley 1994 and Le Vine 2002)

Although Washington's security monologue and recent assault on Iraq may entail a levelling down of the way in which the international community relates to the region, Halliday's caution remains pertinent. Yet despite MENA's economic diversity, with differences in per capita income, economic growth and structure, there are also many similarities. There is a high dependence upon economic rents, whether from natural resources or labour remittances. The region's economies have poor agricultural sectors, with gross investment in this sector falling in the period 1980–92; the result is that evidence of poverty is generally stronger in the countryside than in the towns, and the region is heavily dependent upon food imports.[3] Rents have provided largesse for regime elites, sustained corruption (the use of public goods for private gain) and provided an obstacle to political liberalization and, at different times, succour for radical Islam.

Yet one of the consequences, it seems, of the authoritarian populist regimes that have been common in the region has been a record of low levels of poverty. It is difficult to give a comprehensive account of poverty and income distribution in the MENA region because while there is an increased volume of material on it, very little is comparable. Indeed the World Bank notes that the MENA region is the least productive of survey data (World Bank 2002), although as I shall indicate, the lack of quantitative survey data per se is nothing to lament. The shortage of comparable data accounts for the predominance in the literature of Egypt, Morocco, Tunisia and Jordan, where data are most available and some comparisons can be made because of national income and expenditure surveys, although just how accurate these are is another issue.

There is also the problem of which countries are included in the range of data sets. In World Bank material the category MENA excludes the Gulf countries, while Sudan, Somalia and Mauritania appear as sub-Saharan Africa, for instance. There is also the question of whether to include Turkey – a major actor in terms of foreign and economic policy, population size and control of water flows – and similar doubts also apply to Iran.[4]

According to the World Bank (1995), income growth and equality of income distribution in MENA for the period 1960–85 outperformed all other regions except East Asia. As a consequence the region saw significant improvements in infant mortality rates, life expectancy and other social indicators. According to Ali Ali and El Badawi (2002: 71), who

Table 1.1 Summary of poverty trends in five MENA countries, 1980s–1990s

Country and population group		Poverty			Contraction			Inequality			Breakdown of population (%) c. 1997			Poverty Headcount Index* c. 1997		
		Overall	Urban	Rural	Overall	Urban	Rural	Overall	Urban	Rural	Overall	Urban	Rural	Overall	Urban	Rural
Algeria	Overall	←			←			←			100			22		
	Urban		←			←			?			56			17	
	Rural			←			←			←			44			28
Egypt	Overall	←			←			←			100			24		
	Urban		←			←			=			44			23	
	Rural			←↑			←			←			56			24
Jordan	Overall	←			←			=			100			12		
	Urban		←			←			=			79			10	
	Rural			←			←			=			21			18
Morocco	Overall	→			→			=			100			19		
	Urban		→			→			=			54			12	
	Rural			→			→			=			46			27
Tunisia	Overall	→			→			?			100			7.6		
	Urban		→			?			?			61			3.6	
	Rural			→			?			?			39			14

* Poverty Headcount Index is the percentage of people within the group falling below a defined poverty line. The poverty line used is based on the costs of minimum food and non-food requirements in the named country.

Sources: Poverty Headcount Indices from Adams and Page (2001: 29); population breakdowns calculated from the Headcount Index data. Data for Algeria are from Belkacem (2001) and refer to 1995.

use their own calculations for a poverty line approach to measure the incidence of poverty:

> about 22 per cent of MENA population were living below a poverty line of US$51 per person per month in the early 1990s. At the other extreme, 52 per cent of Africa's population were living below a poverty line of US$42 per person per month.
>
> (Ali and El Badawi 2002: 71)

Adams and Page (2001), whose work is cited as a major source for the Arab *Human Development Report*, stress that MENA has the lowest incidence of poverty for a developing region, defined as US$1 or US$2 per person per day, except for the old socialist economies in Europe. These measures indicate an increase in poverty, with 29.9 per cent of people in MENA living on US$2 and 2.1 per cent on US$1 per person per day in 1998, compared with 22 per cent and 1.8 per cent respectively in 1996 (Adams and Page 2001: 24). The region is also seen to have the lowest level of absolute poverty in the world, although it is likely that chronic poverty is eclipsed by the presence of Islamic and social welfare and/or coping mechanisms that obscure the persistence of poverty.

The AHDR explains the relatively low poverty levels in the region as a product of egalitarian income distribution practices (UNDP 2002a: 90) and the ability of the poor to draw on periods of relative prosperity from 1970–1985. Adams and Page (2001) note that MENA has one of the most equal income distributions in the world, with a Gini coefficient of 0.364 for 1995–99.[5] This is the result of high shares of income accruing to the bottom quintile of income distribution, namely 7.2 per cent – the same proportion that accrues to this group in the OECD countries.

Economic growth does not *ipso facto* lead to less poverty. One need only look at the case of Brazil in the late 1960s and early 1970s – a period when the country witnessed unparalleled economic growth but when the income inequality remained the third-worst in the world – to see this. Other authors have noted that fluctuating growth rates in Egypt in the late 1980s and in 1993–95 led to sharp increases in poverty (Kandeel and Nugent 2000). It seems that the speed with which economic growth reduces income poverty 'is largely a function of the distribution of income' (Adams and Page 2001: 4).

The highest incidence of poverty was recorded for Mauritania, where 39 per cent of the population lived below a poverty line of US$33 per person per month, and the lowest incidence was recorded for Egypt, with 14 per cent living below US$ 42 per person per month (Ali and El Badawi 2002).

Table 1.2 Poverty trends in five MENA countries, 1980s and 1990s

Country	Poverty trends	Growth and expenditures (in the economy as a whole)	Distribution and inequality	Poverty profile
Algeria	A doubling of both urban and rural poverty, 1988–95	Negative growth as a result of collapse in oil prices in 1985. Improvement since 1995.		Most of the poor live in rural areas but the share of the urban poor has increased.
Egypt	Overall poverty increased sharply in the 1980s and remained fairly steady in the 1990s. The increase was more marked in the rural population than the urban one, where the growth of poverty was steady but slower.	Mean expenditures declined as poverty increased.	Rural poverty was associated with increasing inequality but, for the urban population, increasing poverty was slightly mitigated by greater equality.	Poverty rates are fairly similar among the rural and urban populations but have been growing faster in the rural population.
Jordan	An overall increase in poverty over the period, but sharpest in the late 1980s and early 1990s, especially in urban areas. Poverty decreased slightly after that.	Poverty was associated with declining mean expenditures, which was especially marked in the late 1980s and the period of the Gulf Crisis.	There seem to have been trends towards greater inequality during the times of contraction in the late 1980s and early 1990s, but towards greater equality at other times.	The population is mostly urban, but the proportion of people in poverty is relatively high in the rural areas. Women have much poorer access to economic opportunities than men.

Table 1.2 continued

Country	Poverty trends	Growth and expenditures (in the economy as a whole)	Distribution and inequality	Poverty profile
Morocco	Poverty fell sharply in the 1980s but rose almost as sharply in the 1990s. The overall reduction in poverty was slightly more marked in the urban population than the rural.	The decline in poverty occurred alongside economic growth. In this agricultural economy, growth was inhibited at times of drought.	Levels of inequality remained fairly steady.	There is a much higher proportion of poor people in rural areas than in urban areas. Poverty affects the rural population much more than the urban population.
Tunisia	Poverty rates fell in the late 1980s but remained steady in the early 1990s.			

Sources: Adams and Page (2001); IFAO (2001: 58–9).

MENA had a period of rapid growth from 1970–85, followed by a period of stagnation from 1985 to the present. While the period of stagnation had not affected the robustness of income distribution and low poverty levels by 2001, according to Adams and Page, it is noteworthy that the level of US$2 per person per day poverty increased from 24.8 per cent in 1990 to 29.9 per cent in 1998 – that is, over the period that marked the introduction of structural adjustment and economic reform programmes. Although Adams and Page (2001) project a decline in poverty over 2000–10 to 14.7 per cent, it is not entirely clear why the decline might take place. Their figures are certainly more optimistic than those offered by, among others, Fergany (2002).

The framework employed by the AHDR, Adams and Page, and most other authors for examining the extent of poverty in MENA is a quantitative measure (see for instance El Said and Löfgren 2001; Ghazouani and Goaied 2001; Morrison 1991; Zouari-Bouattour and Jallouli 2001). It is a measure of Gini coefficients that usually use government-inspired (and controlled) household income and expenditure tables (with often limited sampling and poor methodology) or use the re-examination of time series data from Deininger and Squires (1996), using model-building techniques to tweak the sensitivity or accuracy of data and thus results. The preoccupation with model building is the preserve of econometrics specifically, but also more generally a brand of development economics that seems to shy away from considering the relevance or serious integration of qualitative material to inform analysis of income distribution or poverty.

There are exceptions to this. Belkacem (2001) has examined the historical context in Algeria within which certain continuities and discontinuities of poverty have taken place, and Khasawneh (2001) has explored the strategies for poverty alleviation in Jordan, examining competing perspectives on poverty-line definitions of 'abject poverty' and 'absolute poverty' related to access to minimum nutritional requirements. Khasawneh noted the increased severity of poverty in Jordan over the period 1987–97, and the main characteristics of the poor that are evident in other accounts of MENA poverty (such as Haddad and Ahmed 2003). These characteristics are:

- higher rates of illiteracy among the poor (about 42 per cent of the adult poor are illiterate in Jordan)
- the fact that the poor were often not without work, but were employed in the informal sector where remuneration was extremely low, so that poverty was indicative of low wages rather than simply unemployment (although this category ignored 'lumpen' elements who are destitute or near destitute)
- poor families with heads of household employed in the private

sector being poorer than those with work in the public sector; and the fact that, despite higher rates of poverty in rural Jordan, about two-thirds of the poor are urban-based (Khasawneh 2001: 12).

While Khasawneh recommends the need for a comprehensive survey of poverty-related issues, he also suggests the need for an understanding of the broader context within which poverty levels in Jordan increased between 1987 and 1992 and declined from 1992 to 1997. He asserts that poverty levels fell in the latter part of the 1990s (although this is contested elsewhere) because inequality fell. Avenues for economic growth were clearly problematic for the Jordanian economy, as they were elsewhere in MENA. Restrictions on growth in Jordan were identified as resulting from national institutional constraints and the external orientation of the Jordanian economy in relation to education and industry, including the historical demand for Jordanian teachers and engineers (leading to a 'brain drain') which has declined as regional economies have contracted.

In other analyses within the region, El Khoury (2001) has indicated the presence of economic inequalities across religious divides in Lebanon, while Collicelli and Valerii (2000) have tried to build a model that accounts for different levels of poverty within different geographical (spatial) settings and correlates complex phenomena. This view suggests the need to look at 'inter-related factors responsible for the conditions of hardship in a given social and territorial context' and does attempt to move beyond merely quantitative data to assess poverty levels.

The evidence: a critique

One explanation that is regularly offered for the perception of relatively equal income distribution in the MENA region in the last 30 years is the ideology and political and economic practice promoted by regimes to redistribute assets, notably land, and also to bolster employment with government jobs, provide food subsidies and impose tariffs on luxury commodities – those things that have to be jettisoned with economic reform and structural adjustment. MENA has been fortunate in that the benefits of the boom years of the 1970s were preserved to an extent by those who benefited from them, mainly labour migrants who accessed remittances that were gained from the region's oil sectors. Those remittances, it seems, accrued mostly to those at the bottom of the income scale or 'indirectly through their impact on the labour market' (UNDP 2002a: 90). Any tampering with employment opportunities and migration is thus likely to hinder the ability of the unemployed to find work, or of migrants to fulfil their dual role of working in the town and countryside, at home and abroad. We should note, however, that the idea of a great Nasserist heyday (in Egypt's case), which had lasting consequences on income distribution, has been contested. The work of Abdel-Khalek and Tignor (1982) noted at best a marginal improvement in income distribution from 1958–75, despite real changes in the mechanisms for generating wealth, namely land and factory ownership (cf. El-Ghonemy 1998).

Despite the assembled evidence supporting the relatively even distribution of income and low levels of poverty within MENA, there is a need for caution. For the same reason, a degree of circumspection is required regarding the evidence presented in Table 1.3. Indeed, in general, the causes of poverty, policy prescriptions and the political implications of the evidence presented in the literature should be treated with care.

The caution regarding the data and prescriptions regarding the way in which poverty is characterized in MENA relates to four major issues which I further elaborate in the conclusion to this chapter.

First, we need a degree of perspective in relation to the acclaimed performance of the MENA economies. While there has been seen to be a period of improved economic performance, despite (or because of?) economic reform from the late 1980s, the real purchasing power parity of the average Arab citizen fell between 1975–98, from 21.3 per cent to 13.9 per cent, or one-seventh, of that of the average person in an OECD country (UNDP 2002a: 89).

Second, there seems to be an increase in uneven development in the MENA region. There is greater inequality between the rich (Gulf) countries in the region and the poorer low-income countries. Middle-income countries moved closer to the richer countries in the 1980s and 1990s as the economic performance of countries like Kuwait, Saudi Arabia, the United Arab Emirates and Qatar declined relative to Syria, Morocco, Jordan, Sudan and Egypt (UNDP 2002a: 89).

Third, there is variation within the region regarding the relatively low levels of absolute poverty, income inequality and contrast between town and country. Income inequality in Jordan, Egypt and Iraq increased from 1980 to 2000, and in Egypt that increase was very marked in the country-side and larger cities. There has also, of course, been a complete implosion of poverty levels in Palestine – a case that (like Iraq, but for different reasons) deserves particular attention beyond the scope of this book. Fergany (2002) argued convincingly that the most-used poverty-line measure (the cost of a minimum basket of commodities) underestimates the extent of poverty. Using that measure, poverty in Egypt doubled between 1990 and 1996 to 44 per cent, or about 30 million people. Using the crude US$1 a day measure, Fergany demonstrated that figures from the 1991 HIES (the Egyptian Household Income and Expenditure

Table 1.3 MENA poverty

Country	GNPpc (WB) US$	GNPpc at PPP	Real GDP	Gini + year 1950s–60s	Gini mid-1980s	Gini mid-1990s	Under-5	Adult literacy	Life/mortality expectancy
Algeria	1550	4753	2.4	0.516 (1965)	0.401	0.367	48.6 (1992)	65.5	69.2
Bahrain			5.3		0.394	0.350	16.7 (1995)	86.5	73.1
Egypt	1400	3303	5.1	0.429 (1950)	0.443		54.3 (2000)	53.7	66.7
Iran	1760	5163		0.470 (1969)			–	–	–
Iraq			4.0	0.568 (1956)	0.560		–	53.7	63.8
Jordan	1500	3542	3.9		0.375	0.378	34.2 (1997)	88.6	70.4
Kuwait			3.9				17.2 (1996)	80.9	76.1
Lebanon	3700	4129	–0.6				32.2 (1996)	85.1	70.1
Libya			2.6				30.1 (1995)	78.1	70.2
Mauritania	240	693	5.0				–	41.2	53.9
Morocco	1200	3190	0.9	0.500 (1965)	0.446	0.395	45.8 (1997)	47.1	67.0
Oman			5.1				20.0 (1995)	68.8	71.1
Qatar			7.2				15.2 (1998)	80.4	71.9
Saudi Arabia			4.9				29.0 (1996)	75.2	71.7
Sudan			6.9				112.7 (1993)	55.7	55.4
Syria	970	2761	0.6				41.7 (1993)	72.7	69.2
Tunisia	2100	5478			0.406	0.400	43.6 (1994)	68.7	69.8
UAE			6.9				43.6	74.6	75.0
Yemen	350	688	5.1		0.444	0.232	104.8 (1997)	44.1	58.5

Sources: Adams and Page (2001); Economist Intelligence Unit Country Reports (2000) www.economist.com/countries/; UNOP (2002a); World Bank (1999).

Survey), 94 per cent of the population in the countryside and 80 per cent in the towns should be considered poor. He actually estimated that a majority of the population were living on less than half the measure of US$1. Using the 1995 HIES survey in constant 1990 prices, he estimated that 90 per cent of Egyptians were poor, with rural poverty pervasive but a greater relative rise in urban poverty (Fergany 2002: 213–14). These figures are at odds with those presented by the government of Egypt's statistical office, CAPMAS, and it seems likely that the government may have been economical with the facts.

A useful starting definition of poverty is 'human capability failure'. This is more comprehensive than the simple expenditure surveys that dominate the literature. Fergany, for instance has argued that expenditure measures underestimate poverty, and that while household income and expenditure seem to have risen by 40 per cent (in urban areas) and 20 per cent (in rural areas) from 1990to 1996, real income, allowing for inflation, fell by 14 per cent in the cities and 20 per cent in the countryside. The decline in mean expenditures occurred while there was an increase in GDP per capita of 37 per cent from 1981 to 1996 (Adams and Page 2001: 13). A major challenge in alleviating the vulnerability of the poor relates to employment possibilities: Egypt needs to create 900,000 jobs a year to employ new entrants to the job market, as well as trying to absorb the stock of unemployed and under-employed. The government must create employment at a time when, although overall population growth is declining, that decline is more than offset by the increase in population of working age.[6] Globalization does not offer labour-intensive production, and policy makers and donors do not support it either.

Using the headcount index of those living beneath a poverty line, poverty has increased in Egypt and Jordan since 1980 and average per capita expenditures have fallen, dramatically so in Jordan, suggesting an important reason for the increase in poverty rather than the increase in income inequality. The poverty gap index, the measure of the extent to which average expenditures of the poor fall short of the poverty line, has also increased for Egypt and Morocco. Morocco and Tunisia seem to have withstood the boom–bust oil cycle better because of the opportunity for people to migrate to Europe, which in recent years has been much reduced because of restrictive immigration policy in the EU.

However, the question has to be raised: just how useful is the poverty-line method for assessing poverty? Can different poverty lines be generalized across geographical areas, and how accurate is the World Bank's use of the term 'purchasing power parity' (PPP)?

The most often-used poverty line is US$1.08 in 1993 prices; PPP converts the dollar to a local currency equivalent. The US$1.08 is a recent revision of the World Bank's previous US$1.02 PPP at 1985 prices, although no justification for the shift has been given by the World Bank. This mechanism for trying to assess the different levels of poverty in different country locations has recently been dismissed as arbitrary and grossly inaccurate (Reddy and Pogge 2003: 6). Moreover, World Bank poverty figures – and by extension many of those referred to throughout this book – are not just arbitrary in the choice of poverty line, but also misleading and inaccurate. Reddy and Pogge argue that World Bank PPP figures extrapolate from limited data, masking the real levels of global poverty. PPP assumes poor people have the ability to buy goods and services in their respective economies, when the reality is that basic goods and staples tend to be more expensive in poor countries, while services (because of the lower wage component) tend to cost less. Summarizing this argument, Monbiot (2003) has noted that a more accurate account of poverty levels in the Global South would be to measure 'only the cost of what they [the poor] buy, rather than what richer people in the same economies buy' (*Guardian*, 6 May 2003). In other words, calculations of poverty which average all goods and services that are purchased in a country can give the impression that people at the 'bottom of the heap' are much wealthier than they actually are.

Significantly, Reddy and Pogge do not argue that all attempts at comparing 'income poverty levels across time and space are doomed to fail' (Reddy and Pogge 2003: 32). Instead, they argue the need for an approach that measures poverty on a world scale by using the equivalent 'of the poverty measurement exercises conducted regularly by national government' (Reddy and Pogge 2003: 33) – presumably without the errors, secrecy and reluctance common in MENA – to come clean on what the 'real' levels of poverty are. Specifically, the ditching of PPP would enable greater transparency and definitions of poverty in terms of 'elementary capabilities' or 'in terms of the characteristics of commodities (e.g. nutritional content)'.

Reddy and Pogge continue:

This core conception should be used to define at the national level minimal income thresholds derived from this core conception, appropriately adjusted to take account of relevant inter-regional and inter-group variations in the ability to transform commodities into capabilities. These thresholds should then be applied to available survey data so as to determine whether individuals have sufficient incomes to escape poverty. Such a procedure can produce consistent estimates of poverty that are comparable across space and time.

(Reddy and Pogge 2003: 33)

There is a fourth issue that we can introduce regarding the ways in which calculations of inequality and poverty are made. This relates to the dependence upon income and expenditure surveys and reliance upon the Gini coefficient to denote income distribution and poverty. The Gini coefficient does not give a very full picture of inequality. Expenditure surveys say nothing about savings or savings habits, and we need more nuanced qualitative data about the management of poverty: distributional indicators that include reliance upon kinship and village networks, urban strategies to manage destitution, and so on. We also need tools to investigate poverty, income inequality and political mobilization that help build a picture of the dynamics of wealth and poverty creation. Such a dynamic approach to understanding poverty in MENA, and elsewhere, is rare.

One approach that has raised the issue of understanding not only what creates poverty but also what helps facilitate the movement of people in and out of it has stressed the need for further qualitative work (Haddad and Ahmed 2003). One purpose of collecting this type of data would be to see what happens to households over time. Work on Egypt suggests that the chronically poor are mostly found in urban households, while transitory poverty is most common among those with land or with elderly household members. The intractable nature of chronic poverty leads the authors to call upon the government of Egypt to 'improve the asset accumulation process for the poor' (Haddad and Ahmed 2003: 80).

The future of poverty: an alternative perspective

What does the evidence indicate for the futures of poverty, income distribution and vulnerability in MENA, and what lessons can be learnt for experiences elsewhere in the Global South that I explore in the rest of this book? What can be learnt from some of the perspectives reviewed here? And what impact is the Western drive to target authoritarian regimes and remove perceived political backwardness, as well as post 9/11 US military adventurism, likely to have on the chances of limiting an escalation of poverty during a period of economic reform?

It is important to address at least five issues, which extend the criticisms already made of the ways in which debate about poverty and income distribution has been retained as the preserve of neoliberal economics.

The first is that in the literature on poverty and income distribution in MENA, there is a preoccupation with asset building as the vehicle to reduce poverty. This is misplaced. Access to assets might be important, but so too are the social and productive relationships that generate income from them. As Whitehead (2002) has noted in the African context, it is important not to allow neoclassical economics to tear assets and capital 'out of their relational context'. Livelihoods analysis seems not yet to be influential in MENA studies, but there are lessons to learn from the interdisciplinary approaches used in other geographical regions. Not the least of these is to try to examine the dynamics of rural poverty creation and the way in which the lives of the poor enrich the wealthy. This also requires analysis of the ways in which households are organized and gender relations are constructed and reproduced. My concern to downplay the idea of asset building in MENA as a vehicle to reduce poverty also suggests the need to strengthen analyses of the character of politics, the way in which it is conducted, in whose interest decisions are taken, and wherein might lie the influence for policies that shape class and power – and thus the possibility for political opposition.

Second, there seems to be a preoccupation in the literature with education and the improvement of skills as a vehicle for reducing poverty. In the African context this is asserted further in the Africa Commission, which I discuss in Chapter 2. In itself there seems little wrong with the proposition about the importance of improving educational opportunity (El Kogali and El Daw 2001; El Laithy 2001). Kandeel and Nugent (2000) have argued that educational differences are the most significant determinants of poverty and inequality, and these differences account for why inequality in incomes can fall while poverty increases. Yet the point, surely, must be broader than the increase of education provision *per se*.

The debate about education and skills development must be linked to the use for which such development is intended. If, as seems to be the case, the improvements in education budgets are intended to accelerate the further incorporation of people into the global economy, this must be resisted. There is little in any of the empirical evidence or the assertions or commentaries of, notably, the World Bank, or in much of the work of the Economic Research Forum for the Arab Countries on Iran and Turkey, for example, which provides a robust and coherent argument for the benefits of globalization accruing to MENA.[7]

Discussions about improvements in education only occasionally include a gender distinction. Where this does accompany one set of proposals that has interestingly reflected on poverty, human capital and gender in Yemen and Egypt, there appears to be a new orthodoxy, namely declaring the need for 'policies that empower women ... necessary for poverty reduction and human capital development' (El Kogali and El Daw 2001). Policies need to target women-headed households to enhance 'their access to resources', but just how these policies might be possible and deliverable, and what the shift in political and power relations would need to look like to ensure their meaningful success, is not discussed beyond a sense of the need for 'an active role of the community [that is] critical in the design and implementation of educational policies' (El Kogali and El Daw 2001: np).

Expenditures on education have increased almost universally across the region, but improving education and 'standards' is not only about budgets or even school building programmes. It is about what is taught and how it is delivered, and what the gender and regional dimensions to that strategy look like. In other words, it is about whether it is possible to meaningfully empower women and children through education that goes beyond the improved provision of skills and training in the hope that employment may follow.[8]

Third, the literature is preoccupied with the organization of local and national markets to increase the incorporation of the region into the world economy. According to the World Bank (1995), the driving force for economic growth and thus poverty reduction is trade. It is the quintessential position of the IFIs that realizing the growth potential for countries in MENA depends upon the more efficient operation of markets in general and their outward design in particular. The reification of markets, however, does little to unravel the way in which they are vehicles for exerting economic and political power. They require structures and strategies for regulation, and they are not neutral in their design and outcomes.

Fourth, occasional voices do look at local ideology (Islam) as the vehicle for promoting alternative ethical systems, and try to incorporate more holistic views of poverty (Sirageldin 2000). Yet what seems to be an attempt to explore the dynamics of poverty creation can easily become an ahistorical and idealistic approach that offers the principles of a suggested Islamic ethical system prescribing individual freedom and human dignity, together with poverty alleviation strategies based on 'the principle of promoting economic growth with productive equity [sic]' (Sirageldin 2000). There is no hint of an understanding that the production of wealth leads to the production of poverty.

This leads to the fifth observation regarding the ways that poverty and vulnerability are usually structured and construed in the literature. As we have seen, the discussion of poverty and income distribution is almost entirely dominated by neoliberal economists employing narrow, often simply quantitative, techniques to investigate complicated political and social, as well as economic, issues of inequality. This problem is highlighted by Mitchell:

> The role of economics is to help make possible the economy by articulating the rules, understandings, and equivalences out of which the economic is made.
>
> (Mitchell 2002: 300)

We too often talk about the binaries of wealth and poverty, the global and the local, nature and technology. In so doing we undermine and fail to recognize that these supposed binaries are 'uncertain forms of difference constituted, and at the same time undermined, in the political process' (Mitchell 2002: 15).

It seems that within poverty/vulnerability monologues, the need to understand the political conditions necessary to improve income distribution and reduce chronic poverty is ignored. As Mitchell notes, it is important to recognize that economic transactions do not take place only in the market but also, for example, through networks, kinship, marriage, ties of affection and so on that are not 'backward' and do not on *a priori* grounds inhibit growth and development.

I have already mentioned some of the difficulties inherent in the way in which economists seek to measure poverty and inequality, but there are also issues relating to what specifically is measured: is it monetary earnings alone, or do we need instead to set financial remuneration alongside non-financial social relationships in assessing what we understand by poverty, seen in terms of people's capabilities to sustain and reproduce themselves and others linked to them?

In relation to the overwhelming concern of donors and governments to integrate MENA into a 'globalizing economy', we need to examine how the belief in this need for greater incorporation in the world economy, proclaimed in virtually all strategies for poverty alleviation, has been generated and by whom, and in whose interest it operates. We need to guard against assuming the forces of the economy and politics have internal logic and coherence with an internal rationality (Mitchell 2002). When discussing vulnerability and poverty, we also need to look at the ways in which the social and class forces that are impacted by poverty, and which have helped shape the form that it might take, are created and reproduced. That discussion has recently taken the stylized form of voices from 'the Arab street' or Arab masses (Bayat 2003).

This narrative should not be couched in terms of 'the mice' versus the lions (see Fisk 2003), but should address the way in which opposition and resistance to poverty – and opposition to the MENA states' failure to promote any meaningful notion of citizenship, broadly defined – takes many different forms. In so doing, opposition politics, both formal and informal, affects the construction of what is possible in the debate about reducing poverty and the policies that are possible to redress inequality. I pursue this theme in Chapter 7.

Recent examples of MENA opposition, expressed through street protests and ballot boxes, are not simply responses to cost of living increases, and neither can they be written off as a rise in support for Islamic opposition. Roberts (2002: 1–3) has noted that in the case of

Algeria, for instance, many such protests can more accurately be described as an opposition to 'the systematic and contemptuous violation' of people's rights 'through constant abuse of power and arbitrary rule'. In the Algerian case the support for Islamist politics after 1989 might thus be viewed as a 'conjunctural mode of expression of a preexisting social demand for good government which was not itself premised on adherence to contemporary Islamist doctrines' and had its roots in the early 1980s (Roberts 2002: 1).

Clearly one of the issues and themes that I raise here and which might be pursued is the possible relationship between political mobilization and economic austerity, the conditions under which support for Islamist opposition emerges and the type of solidarity it might engender, including a trend towards the growth of individuals' preoccupation with personal piety; a growth of violent anti-Western jihadi activity, and the domestication/routinization of political Islam in the form of legal and constitutional parties at the national level – Algeria, Morocco, Turkey (compare the views of Bayat 1997, 2003; Pratt 2002; Roberts 2002; Walton and Seddon 1994).

Poverty and politics

There seem to be at least two strong narratives that are emerging in MENA relating to its location in the post 9/11 world order. At the core of one is the idea of the end of the national economy and the emergence and dominance of globalization, a new world society in the new information age, where the benefits of poverty reduction, economic growth and modernization will only be delivered if hitherto closed and inward-looking economies open up to the forces of economic liberalization, namely financial capital.

A second narrative is that the globalization that is presented is nothing more than the continued (but transient) capitalist (uneven and combined) development. This latter interpretation can help explain a process of what Ferguson (1999: 236) has called abjection: 'a process of being thrown aside, expelled, or discarded'. In MENA, a process of being thrown aside is progressing to reincorporation and resubordination to the interests of capital in general, and US capital in particular. The reincorporation is paralleled, or perhaps more specifically driven, by the most naked imperialist military aggression of recent decades. In addition to Iraq (and further afield, Afghanistan), and the enormous diplomatic missions in Israel and Egypt, the USA has troops in twelve countries in the region and in central Asia, ensuring that 42 per cent of world oil reserves are preserved for Western access.

Helping to structure and explain the military presence, beyond the rhetoric of a war on terror, is the increasing ideological assertion of the virtues of neoliberal economics and a state role of regulating labour on behalf of capital. In these new circumstances of neoliberal hegemony, 'poverty is everywhere re-badged as social exclusion' and underpinned by individual inadequacies (Radice 2006). This provides the rationale for avoiding the need to establish the historical context in which the authoritarian populist regimes of MENA have delivered comparatively low levels of poverty and better levels of income distribution than many other parts of the world.

Little is said about the consequences of the US and coalition regional agenda, which is likely to threaten regime stability during the war on terror. Yet even the erstwhile World Bank President, John Wolfensohn, noted that while it might be 'meritorious' to knock off the heads of fundamentalist organizations, it does not address the 'question of fundamental stability', namely the growth of poverty and the failure of international policy makers and politicians to link poverty with terror.

My pessimistic characterization of MENA's contemporary position in the world economy, and the impact that the war on terror will have on the region's poor, suggests an undermining of historical social contracts that are in the process of being replaced by economic adjustment and the Western drive for limited rather than grassroot political opening. In indicating this I am not marginalizing the importance of political struggles and the possibility for social transformation. Le Vine (2002) has noted the need for Arab voices to join the 'global conversation on building alternatives to the existing systems of economic, political and social power', of the need for Arab voices to be heard in the international anti-globalization movements in spite, or because, of the region's role in the war against 'terrorism'.

It is important that local social and class forces within MENA contest the inherited and dominant wisdoms of the international actors and players of globalization. The IFIs, for instance, are content to continue to access key resources in the MENA, sustain rentier economies (albeit slightly transformed) and provide external assistance, and also to get increasingly vexed about the twin threats of Islam and demographic pressures that may entail continued migration to Europe and threaten Jewish control of Israel. It is thus important for local political forces to conjure up an alternative modernity to that peddled by international capital via Washington's neoconservatives.

Two questions might increasingly come to preoccupy work on poverty in MENA. First, if MENA has good income distribution levels and relatively low levels of poverty (notwithstanding my criticism of the evidential base for this), this complicates the issue of autocracy and the Western drive to remove political 'backwardness' in the region. In particular, the characterization of autocracy and the West's attempt to promote (limited) political liberalization, whatever that means, will impact adversely on the social contract that autocratic rulers have accepted regarding the delivery of basic services. How are the dubious gains of Western-style freedoms then to be set alongside not only market reforms but also political reforms?

Second, if my characterization of MENA's uneven incorporation into the world economy and the post 9/11 military and political architecture mapped by Washington is accurate, future research to highlight the impact of this and the way in which regimes in MENA will reproduce it, and be challenged by domestic political forces, needs to adopt a radical agenda. That might explore the political economy of aid and trade, political and economic liberalization, and also the internal mechanisms of power and politics, shifting ideological formulations of, among other things, Islam and state–citizen relations, and the character of local labour regimes in town and country.

Mapping the alternative to neoliberal explanations for poverty will clarify the fault lines within the region and show how strategies for greater equity might be delivered, and by whom. We can now turn attention to the characterization of poverty in sub-Saharan Africa, and an analysis of the most recent strategy for development that was offered by the Africa Commission.

2 Commissioning Africa for globalization: Blair and the G8's project for the world's poor

When UK Prime Minister Tony Blair announced in February 2004 the establishment of a Commission for Africa (CFA), he declared that it would 'be a comprehensive assessment of the situation in Africa and policies towards Africa' (www.pm.gov.uk/output/pages5425.asp). Publication of the report in March 2005, to coincide with Blair's chairmanship of the G8, noted that it constituted '*a coherent package for Africa*' (CFA 2005: 13, emphasis in original).

In many respects Blair was to be congratulated on keeping the international community's attention on the world's poorest continent. Yet it quickly became clear, even during the commission's deliberations, that the challenge was too great to deliver policy to transform both the immediate suffering of the poor and longer-term economic growth. Africa is slipping away from meeting the UN millennium development goals and it is unclear whether the CFA will help ensure that they are met.[1] In sub-Saharan Africa, 19 out of the 35 countries were well behind the target for lowering under-five mortality rates, and this included South Africa which since 1995 has plummeted almost 20 places in the Human Development Index (World Development Movement 2004).

This chapter explores the misguided underpinnings of the CFA and its policy agenda. It also examines the failure of the G8 meeting in July 2005 to meet public expectations of making poverty history. I also indicate that even if the public optimism for action had been stronger, it would still have been insufficient to shift Africa's continental fortunes.

For all the hype and brouhaha, Africa 2005 did little other than reinforce Western prejudice about the continent. The hype and publicity about the need to 'make poverty history' drew largely on a chauvinistic and racist ideology of the powers of the West to civilize, to redeem and to care for wayward 'savages' who still continued, more than 40 years after independence, to rule ineffectively for themselves. At its most crude, the CFA and Blair proffered a paternalistic attitude represented in Bob Geldof's TV series on Africa and captured too in his achievement in providing only limited space at Live 8 for black musicians at the Eden Project sideshow, a long way from the main music action in London.

At its more subterranean and sinister the guise of paternalism and religiosity was a cover for the continued subjugation of Africa and for the power of the West to shape development agendas and prescriptions. That was revealed by the persistent focus in the CFA on Africa's weak state capacity and lack of political accountability (CFA 2005: 14), and the reluctance of the commissioners to understand and seek to redress the imperialist networks of historical adverse incorporation of Africa into the contemporary world of global capital. Blair's hand-wringing about the need to change the EU common agricultural policy and boost trade in and from Africa was an added mask on the face of the continent's impoverishment caused by the interrelationship between the continent's combined and uneven development and the exploitation of its resources from foreign capital.

Meanwhile, the constant references to corruption in African governments, not withstanding Hilary Benn's rhetoric to the contrary in September 2006, became a standardized pathologizing of African politics. Yet in contrast to the representation, there was evidence that corruption was diminishing and some African politicians began to leave office, suggesting a deepening of democratic practice.

It was clear even after the initial announcement of the creation of the CFA that yet another commission on Africa, or more generally on the persistent and growing inequality between the rich Northern and poorer Southern countries of the world, would be unable to make progress with strategies to mediate worsening disparities in income and wealth. That was because of a fundamental shortcoming of the thinking behind the CFA, reinforced later in 2005 by the Gleneagles meeting of the G8. Blair, his Chancellor Gordon Brown and their New Labour colleagues' demanded that Africa become more integrated in the global world economy to take advantage of the presumed benefits of globalization.

Their preoccupation with the benefits of globalization denied at the outset of the CFA the opportunity to argue that it was precisely the way in which Africa was integrated into the world economy, rather than its absence or refusal to take part, that had contributed to the continent's predicament. The CFA, the G8 and the personal bonding of Messrs Geldof and Bono with Blair and Bush, promoted the idea that the West could and should save Africa and that promoting a business partnership with Africa was the only meaningful strategy to pursue. Thus Bono and Geldof's strategy of glad-handing the neoconservatives in the United States and New Labour in the UK did nothing to expose the reasons for Africa's crisis other than to heap blame on poor capacity, war, poor education, corruption and the need for more trade. These were not explanations of crisis, only a shopping list for future palliative care dependent upon increased flows of aid.

Bono and Geldof's personalized strategy of making friends in high places did nothing to publicize the West's role in promoting a crisis that it now charged itself with resolving. And it certainly did nothing to refute the spurious notion that Western business and new partnership with African elites were necessary to promote development. It was disingenuous to hide behind Bush and Blair's strategy of promoting business associations to shape African development. That view failed to understand that business engagement was part of the problem, not the solution, and it fundamentally served to obscure the way in which the power of the North to control and shape the meaning and understanding of development took on a new and aggressive character. This was fashioned in the United States by Bush's *African Growth and Opportunity Act 2000* (www.agoa.gov accessed 7 February 2006), which promoted the need for African states to advance market reform and secure property rights.

USAID was tasked with promoting the market-friendly environment, and responsibility for strategy implementation was given to the Corporate Council on Africa. That organization, established in 1993, had as its main aim the promotion of commercial relationships between the United States and Africa (www.africacncl.org accessed 7 February 2006). In the UK, Blair promoted the importance of business and multinational companies as the salvation for African poverty. In July 2005 he opened the Action for Africa Summit, chaired by Sir Mark Moody-Stuart, the head of Anglo American. Other major international corporations were also represented, Shell, British American Tobacco, Standard Chartered Bank and De Beers. The meeting launched the Investment Climate Facility to manage a $550 million fund financed by the UK, the World Bank and members of the G8. Its responsibility was 'to remove real and perceived obstacles to domestic and foreign investment' for the private sector (www.investmentclimatefacility.org; George Monbiot, *Guardian* 5 July 2005: 21).

This chapter argues that the character of capitalism in the twenty-first century is the problem rather than the solution to Africa's crisis, and only when that is recognized would there emerge a glimmer of hope and an idea of what a strategy for the continent's growth and development might look like. In highlighting this I demonstrate why the CFA was an irrelevancy to the poor in Africa, and indeed by early 2006 the Report had already begun gathering dust of the forgotten. Given New Labour's commitment to globalization, the time and the money spent on the CFA would have been as well spent dusting off the findings of the Brandt Commission (1980) or even the Pearson Commission (1969) before it, but those earlier Keynesian formulas for saving the poor were also inadequate. Blair used the gimmickry of summitry as a substitute for hard analysis of the way in which the wealth of the rich in the North is based on the poverty of those in the South.

African crisis: what the CFA and the G8 already knew

Evidence from numerous sources – international financial agencies, NGOs and bilateral donors – confirms the level of human suffering and misery in Africa (World Bank 2000; UNDP 2003; Oxfam 2003). Thirty of the UN's 'low human development' countries are in sub-Saharan Africa, more than a quarter of the continent's poor are undernourished and half of the 719 million population exist on less than US$1 a day. The number of those in extreme poverty increased from 242 million to more than 300 million in the 1990s. Average income per capita is lower than it was at the end of the 1960s, falling by 2 per cent per annum since 1980, and external debt at over US$200 billion is about 10 per cent of all developing country debt.

Africa's debt is also harder to repay. It is a much higher proportion of GDP than in other poor regions, and many countries use more than half of revenue from exports just to service the debt. And reconstruction in many states that have experienced complex political emergencies, war and state collapse has been slow and protracted. That has not least been because of the way in which Western munitions firms market small arms to the continent, fuelling conflict; Congo's conflict was fuelled by more than 800,000 illegal small arms. Not all of the military and humanitarian disasters can be levelled at the doors of the West, however. The Khartoum regime, for example, has been charged with genocide in Darfur, where it has tried to extend its legitimacy among Arab militias that have murdered, raped and pillaged the meagre possessions of an African majority population in Sudan's western province.

Africa is the poorest part of the world and it is getting poorer; the only continent to do so. The total GDP of all 48 countries on the continent combined comes to little more than the income of Belgium, while the average GDP for sub-Saharan African countries (excluding South Africa) is about US$2 billion; no more than the output of a town of about 60,000 people in a rich Northern country (World Bank 2000: 7).

Africa's poverty has created enormous health and social problems. The most significant of these are famine and HIV/AIDS. Sub-Saharan Africa accounts for 11 per cent of the world's population but 24 per cent of the world's undernourished people. As many as 40 million people in the period 2003–06 were in need of famine and food relief in the greater Horn, Ethiopia, Eritrea and also Sudan, and famine has also stalked the region of southern Africa.

Food relief has also been necessary in west and central Africa. Many different causes underpin the continent's food crises as we shall see in Chapter 6. These include drought, economic marginalization, and international and local food policies that undermine food producers and their abilities to sustain a livelihood that can with-stand periodic shocks from poor weather, armed conflict or deleteri-ous national economic policy. There is a continental food crisis because increases in food productivity have failed to keep up adequately with local demand and deleterious trade rules have made it impossible for significant levels of foreign exchange to be earned from the sale of agricultural commodities and other raw materials to purchase food on international markets. This suggests a systemic food crisis in Africa.

That crisis was not helped by the US/UK 'coalition of the willing' to oust Saddam Hussein in Iraq. Chancellor Gordon Brown in the UK put more than £3 billion aside at the start of the war, while the annual bilat-eral aid programme to Africa was £528 million in 2001/02 set to reach £1 billion by 2005/06. Ethiopian Prime Minister Meles Zenawi noted Western hypocrisy, criticizing Western trade policy and the war in Iraq as deflecting attention from the crisis in Africa (*Guardian* 25 February 2003). This is a position he seems to have later readdressed when he became a member of Blair's CFA and quickly signed up to President George W. Bush's war on terror and the US request for military bases in the Horn of Africa.

HIV/AIDS (Human Immunodeficiency Virus/Acquired Immun-odeficiency Syndrome) is exacerbating Africa's fragile economic and social infrastructure and it is having a profound structural impact on the continent's demography and ability to feed itself. Health facilities across Africa are rudimentary as debt repayments have eaten oppor-tunity for social spending, and access to medication is difficult even where there may be money to purchase basic drugs. Sub-Saharan Africa has the world's highest HIV prevalence. More than 25 million people in Africa have HIV or AIDS and as many as 17 million have probably died from the disease in the last ten years. HIV is the most infectious killer in Africa and it has a structural impact in transform-ing the continent's ability to sustain itself. AIDS is reversing gains in life expectancy that rose on the continent from 44 years in the early 1950s to 59 years in the early 1990s. AIDS is now likely to reduce life expectancy to 44 years between 2005 and 2010, and less than half of all Africans currently alive are likely to reach the age of 60. This compares with 70 per cent for all developing countries and 90 per cent for industrial countries (Poku 2002: 532).

In seven countries where HIV prevalence is greater than 20 per cent, the average life expectancy of someone born in 1995–2000 was 49 years: 13 years less than in the absence of AIDS (UNAIDS 2004). The situation is worse where antiretroviral medication is unavailable or where the income of patients is too low to purchase it. The disease has its greatest impacts on those in their most productive 20s and 30s, thus

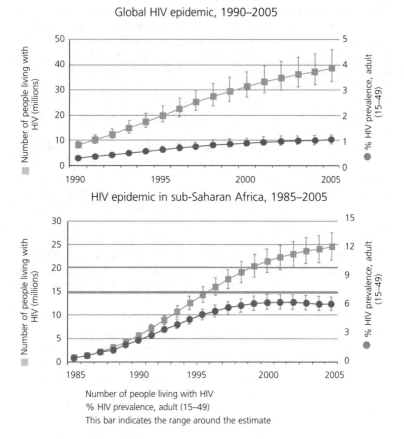

Figure 2.1 Estimated number of people living with HIV and adult HIV prevalence (%) globally and in sub-Saharan Africa 1985–2005

Reproduced with kind permission from UNAIDS (2006) (www.unaids.org).

attacking the continent's ability to drag itself out of the mire of economic crisis and poverty. It impacts too on the continent's ability to feed itself, and affects women and girls more than men. According to UNAIDS, women in sub-Saharan Africa are 30 per cent more likely to be HIV positive than men. African women between 15–24 years old are on average more than three times as likely to be infected than their male counterparts and this is often due to male sexual violence

(UNAIDS 2004: 40) this thus indicates the importance of gender awareness rather than just state-orchestrated sex education or condom supply as a means to reduce infection rates of women, and the importance of confronting male violence (Schoef 2003).

The vicious cycle for high-prevalence countries is the link between food shortage, malnutrition and AIDS. In Zimbabwe, for instance, adult HIV prevalence is about 25 per cent, and by 2000 the disease had killed up to 10 per cent of the country's agricultural workforce. There are direct links between the ability of countries to manage drought, poor economic conditions or other critical issues affecting food security and the level of HIV infection. AIDS may cluster in households, attacking people of prime working age; the resulting need to care for breadwinners who are no longer able to bring in income to sustain the family drives coping strategies among those still able to focus on producing less labour-intensive non-cash crops. In turn this reduces abilities to fund the purchase of food during crisis. And the desperate spiral exacerbates as the need to care for sick relatives can reduce the abilities of the fit to carry out agricultural work or seek off-farm wage employment. Also, family members spend more than is 'rational' on medication that may or may not help the sick person, including those from traditional sources, or on expensive antiretrovirals which undermine household food security

Blair's commission: to Africa's rescue?

The CFA was trumpeted as an opportunity to 'take a fresh look at the challenges Africa faces'. Its job was to look at 'the facts on Africa', make an assessment of policy, of what has worked and what has not and what more could be done. There were 17 commissioners, politicians and 'opinion formers' supported by a secretariat that collected evidence from public meetings and a 'wide range of experts'. The intention was that the CFA's findings would 'help inform' the UK's agenda for Africa during its G8 and EU Presidencies in 2005.

If Bob Geldof is to be believed, he was instrumental in getting Blair and Brown to talk about the need for a Marshall plan for Africa. Initially underwhelmed with the idea, Blair warmed to the suggestion that a commission might well reignite the concern he has often expressed that Africa is a 'scar on the conscience of the world'. Geldof expressed the need for strong representation on the commission from Africa and he has calmed the previous shrill indignation that was evident at the time he convened Live Aid in 1985.

Revisiting Ethiopia in 2004, Geldof was struck by how bad people's lives continued to be, and he has contextualized Africa's worsening economic and social conditions in historical terms of the impact of colonialism, misdeeds of the continent's dictators and unaccountable international financial institutions, drawing the conclusion that 'Africa is fucked'. Aid has done little, the West has 'a hypocritical notion of economics and there is confusion about the view of human rights in Africa and the benefits of globalization' (Geldof 2004). Geldof, it seemed, was the conscience of the CFA but he could not, or simply did not, understand the power of finance capital. Blair was certainly deaf to the idea of having a broad-based commission.

The Africa commissioners were primarily chosen for what they offered from the world of business, although they included the President of Tanzania and the Prime Minister of Ethiopia, who not only became an advocate for US interests in Africa but also became an auto-cratic leader at home. Other commissioners included the executive secretary of the Economic Commission for Africa, K.Y. Amoako, and the executive director of UN Habitat, Anna Kajumulo. By far the most significant interest represented on the CFA was from the world of business:

- Canadian and South Africa Ministers of Finance and the Governor of the Bank of Botswana[2]
- the chairman of FATE, a Nigerian charitable foundation that 'promotes entrepreneurship among the youth of Nigeria'
- the Group Strategy and Development Director of Aviva PLC – the world's seventh largest insurance group and the biggest in the UK.

Also present was Michel Camdessus, an honorary Governor of the Bank of France and President Chirac's personal representative on Africa. Camdessus was infamous in Africa and elsewhere as the erst-while Managing Director and Chairman of the Executive Board of the International Monetary Fund 1987–2000. Under his tutelage Africa was forced to comply with tough debt rescheduling which drew money away from health and education budgets, and he also oversaw finan-cial crises in South-East Asian growth and helped deliver market chaos to the former Soviet Union.

After the Commission's first meeting in May 2004 Blair noted that: 'We got through the stuff we needed to get through.' But to get a clearer idea as to just what that 'stuff' was and what kinds of conclusion Blair and his new friends came up with we need to take a brief and broader examination of the UK agenda and the role given by New Labour to globalization in promoting development in the Global South.

Geldof's initiative for a Marshall Plan for Africa fell neatly into Blair's lap following the PM's contentious decision to follow the United States into Iraq. Blair additionally failed to keep on the international agenda a strategy to resolve Israel's continued occupation of Palestine, leaving his foreign policy a subject for considerable criticism. Thus the formation of the CFA became partly an attempt to salvage some of Blair's international reputation and deflect attention from the continuing violence and disruption in Iraq. But he was also driven by a feverish clamour among activist and advocacy groups like Jubilee 2000 and Make Poverty History to do something that would significantly reduce Africa's debt burden.

Blair likes the world stage and thinks it is where he performs well; he promotes, just like Margaret Thatcher, his predecessor in Downing Street, a view that the UK can punch above its weight in an international forum. Underpinning Blair's conviction politics and inflated view of the UK's role in the world is his faith that globalization can work for the poor. This indeed was part of the title of the UK government's 2000 White Paper, and helps explain why the CFA was full of business people rather than advocacy groups, those seeking access to grassroots in Africa or activists aware of the damage that Africa's position in the capitalist world economy has produced (HMG 2000). Blair ignored the urgings of Nelson Mandela, expressed at the 2000 annual British Labour Party Conference, that globalization had to be understood as not simply involving economic liberalization but also as having ideas about international equality and solidarity. Blair and New Labour repeated the mantra that globalization was the only game in town, and that 'partnerships' with Africa were the way forward for the world's poorest continent.

The mistake here is to imagine that Africa's problem is its marginalization from the global world economy. Like MENA, which we examined in Chapter 1, Africa is characterized as a continent on the periphery of global economic activity. The problem, however, is not that the continent is insufficiently integrated with globalization; it is that Africa has been integrated in a particular way that has underdeveloped its resources of people and raw materials. That underdevelopment has been the outcome of its historical struggles with the way in which the world economy has been created. It has also been shaped by the particular histories and political economies of African social formations and local classes in their interaction with the world economy and nationally in the construction of local economies.

In the current phase of capitalist development, which might be called 'globalization' – although this is an unsatisfactory term for many reasons – the poverty of most Africans has mounted immeasurably, in particular since the mid-1970s. Herein lies a problem that the CFA was simply unable to consider: policies that focus on the interests of Western and sometimes local African capital rather than the wellbeing of rural and urban poor, of those in work and those without it, and of those with little chance of finding future work that will raise and sustain standards of living, welfare and health. At best it seems the problem confronting IFI policy makers and the CFA was one of obfuscation. At worst, however, it became deceit for we shall see in a moment that, while the CFA and the G8 in 2005 announced policies to ameliorate the poverty of the most poor by promoting debt relief, and longer-term strategies for reconstructing the continent by promoting infrastructural assistance and investment for education, the overwhelming tenor of reform was to promote state governance reform and trade liberalization.

The real strategies to develop the continent, to remove the obstacles to trade and expansion of powers and skills, expertise and knowledge, wellbeing and economic growth are policies that will attack the profitability of Western interests, corporations and individuals who benefit from African misery. That is because by far the most dominant mechanism used by the West to extract African wealth is the persistence of strategies of primitive accumulation. This can be characterized as a mechanism of super-exploitation where 'normal' capitalist exploitation of commodity exchange or surplus extraction through the wage relation is less important than the dominance of plunder through raw material extraction and control of labour (Bond 2006; Harvey 2003; Perelman 2000; Chapter 4).

Our common interest

The CFA stressed that 'it is in our common interest to make the world a more prosperous and secure place.' It also noted that the starting point for the CFA was 'the recognition that Africa must drive its own development' by creating 'the right conditions for development'. If those conditions were not met then 'any amount of outside support will fail' (CFA 2005: 1). The recognition that Africa must drive its own development is crucial in the defence of self-determination and national sovereignty. Yet as the report unfolds, and the central role for private business becomes the key for redressing the continent's ills, Africa's abilities to confront the power of capital in general and the power of extractive industry capitalists in particular shrinks.

The CFA had five main arguments that constituted its 'coherent package for Africa'. These amounted to the need to build governance and accountability structures at the national and also regional levels in Africa. Here the African Union and NEPAD (more about that later) were to be central in ensuring that donors did not always put their own imprint on reforms as 'improving accountability is the job of African leaders' (CFA 2005: 14). The second concern was the need for peace and security. African leaders were tasked with taking control, preventing and managing conflict, using aid better and facilitating improved mechanisms of mediation and peacekeeping. Third, in promoting the importance of poverty alleviation and provision for basic human rights, the CFA promoted the importance of 'investing in people': the provision of basic education, 'rebuilding systems to deliver public health services' and funding improved sanitation and improved ability to deal with 'the catastrophe of HIV and AIDS' (CFA 2005: 15). The fourth concern of the CFA was the need for growth in Africa in order to reduce poverty. Economic growth of 7 per cent was needed to reduce poverty but that is little in evidence anywhere on the continent, apart from the exceptional case of Botswana. At a celebrated growth of just 3.8 per cent, for just 16 countries in sub-Saharan Africa, there remains a long way to go before growth can eat into extensive and systemic poverty.

For growth to promote poverty reduction the CFA required changes in governance. The intention was to make an investment climate stronger and to achieve massive infrastructural development: a doubling of spending on roads and irrigation, highways and rail networks, rural development and slum upgrading. Agricultural development was particularly identified as necessary for poverty reduction and to help small enterprises, women and the young. A target of US$20 billion a year on investment in infrastructure was identified. Developed countries were to provide an extra $10 billion a year up to 2010 and a further increase to $20 billion in the following five years. Crucially for the CFA, the build up in aid to $20 billion per annum by 2013 could raise GDP in 2015 by 4.5 per cent above what it would otherwise be. 'This would result in, by 2015, a poverty rate that is close to 2.5 percentage points lower than would otherwise have been the case, equivalent to around 20 million' people (CFA 2005: 235). The focus on infrastructural development was seen by one commentator as 'probably the biggest single development story of 2005' (Maxwell 2005: 485).

The final area examined by the CFA was trade. It argued the need for improved African 'capacity to trade', with the need for better quality of goods produced and streamlined bureaucracy within and between African trading partners. But the CFA also argued the need for rich nations to 'dismantle the barriers they have erected against African goods, particularly in agriculture', and thus the need to 'abolish trade distorting subsidies' (CFA 2005: 16).

The mechanism for supporting these reforms, innovations and investments was increased aid: an additional US$25 billion per annum to be implemented by 2010 and a further increase in international aid budgets of US$25 billion a year by 2015. This increased aid was dependent upon two factors, in addition to whether it could by raised by donors. The first was the importance of good governance in Africa, the need to ensure improvement in openness, accountability and democratization, and the second was an improvement in the quality of aid. The CFA stressed the need for more grants rather than loans, less attached or tied aid and the importance of the IFIs prioritizing African development and giving Africa a stronger voice in decision making.

The implication from the CFA was the need for urgency: urgency to act quickly from 2005, to commit funds for Africa and if necessary to front-load aid through Gordon Brown's initiative of the International Finance Facility and 100 per cent debt cancellation 'as soon as possible'. That was necessary for Africa to meet the millennium development goals in 2015. Additionally the CFA called for a new kind of partnership based on 'mutual respect and solidarity and rooted in a sound analysis of what actually works' (CFA 2005: 17).

Whose common interest?

It seems that all parties to the year of 'Africa 2005', government and non-government alike, signed up to the idea that it was in the common interest that Africa's crisis should be addressed. The common interest became inscribed in the title of the CFA, an interest that had a moral imperative from Blair that provided a veil for the economic interests of the G8 and security concerns that a poor and potentially increasingly lawless Africa might pose problems for European security.

Western policy makers had been here before of course with the Brandt report of 1980 that spoke of a common crisis, a report that stressed the importance of Southern markets for Northern commerce (Brandt 1980). The erstwhile German Chancellor Brandt had tried to build on the proposals of Nobel Peace Prize winner Sir Lester Pearson before him. Blair, much like Robert McNamara at the World Bank in the 1970s, implied that a brilliant new idea would emerge from another commission of enquiry into poverty that would have the power to solve stubborn economic and social problems. The parallels are strong between McNamara, reflecting on Pearson and initiating Brandt, and Blair establishing the CFA. Both McNamara and Blair were short on detail and long on the need for broad understandings of the size of the problem, on moral outrage and confidence that the global economy (international as it was viewed in the1970s) could resolve inequalities between the North and the South, that there is benefit for the North and the South in so doing, and that the establishment of a high-level commission is the way to generate the policies that will create a more just and equitable world (McNamara 1973; *New York Times* 29 September 1977: D1; *Economist* 15 January 1977: 82).

Even the anecdotal moral outrages were similar. Geldof noted how the United States spent three times as much per annum on pet food as it did on treating HIV/AIDS, while Brandt had drawn the parallel of the cost of one tank representing the spend on 1,000 classrooms for 30,000 poor kids.

There were three main misconceptions about the findings of the CFA, and one fundamental systemic problem that flawed its entirety. The fundamental problem was its singular lack of historical analysis as to why Africa was in the mess that it sought to redress. The failure to understand the history of poverty made it impossible to transform it: the CFA could not recognize that capitalism prevented African prosperity. Although the CFA mentioned the culpability of the West and the IFIs in the continent's predicament, unsurprisingly it did not offer a strategy to redress it.

The CFA adhered to an ahistorical narrative that persisted with the use of neoclassical frameworks to account for the status quo. A leap of faith was then made to argue that the economic system that has overseen and generated global inequality could be used to shift the global hierarchy of inequality. Thus the CFA became concerned with issues essentially of aid, debt reduction and trade. These three areas of misconception had been profiled long before the CFA. None of these issues alone or collectively would prevent the persistence of Africa's uneven incorporation into the world economy. Improvements in them could reduce some suffering and for that reason they could be supported. Yet failure to understand why and how Africa has been adversely incorporated, and why that would not be structurally addressed by the CFA palliatives, relegates the report and Blair's place in history to the sidelines. The sidelining began in July 2005 at the Gleneagles G8 summit.

Aid

The G8 summit was previewed as the moment when the major industrial capitalist states would usher in a Marshall plan for Africa. Yet the hype around the rhetoric of the G8 doubling aid to $50 billion was misplaced. Africa in 2005 was certainly not the Europe of 1948, although the parallel with problems of order and security could be made (Elliot, *Guardian* 6 July 2005). Oxfam reported that the $50 billion was not all new money and that in any case the increased assistance was not due until 2012. Temporizing on increasing aid has been a common theme among Western donors. Indeed, instead of the CFA the leaders of the G8 might have been better informed about their 'moral' duty to raise foreign assistance if they had revisited the Brandt report.

There is a continuous development thread predating Brandt and stretching forward to the contemporary period: namely, for the industrialized countries to commit 0.7 per cent of their GDP to Official Development Assistance (ODA). The UN General Assembly called for this in 1970 and most donors, except the United States, agreed to try to achieve it. Yet 35 years after the declaration only Denmark (0.96), Norway (0.89), Sweden (0.83), the Netherlands (0.81) and Luxembourg (0.77) had reached that level.[3] The UK Labour Party reiterated its commitment to the 0.7 target in its 2001 manifesto but remained far from achieving its promise. Assistance peaked with the Callaghan government of 1979 at 0.51 per cent of GDP, which dipped to 0.24 per cent in 1999, two years after Tony Blair's landslide victory.

Overseas assistance was not on Blair's agenda until the 2004 spending review made much of the promised improvement of ODA to almost £6.5 billion by 2007–08, a real-terms increase of 140 per cent over the 1997 level. UK treasury officials indicated that with this level of increase the UK would reach the target of 0.7 per cent of GDP by 2013, just two years ahead of the timetable for the Millennium Development Goals to have been reached (www.hm-treasury.gov accessed 26 July 2004).

UK International Development Minister Hilary Benn suggested that by 2008 ODA to Africa from the UK would be £1.25 billion per annum. An additional £1.5 billion would be spent on HIV/AIDS work over the three years 2004–07 but that was for the entire developing world, not just Africa. There therefore seems little to celebrate when Blair's attempt to rid the scar from the world's conscience, by improving ODA, has not yet reached the levels of the Labour government of 25 years ago, and that struggle to get over £2 billion ODA to Africa looks very poor set alongside Chancellor Brown's swift access to funds to wage war in Iraq at the start of military action.[4]

The euphoria of the G8 trumpeting the promise to double aid to $50 billion needs to be set against NGO concern that less than half of that was new money, and the lack of clarity as to whether it included $20 billion already pledged for HIV/AIDS by 2010. The Make Poverty History Campaign suggested that only $16 billion was new funding. Moreover, the $50 billion included an amount that was a contribution towards multilateral debt reduction. The continued temporizing over getting ODA to represent 0.7 per cent of G8 GDP was likened to 'waiting five years before responding to the tsunami' (www.eurodad.org/articles/default.aspx?id=638 accessed 15 February 2006).

The Gleneagles promise of increased ODA also needs to be set in a context of the cost to the Global South of repeated shortfalls in the UK commitment to meet the 0.7 per cent of GDP target for ODA. Coupled with the cost of UK militarism in Iraq, *World Vision* reported, 'Britain's "miserable" failure to meet promises on international aid has cost the world's poorest nations £9.5bn in three years'; and this at a time when Gordon Brown made repeated statements about the need for the international community to boost ODA from $50 billion to $100 billion (Morris, *The Independent*, 28 July 2004).

Despite the hype about increased ODA from the G8 to resolve Africa's problems (and in fact in many respects Blair was muted in his overall assessment of what the G8 achieved for Africa), rich Western countries continued to spend more than 25 times as much on defence as they did on ODA. Since 1990 ODA to the world's poorest African countries increased by just $3 a head, yet per capita incomes in the G8 rose by $6,000. For every £1 spent on development by the UK £8 is spent on defence. And while the UK aid budget doubled between 1990 and 2003, from $11 to $22 per head, that represents just one-fortieth of defence spending. Defence spending by the G7 (the G8 minus Russia) at about $600 billion a year is ten times the level of spending on aid not just in Africa but also Asia, Latin America and poor countries in Eastern Europe.

If ODA is seen as the Western panacea to poverty in the Global South, the G8 needs to transfer some if its prosperity since 1990 into overseas aid: it has not. France, Japan and Canada spent less on aid to Africa in 2005 than they did in 1990 (UNDP 2005). In short, the promise of an additional $50 billion fell far short of $90 billion seen as necessary to meet the millennium goals noted by the Millennium Development Project Report or the $200 billion seen as necessary by other observers (*Guardian* 19 September 2005). It was also a concern for NGO and activist groups that conditionality would be attached to ODA, and despite the rhetoric of letting Africans decide for themselves about the use of funds, UK and US governments would link ODA to donor company interests. Support from the US Millennium Challenge account, for instance, is conditional upon US company access, and major US firms have protested against World Bank assertions that local firms can even bid for contracts.

Debt relief

The G8 also failed to deliver on debt relief. The celebrated breakthrough of 100 per cent debt cancellation that ran ahead of the July meeting covered just 18 heavily indebted poor countries (HIPCs), with a possible additional 20 to follow. There was no mention of debt distress experienced by middle-income countries for example. While about $1 billion would be saved by the eligible HIPC states there were more than 60 countries that paid at least $10 billion a year in debt servicing and desperately needed relief if they were to approximate to the millennium development goals. There was as least as much smoke and mirrors about debt cancellation as there was about increases in ODA. And there was much conditionality attached to the generosity of relief.

Debt cancellation applied to the debts of the IMF, World Bank and African Development Bank but omitted money owed to 19 other multilateral creditors. Thus five countries in Latin America were left to pay the Inter-American Development Bank $3.3 billion in debt servicing in 2005–15 (*Independent on Sunday* 10 July 2005). The debt deal still left Africa $200 billion in debt, with the developing world as a whole paying the rich world $100 million daily.

There was also a big problem with the delays in actioning the debt reduction packages by the IFIs and deciding a cut-off date for the figure of debt that was eligible for relief. The IMF began delivering debt cancellation after January 2006, but the World Bank was unlikely to follow until midway through the same year, 18 months after the first agreement by G8 finance ministers which predated Gleneagles in February 2005. Only debt stocks that had accrued by December 2003 were eligible for cancellation by the International Development Administration, the soft loan affiliate of the World Bank. The IMF, however, set the cut-off date at the end of 2004.

Total nominal IDA debt cancellation might total $25 billion but does not represent 100 per cent of countries or 100 per cent of debt cancellation (www.eurodad.org/articles/default.aspx?id=673 accessed 10 February 2006). Most challenging of all, however, was that first of all the IFIs required reimbursement by donors for the debt they wrote off. The IFIs simply argued that they did not have sufficient liquidity to take the hit of diminished credit flows. It was the continued dominance of conditionality however that undermines the generosity, real or otherwise, of the debt reduction. Debt cancellation is linked to meeting IFI strictures for implementation of poverty reduction strategy papers (PRSPs), linking debt reduction with investments in poverty alleviation and, centrally, the provision of a policy infrastructure conducive to accelerated private capitalist investment. Thus the 'old' conditionalities of the structural adjustment years of the 1980s and early 1990s continue with the 'new' policies of declared poverty reduction. Privatization of services and improved access by foreign and domestic private investment are seen as the key to growth in Africa and elsewhere in the Global South. Thus at the start of 2006 the IMF delayed debt cancellation to Ethiopia, Madagascar, Rwanda and Senegal and also Nicaragua because of concerns that IFI conditionalities were not met (see for instance Berthelemy et al 2004).

Trade

The final major area of shortcoming that emerged from the rhetoric of the CFA and G8 summitry was trade. There was barely agreement on reductions in rich country export subsidies and considerable delays in terms of when reductions might happen, 2010, 2012 or 2015. One set of figures reinforces the deceit about improvements in aid and development opportunity for Africa compared with the reality of continued subjugation: OECD countries subsidized farm exports by $350 billion in 2003 compared with the $22 billion in aid they offered to Africa. The UN estimates that 'unfair trade rules deny poor countries $700 billion every year,' which far exceeds any palliatives of Western conscience of debt relief or increase in ODA. And while the EU and the United States are pushing 'partnership' deals with countries in the Global South that will be offered preferential trade relations, they are piecemeal and are structured around rich country strategies to liberalize Southern economies for Western capital penetration. Instead of global free trade, the mantra of the WTO and the rhetoric of US and EU ministries, bilateral free trade deals seem to be at the top of G8 country agendas. The EU is pushing such arrangements with the 77 Africa, Caribbean and Pacific countries, and the United States promotes the same with its trading 'partners'.

Commissioning poverty: an African response – a return to the future

It might be naïve to have expected innovation from the CFA or action to deliver effective and sustainable poverty reduction from the G8, but government and international agency pronouncements need to be set against the outcomes of policy initiatives. One overriding factor seems to have escaped the hyperbole of Blair, however. Simply put, a change in policy to genuinely bolster opportunity for Africa's poor held:

> No attraction for those who currently own Africa's debt, buy Africa's exports or arrange official capital assistance flows. Such ideas could come to seem rational only in a world that was in the process of rejecting the currently predominant ideology of the market. While this world must surely come, it is not yet in place, and meantime the African tragedy will unfold.
>
> (Leys 1994: 9)

Blair needed to do something special to persuade the G8 and EU in 2005 to pursue policies that would undermine the efficacy of their national economies: he could not and did not succeed in making G8 leaders subordinate national capitalist failings/interests to international outcries of Africa's felt needs. And neither was he able or willing to propose policy initiatives that would alter the international architecture of the world economy to challenge the hegemony of finance capital. Blair was also frustrated in delivering the much vaunted international financing facility, the brainchild of his Chancellor Gordon Brown, which was intended to usher in accelerated ODA to Africa.

The CFA and G8 initiatives continued to be steeped in the neoliberal bias of the age that glorified opportunity for international capital, and particularly finance capital. It is an age that declares the importance of increased participation in global economic activity, but it is Africa's participation in global activity that has shaped the continent's decline. The promise then is not that the African tragedy will be transformed but that the continent will continue its slide towards 'capitalism-produced barbarism' (Leys 1994: 1).

The tragedy is the worse because of elite African capitulation to the global neoliberal agenda. There has always been African resistance to Western characterization of Africa's development failures. That continues with workers and civil society and other popular organized and informal opposition to economic adjustment, corrupt political rulers and external prescriptions for rehabilitation.

Until the twenty-first century, African leaders had at many different times offered a critique of neoliberal views of crisis that had inevitably blamed Africans themselves for the problems they had. Indeed Africans have endured corrupt authoritarian bureaucrats, poorly conceived development projects and many other failures. But the constant reiteration that neoliberal market policies will *ipso facto* deliver growth and equity, development and inclusion, poverty reduction and more else besides is folly. It is not that markets are good or bad, but that that 'some countries or regions have the power to make the world market work to their advantage, while others do not, and have to bear the cost'. This power may be seen to lie in good or bad luck that has 'deep roots in a particular historical heritage that positions a country or a region favourably or unfavourably in relation to structural and conjunctural processes within the world system'. Africa's tragedy can broadly speaking be linked to a 'pre-colonial and colonial heritage which has gravely handicapped the region in the intensely competitive global environment engendered by the US response to the crisis of the 1970s' (Arrighi 2002: 16).

Placing Africa's crisis in the context of the global economic crisis does not absolve African elites from past mistakes, but it does help explain how and why some of those mistakes have occurred and what role the global hierarchy of states plays in keeping Africa in a subordinate position. African leaders have moved, albeit gradually, over the last 35 years to accept the neoliberal agenda that has been set for them by the IFIs and major bilateral donors. The embrace of the neoliberal agenda was cemented by the triumvirate of Presidents Obasanjo of Nigeria, Mbeki of South Africa and Bouteflika of Algeria. Asked by the

OAU to explore how Africa can escape its debt burden, these three presidents initiated the New Economic Partnership for African Development (NEPAD). Adopted by the OAU (renamed African Union in 2001), NEPAD promoted the idea of 'enhanced partnerships' between donors and African states, whereby the latter try to determine the important development projects and donors pool funds to ensure liquidity and the policing of governance and project management (www.dfa.gov.za/events/nepad.pdf).

NEPAD is the culmination of a period of movement by African leaders to meet with and agree to the IFI characterization of the continent's economic crisis. It has been met enthusiastically by Western leaders, and was much endorsed by the CFA and the World Bank. For many years African governments have been encouraged to take ownership of economic reform, cemented further by the PRSPs. The World Bank sees this as African countries taking 'more effective ownership of their own development', and the emphasis on partnerships that underpins NEPAD and PRSPs is seen as being at the heart of African strategies for greater transparency and accountability (www.web. worldbank.org accessed 7 February 2006). Here, the idea of ownership and partnership is very one-sided. The IFIs relinquish formal ownership of reform programmes, but impose conditions on the ways that host governments manage 'local policy initiatives' and disgruntled populations. The partnership agreements prioritize the liberalization of African economies that has taken place three times more quickly than tarriff reductions in the OECD. The losses from trade of these economies are estimated to have been $270 billion since 1975, and the emphasis on attracting foreign investment erases opportunities for local sourcing and retaining local value added. Such ownership makes it easier for donors to blame residual state intervention as the continuing cause of Africa's crises.

We can thus reject the characterization of Africa's crisis as rooted in 'the manner of governing' and 'difficult geography' (CFA 2005: 105–6) and instead recognize the historical context of the continent's adverse incorporation into the world economy. The economic crisis did not emerge until the mid-1970s, although the elements of failure were built into post-colonial settlements rooting the new economies in old trading and commodity dependence that benefited Europe and industrial countries.

The crisis of the mid-1970s emerged after good periods of economic growth and improvements in productivity. The crisis resulted and culminated in, among other things, a fourfold increase in the price of petroleum, a dramatic decline in raw material prices, increases in the cost of imported manufactures, and tariffs on the continent's exports levied by industrial countries to defend inefficient European and US agricultural interests. These externally driven causes were exacerbated as Thatcher, Kohl and Reagan came to power in the 1980s and drove up the cost of borrowing at a time of liquidity crisis in Africa, and the debt trap, so to speak, was complete.

African leaders responded with the Lagos Plan of Action, proposed by the Organization of African Unity (OAU) in 1980. It emphasized the external causes of the crisis without entirely exonerating people in Africa. Yet the IFI response to the Lagos Plan was very much to stress internal African inefficiencies rather than external market conditions. The World Bank's Berg Report, as it became known, blamed African leaders for the continent's plight and the policy failure of not getting the prices right: the African state was too big and too inefficient and corrupt (World Bank 1981).

By the mid-1980s, African elite response was to capitulate on the issue of getting markets reformed. A new OAU-authored document in 1985 was clearer on the mix of internal and external factors and won UN support for the need for the West to reduce protectionism and the debt burden and raise the prices paid for Africa's raw materials, including agricultural produce (OAU 1985).

The persistence of debt, however, and the dominance of structural adjustment led the 1980s to be seen, not only in Africa but elsewhere in the Global South, as the lost development decade. While it was relatively easy to destroy African state capacity, slash public expenditure and humble worker and peasant opposition to IFI policy, it proved much more difficult to generate economic growth. More than 30 countries in Africa embraced structural adjustment and as a result average incomes fell by 20 per cent in the 1980s and open unemployment quadrupled to 100 million; investment levels fell to levels lower than 1970 and the region's share of world markets fell by half to 2 per cent.

African elite response to economic adjustment in the 1980s was to offer an alternative framework for reform (ECA 1989). The IFIs ridiculed it, tried to block media attention surrounding its launch and failed to understand it as a document that tried to grasp the reality of the excesses of some African political leaders while also arguing for a further reappraisal of Africa's position in the world economy (ECA 1989). Although the World Bank response to Africa's alternative framework, and wider criticism of structural adjustment, was to say that there was a shared responsibility for the continent's decline, structural adjustment programmes (SAPs) persisted and African leaders were subordinated to the IFIs by debt, poverty and the recurrence of famine. African leaders and elite policy statements in the late 1980s and throughout the 1990s have seen a gradual and persistent shift towards neoliberal formulae for African development.

NEPAD was the culmination of the move by African leaders to embrace neoliberal orthodoxy (de Waal 2002; Owusu 2003; Chabal

2002; Loxley 2003). It meets many of the issues raised in a World Bank document in 1999 which followed John Wolfensohn's appointment as President in 1995, when poverty alleviation became an IFI rhetorical concern (World Bank 1999; compare Bond and Dor 2003). The World Bank's Comprehensive Development Framework (1999) stressed the importance of partnerships between donors and states, and emphasized that poverty strategy reduction papers, drafted by governments that want new donor and IFI assistance, would form part of all development agendas. IFIs were to also supervise governance reform in Africa. The IFIs and African advocates of NEPAD now share the same prescriptions for Africa's development. Optimists speak about an African renaissance (Cliffe 2002; Cheru 2002) and new partnerships to celebrate the potential for African economic development, but are seldom in a hurry to declare hope. Is there any understanding that Africa's economic ills go beyond problems of liquidity? This is solvable, it is declared, by improved ODA.

African 'insolvency' resulting from African's mismanagement of bountiful resources can be resolved equally easily by improving African state capacity. Amid all of the nonsense delivered by the CFA, IFIs and G8 countries there is no mention of Africa's weak political status *vis-à-vis* the West. There is no mention of the way in which externally driven reform has become so internalized by submissive African governments that the prospect of the much vaunted recognition of national circumstances seems forever forgotten. And it is with the failure to understand and try to resolve inequalities of power to shape economic reform that African leaders relinquish identity and submit to the externally driven and locally assisted primitive accumulation of the continent. The World Bank has spoken about the vision of 'hopeful realism', noting the return of positive economic growth (4.1 per cent for the continent in 2005), but the hope for accelerated growth and participation of the poor in decision making is empty rhetoric that provides an escape from the realism that is seen to be so important.

Fundamentally international policy makers failed to understand that Africa in the 1980s could simply not meet the needs of even very limited economic development. And they failed to understand why that was the case: a dramatic change in the fortune of Africa in the world economy after 1970, and SAPs that erased strategies of import substitution industrialization in Africa that were still only in very preliminary stages of development. The IFIs have singularly failed to understand the importance of why African economies failed to grow and why IFI prescriptions failed. This was because:

The singular concentration on 'opening up' the economy has undermined post-independence efforts to create, albeit lamely, internally coherent and articulated economies and an industrial structure that would be the basis for essential diversification of Africa's export base. The excessive emphasis on servicing the external sector has diverted scarce resources and political capacities away from managing the more fundamental basis for economic development. ... SAP, owing to its deflationary bias, has placed African economies on such a low-growth trajectory, which has then conditioned the levels and types of Africa's participation in the global economy.

(Mkandawire 2005: 174)

It is convenient for IFI ideologues to forget the SAP years, to argue the need to look forward rather than back and to continue to absolve themselves of responsibility for Africa's crisis. Yet the consequences of SAP are so extensive, and the political conditionalities that have replaced economic reform with PRSPs are so similar to reforms of the 1980s, that the continuities of the IFI-led agenda of the twenty-first century need to be addressed. The G8 continues to define what African development will be. Africa's debt burden ensured that its states became supplicants to the IFIs, and this despite the failure of SAP to promote growth in Africa. Moreover, the IFIs have striven to replace an emphasis on economic reform per se, reforms that failed to do anything other than stabilize economies and push them into the abyss of negative growth and collapse, with demands for political reform. Thus 'governance states' became the key to the second generation of IFI reforms in Africa (Harrison 2005).

Western preoccupation with governance reform in Africa is not new (World Bank 1992). The idea that Africa fails to develop because of its political shortcomings can be traced back to the ideology of post-Second World War modernization theory. The difference between the twenty-first century and the 1950s, however, is that the evidence for economic collapse and political turmoil in Africa is overwhelming. So too is the direct involvement in those failures by the IFIs. Thus in the contemporary period IFIs address perceived political failings in the capacity of public administration, civil service reform, the transparency of the judiciary, and more general resource management techniques. The rationale was that if economic reform continues to fail, it is not the policy that is flawed but its implementation due to poor African state capacity.

The importance of the need for capacity reform is advanced further by UK and other governments that are concerned with the idea of fragile states (Torres and Anderson 2004; Vallings and Moreno-Torres 2005). There are apparently 46 fragile states with 870 million people, representing 14 per cent of the world's population. They are defined as fragile because of weak capacity and lack of political will. In such states children are less likely to go to school, and there is chronic illness and poor growth. These states, such as Liberia, Sudan and Sierra Leone, are concerns for Western donors because they can spread insecurity, but the list goes further to include countries without conflict where the poor have difficulty sustaining themselves; Angola, Burundi, Cameroon, the Central African Republic, Kenya, Eritrea, Sierra Leone, Sudan and Gambia.

The terminological slippage of the term 'fragile' is made worse by the Department for International Development's (DfID) formulation of states that exhibit 'good enough governance' (Grindle 2002). These are states that are still eligible for the generosity of ODA because they can protect people from harm but where there is still corruption and underfunded capacity. Here the securitization of aid seems paramount (Abrahamsen 2004; Porteous 2005). Just ten years ago humanitarian assistance did not have such an overt security agenda, but especially (but not only) because of 9/11, UK and other G8 ODA has the overriding agenda of prioritizing and improving national and international security. At its crudest, the UK military train security personnel in 'fragile' states, Mozambique, Sierra Leone and Liberia (Duffield 2005).

In addition to the state security aspect, however, UK and IFI policy related to the promotion of governance agendas is to confuse the outcomes of policy failure with the causes of policy failure. It is also to gloss over the evidence that Western donors shape so extensively the policy options and the actual characterizations of policy choice available to Africa (what has been labelled the 'false self-evidence' of development discourse promoted by donors and the IFIs) that they determine what agendas are even placed on the table for development options and practices. This has been proven by the way in which corruption and policies to confront it have risen to the top of donor governance concerns (Polzer 2001), where the normal practice for donors is to assert the existence of problems and relationships without evidence: everything from linkage between development and market economics to fragile states and violence. The conviction with which donors then advance the new creeds for development ensure that governments and IFIs, whether the World Bank, DfID or USAID, define situations to ensure that they can then intervene to resolve the problems identified, problems that in fact have not been demonstrated.

On the issue of corruption, for example, if the West and the World Bank had been so concerned about this pernicious feature, it seems only of African society, why was it not eradicated by linkages of governance in the 1970s and 1980s? Why were the most corrupt and bestial regimes of Africa, the Central Africa Republic and Mobutu's Zaire, not bought to heel sooner than the twenty-first century? It was not because those social formations were less corrupt then; it was more that they served the geostrategic interests of the West's fight against communism.

Donors have not suddenly had a Damascene awakening about corruption and its drag on development. It is rather that the historical failings of donor economic adjustment, and the proximity of an easier assimilation by Africa leaders after decades of subjugation to donor funding, lead to greater ease of promoting political conditionality and political power over Africa. The irony of course is that the internalization of economic reform by African leaders has not led and will not lead to new structural transformations or sustained and widespread economic growth. It has already led to the failure to erase the conditions that led to the call for reforms, namely evidence of political elite rent seeking. Privatization of public assets for example has often led to the reinforcement of economic interests of political elites and rarely to the promotion of wider social ownership (Berthelemy et al 2004). The preferential access to state resources by elites has ensured the continued failure to promote national strategies for development and the persistence of regionalist and ethnic agendas (Hibou 2004, 2006).

We can now look beyond the ways in which poverty has been defined and strategies developed by the G8 to ameliorate it. We next consider some of the ways in which poverty has been generated in the Global South, particularly in Africa. I focus on the links between poverty and resources such as labour, land, minerals and food, and how the commoditization of these sustains inequality. Chapter 3 looks at the fundamental importance of labour.

3 Labour across frontiers? Capitalism's struggle for profit and order

This chapter examines the centrality of labour migration to the development of capitalism and the continued benefits that accrue to capital in general. I also explore the conflicts that emerge between capitalists over how labour migration should be incorporated into wage-labour relations. In doing this it is possible to see clearly why European and US politicians and commentators have falsely and erroneously characterized the early twenty-first century as a crisis of asylum seekers, refugees and economic migrants.

I highlight that an impetus for the emergence and sustainability of labour migration was for capitalists to try to move away from a view expressed by Marx that wage levels do not fall below the cost of reproduction and subsistence of the working class. We shall see that one of the horrors of labour migration has been that the strategy of capitalists has repeatedly been to undermine that dictum. They have done so by trying to ensure that non-capitalist societies pay the cost of the reproduction of labour, and this in some circumstances led to employers of labour paying migrants below the cost of subsistence: the assumption being that the worker's family provides its own subsistence.

There have been instances, such as South Africa, where state power during the apartheid era was used to enforce such a system with the strategic aim of promoting a rapid accumulation of capital. Elsewhere, in the United States for instance, the ambiguous and uncertain fate of migrants, notably in the agribusiness sectors in California where appalling wages are often well below costs of subsistence and reproduction, the state periodically intervenes. It is an intervention that questions not the morality of below-subsistence wages but the illegal status of migrants. There are, as we shall see below, occasional amnesties for those migrants but the recognition is never far away that it is usually much more difficult to pay below subsistence wages to 'legal' citizens than it is to illegal migrants.

In exploring capitalist strategies to push down the wages of labour migrants, I also highlight the contradictions that states are confronted with in the West. This is that, while at different times it is important for sections of capital to super-exploit foreign workers, governments in the EU and the United States are pressured to moderate xenophobic populist bigotry that calls for clampdowns on immigration and asylum.

A global migration crisis?

The total number of international migrants has more than doubled since 1960, from 76 million to about 175 million.[1] But even though world population only doubled from 3 billion in 1960 to 6 billion in 2000, international migrants represented only 2.9 per cent of world population compared with 2.5 per cent in 1960 (IOM 2005: 379). Despite this small proportion of the world population, the perceived problems for developed countries are expressed by media and politicians in those countries as a struggle to maintain stability as the economically poor and socially desperate in the world's poorest countries struggle to gain entry into the 'modern' societies of the EU and North America. These siren appeals to keep the poor from the gateways into Europe have been intensified following security concerns after the 9/11 attacks. Yet evidence suggests the greatest increase in migration since 2000 has taken place in East and South-East Asia. Migration is also seen as crucial to maintain economies of low fertility levels in the United States and Europe.

The much vaunted era of 'globalization' has readily welcomed the flow of international capital, but not of people. And while a fear of foreigners has been exacerbated by attaching labels of criminality to certain types of migrants, notably those seeking asylum and those without documentation, assumptions are made that the contemporary 'crisis' of migration is new and has negative consequences for advanced capitalist countries. But migration has been central to the way in which capitalism has developed and it has been an indicator of the way in which states have been organized hierarchically.

It is important to understand the international context of migration as a dynamic of global poverty and the global power of major capitalist states and capitalist employers of labour. Central to this understanding is the knowledge that most migration takes place within Southern countries and between neighbouring states in the Global South. Dominant Western media recount the tales of the fate of migrants who die while they are being transported into Europe or the United States. Most political focus is upon Europe's inability to cope with labour migration especially after 1990, the break-up of the former Soviet Union as well as Yugoslavia, and 'state collapse' in sub-Saharan Africa. The crisis of migration is thus seen to be a crisis for developed Northern countries suffering from 'swamping' by foreigners and the lawlessness and excessive demand for EU and US social service provision.[2]

In contrast migration for millions in Africa and elsewhere is a strategy for survival and the transformation of livelihoods (McDowell and de Haan 1997). There is nothing automatic about the poor simply moving en masse to the Global North. If this was the case, swamping really would have happened many decades ago. It is not migrants from poor countries that dominate the figures for global migration, as most international migrants originate from middle-income countries like the Philippines and those in North Africa (de Haas 2005). We need to look to other reasons to explain why the language of 'swamping' by international 'scroungers' and the untruths about threats from a deluge of 'bogus' asylum seekers are used by Western policy makers to shore up the political fiction that the West's ills are shaped by an influx of the global poor.

In 2002, Northern fear of asylum seekers, and immigration issues more generally, led Canada, Germany, the Netherlands, the United States and the UK to spend US$17 billion trying to stop immigration: that amount of money was two-thirds as much as those countries delivered in official development assistance (Martin 2003: 5). Aid budgets in this context are another aspect of serving Western interests. This time the self-interest of the imperialist states is to restrict movement of people in poor countries to more productive Northern economies. The foolishness of Western policy makers here is to fail to appreciate that labour migration and the movement of people seeking asylum has always been an integral part of capitalist development. The biggest forced movement of people, from Africa to the Caribbean, for example, was the bedrock upon which capitalist development in Europe was founded, and the commoditization of land and labour in West Africa and elsewhere.

This chapter explores how the character of capitalism has been shaped by the role of migration and the purchase of labour power or the wage–labour relationship. The position of non-national workers is shaped by the demands of 'capital in general' to increase value and of conflicts with particular sections of capital for a segmented labour market, divided in large part by workers who do not 'belong' in the host country, whether they be temporary or long-term labour migrants or asylum seekers.

Capital needs supplies of labour, and supplies with the necessary skill mix to do the work that is required by capitalists. Yet capitalists are not unified in their labour needs. Many may require abundant supplies of cheap and unskilled labour that need less training, or receive it on the job if these people are permanent enough not to leave before the costs of their training are recouped by employers. Other employers need higher-skilled, more permanent workers that are neither temporary nor seasonal. I shall explore this tension between capitalists at a general level, illustrating with reference to conflicts between employers and the state in the United States and elsewhere.

The state is the guarantor of capital's ability to reproduce and expand value and to sustain flows of labour to ensure valorization. Yet the state also responds to the xenophobia of its citizens. And because nation states were partly founded upon the relationship of citizenship with place of birth, politicians are often challenged by the perceived conflict of delivering the interests of capital in general and those of particular capitalists or racial views of citizenship and the right to work.

In short, labour migration and forced migration like asylum seeking pose a contradiction for capitalism in the twenty-first century. And migration is at the heart of the ways in which the poverty of so many is shaped and reproduced in the contemporary world. It is actually a tension at the heart and making of capitalism itself. This is a contradiction between ensuring the reproduction of value on an extended scale for capitalism, and maintaining order and power domestically so nation states can respond to calls to limit 'foreigners' in host countries.

One aspect of the economic internationalization of capital, which has increased the possibility for greater profits for capital, has been the improvement in communications and transport. But these improvements have also helped generate transnational communities that foster multiple identities and multiple citizenships. As Castles notes, 'All this is deeply unsettling both for those who exercise power in national contexts and for populations which feel threatened by globalization' (Castles 1999: 7). Western states' response to this perceived challenge has been to assemble fortress-like 'protection' to their borders. And the rationale to limit the movements of labour was given greater strength after 9/11, the July 2005 bombs in London and the furore over released 'foreigners' not deported from the UK in May 2006. After 9/11 for instance, the US immigration service was converted into the Office for Homeland Security, and the attack served to legitimize US restrictions on the movements of labour. That effectively perpetuated a hierarchically regulated differential world labour market. This is a racially organized international division of labour that helps foster, among Northern workers, the importance of protecting their 'civilization' from people living in the Global South and of keeping people there in poverty.

Xenophobia feeds on and further fuels a transition within the study of the causes and consequences of migration from its possible development impacts towards a security discourse. In doing so it provides cover for the Northern preoccupation with the creation of so-called safe havens or secure zones for refugees (Hermele 1997). During periods of prolonged economic growth, racists have generally greater difficulty in exploiting xenophobia and multi-racial communities are seen as more secure from a politics of hatred. During economic crises however, when there are more acute struggles over employment and access to declining resources, racist attacks on 'foreign' workers increase. Since 9/11 the war on terror, Islamophobia and fuelled fears of 'outsiders' have stigmatized migrants.

Labour migration has been central to the way in which capitalism emerged. Labour migration has also posed questions of order and power for capitalism. In its contemporary form this challenge emerges from the escalation of asylum applications and the trafficking of people into Europe and the United States since 1990. It has taken the unprecedented form in the United States of mass rallies and demonstrations in May 2005 by non-US labour against the horrors of employment conditions for illegal workers without rights and security. Although President G. W. Bush in the early 2000s offered the prospect of an amnesty for 'illegals', that melted away as security issues dominated US and international politics after 9/11.

The persistence of labour migration in all its different forms is a cause and consequence of uneven and combined capitalist development. But this unevenness must not be allowed to veil the conflicts and complexity of struggles that take place within sending and receiving countries. These are struggles in the sending countries relating to who migrates, when and how, and what kind of social and economic consequences there will be for those left behind. In short, why do so many in the Global South stay behind rather than migrate, especially as the explanation so often given for migrants to be in the developed world is that they are attracted by the better standards of living in Europe and the United States (Faist 2000: 6)? And there are struggles in the receiving country between the state and capital over what kinds of regulation and control should be applied to migrants, and between governments and citizens over what rights might be conceded to those seeking employment and safety.

This idea of struggle is important, and we can see how some of it is worked out by reference to the way in which employers in the United States recruit and hire 'illegals' or undocumented workers. It supplements the more innovative discussions of labour migration and forced migration that have used the language of 'turbulence' or 'regimes' of labour (Papastergiadis 2000; Van Hear 1998).

The dominant neoclassical approach to finding the reason for the persistence of labour migration is to explore the motivation of people who migrate. This is usually examined in relation to the 'push' factors of poverty, war, household and other conflict, and the 'pull' factors of economic growth and improved information about potential host countries, as well as the increased presence of traffickers who organize the movements of migrants. These factors are important to document but my focus is elsewhere. The language of push and pull and of forced and voluntary migration is too simplistic. To a large extent all migration is forced: the imperatives driving mobility reduce the possibility for choice. The language of push and pull disguises the significance of the capital relation: the centrality in capitalism for the realization of the capital–wage-labour link wherein labour power realizes value. Migration – whether rural–urban or inter-state – is central to that. It is also important to note that rising incomes in the Global South increase the likelihood of migration for work rather than lessen it. This has a clear policy implication at a time when the EU suggests that increasing aid to sub-Saharan Africa will slow migration to Europe.

Migration and the internationalization of capital

Migration and an international market for labour

There are broadly three major historical periods of labour migration (Faist 2000):

- the age of discovery in the seventeenth to nineteenth centuries
- the white settler European migrations and those of indentured labour from Asia in the mid-nineteenth century to early twentieth century
- the post-Second World War period of predominantly Southern migration to the capitalist North.

This historical process established a world market for labour. The so-called 'age of discovery' can be located as early as the fourteenth century, with European merchant capitalist expansion to West Africa and the East Indies that undermined and transformed indigenous relations of production and social reproduction. The peak of the European colonization and the use of forced labour, within Africa and the Caribbean with transported slaves for the plantations, took place between the seventeenth and nineteenth centuries. At least 2 million European migrants and 12 million African slaves were involved in one of the largest historical movements of people. Probably the same number of slaves died in transit across the Atlantic. And here of course is the dramatic difference between the slave trade and the movements of white, albeit somewhat persecuted and poor, European settlers.

The 'triangular trade' was the name given to activities of mainly British merchants who sold goods produced in British colonies to West Africa. These goods were then exchanged for slaves on the Gold and Slave Coasts of West Africa and the slaves transported to work on plantations in the Caribbean, Brazil and the southern states of America which were owned by Portuguese, Spanish, English, French and Danish merchants. As the acreage of land under cultivation of sugar increased so too did the demand for slave labour (Bean 1975). The triangular trade boosted capitalist development in Britain. 'By 1750 there was hardly a trading or a manufacturing town in England which was not in some way connected with the triangular or direct colonial trade' (Williams 1981).[3]

The second period of large-scale migration from the middle of the nineteenth century to the start of the twentieth century had two major elements. The first of these was indentured or coolie labour. This effectively provided a bridge between slavery and modern day labour migration. Perhaps more than 30 million Indian and Chinese workers were recruited, notably by the British, to work in different parts of the Empire. Indentured workers' labour power was secured under fiercely repressive contracts, often for as long as eight years. During that time such labourers were bound to work for their employers. They were employed on building projects at abysmal rates of pay and with extremely harsh conditions of service. They undercut the price of local labour, which often included released slaves who had won their freedom but not the right to work at wages set by the value of their labour power.

The second major element of migration during the height of industrialization in Europe involved white settlers moving to the Americas, Australia and South Africa. These settlers were a mix of craftsmen, artisans and others, including peasants, political dissidents and religious minorities, who left Europe for what became the Anglo-Saxon settler colonies. Between 1850 and 1914, 50 million Europeans migrated, 70 per cent to North America, 12 per cent to South America and 9 per cent to South Africa, Australia and New Zealand (King 1995: 9).

The post-Second World War period confirmed the 'changing nature of globalization from colonial and imperial expressions of the concept to the spread of economic empires based on the hegemony of capital' (King 1995: 18). While there were clear continuities from the past with regard to labour migration from ex-colonies to the UK, for instance – hence the predominance in the 1950s of flows of labour from India, Pakistan, the West Indies and neighbouring Ireland – other leading capitalist economies in Europe, notably Germany but also France and the United States, became centres of immigration. Labour migration after 1945 was drawn to the UK by the imperative of post-war reconstruction, as cheap labour in construction, transport and health sectors was necessary to promote new rounds of capital accumulation. Other major migratory flows in the post-war period included the structuring of the apartheid South African economy around systemic migration to coal, gold and diamond mines from the Bantustans and neighbouring southern African states. Migration in the early 1970s was driven in the Gulf and Middle-Eastern oil-exporting economies that used petrodollars to fund large-scale construction projects. These were built by immigrant labour as the indigenous labour force was either too small or simply refused menial work.

The different phases of labour migration have overlapped. This is illustrated by contemporary evidence in Brazil, Sudan, Central Africa and also Egypt and elsewhere in the Middle East of indentured labour and slavery. The early phases of migration confirm its centrality for the development of capitalism, the dependence upon coercive, extra-market forms of labour hire and coercive labour relations that have underpinned primitive accumulation and capitalist development and which have never universally disappeared.

Slavery, indenture and wage-labour relations have all been part of uneven and combined capitalist development. They have been a cause and a consequence of the commoditization process of labour and have been central to the growth and character of capitalism and its partic-ular historical development. But discussion about labour migration has focused too much on the increased mobility of labour and increased opportunities for transportation that may have promoted it. That debate has reduced the importance of exploring the crucial role all labour plays in the relations of production that are forged to increase value for capital and reinforce global inequality. Although particular phases of capitalist development cannot be 'read off' from the type of labour recruitment, labour power is a core element in increasing the value of capital. As Karl Marx noted:

> Through the exchange with the worker, capital has appropriated labour itself; labour has become one of its moments, which now acts as a fructifying vitality upon its merely existent and hence dead objectivity.
>
> (Marx 1977: 298)

Marx likened labour to yeast in that when it is thrown into the capi-talist production process it ferments and creates value. It is thus not teleology or functionalism that reports the relationship between migrant labour and the historical spread of capitalism and the persistent poverty of migrants as a category of labour. It is to recognize that without labour, capitalism and the creation of value would not endure. Different phases of capitalism have drawn on different types of labour for value creation as a consequence of struggles between capital and labour, and of the ability of capitalists to transform rela-tions of production in the Global South and to depend, to varying degrees, upon labour migration for economic growth in the industrial North. There is no necessary relationship between the type of exploita-tion of labour and the particular form of capitalism. As Miles has noted:

Migratory processes are [therefore] spatial movements of people to different sites of class relations, difference being understood in the dual sense of either a different position in the relations of production, or in the sense of a historically distinct set of the same relations of production. Migrants are always class agents, and migration refers to the movement of people from one class site to another, both within and between social formations and, therefore, potentially (but not necessarily) from one mode of production to another.

(Miles 1987: 6–7)

The important point is that whenever possible capitalist interests will seek to pay their labour force below the costs of its reproduction and subsistence. Where indigenous systems of production and social reproduction in the Global South are unable to meet the costs of the reproduction of that migrant labour a crisis intensifies. That crisis is usually borne in the rural areas of the Global South. It is from there that most migrants emerge, and the hardship is particularly felt by women in those communities that are under acute pressure to meet the reproduction needs of young male migrants in particular. The labour migrants left in the hands of employers seeking to 'super-exploit' them in the capitalist heartlands are left to fend for themselves in societies where politicians are blind to migrant needs. Under these circumstances – of rural community crisis in the Global South and migrant worker poverty – the lie in globalization theory becomes clear. The impersonal theories of capitalism and markets need to be set alongside the horror of labour migrant experiences and poverty and the destruction of communities in the Global South.

Contemporary movements of labour

The twenty-first century began with one out of every 35 people in the world being an international migrant (IOM 2003: 4).

In 2000, 17.5 million people were estimated to be international

Table 3.1 World population and international migrants, 1965–2050

Year	Total world population (millions)	International migrants (millions)	Migrants as a percentage of total world population
1965	3,333	75	2.3
1975	4,066	84	2.1
1985	4,825	105	2.2
2000	6,057	175	2.9
2050	9,000	230	2.6

Source: Adapted from IOM (2003: 5). Figures for 2050 are extrapolations.

migrants, including undocumented workers, and almost half of all migrants were women. Much of this female labour was employed in low-wage and low-skilled work where workplace conditions were poor and union representation negligible. This included women from Asia working in the Middle East (often as maids and domestics), women from the Maghreb in southern Europe and Latinos in the US domestic and agricultural sectors. As we have already noted the origin and destination of migrants varies.

The biggest movements of labour are within and between countries and regions in the Global South. In 2000, for example, there were 16.3 million international migrants in Africa, representing about 9 per cent of the global migrant stocks (IOM 2005: 33). Official statistics fail to record the huge scale of migration that is internal to countries in the South, although in some cases the figures are inflated in the hope that fears of swamping in the Maghreb from sub-Saharan Africa might lead to greater help from the EU to states like Tunisia, Algeria and Morocco (Keenan 2006). Most migration tends to be regional in nature. One of the largest recent migration systems was a key feature of apartheid: migrants from countries neighbouring South Africa (and from the Bantustans within South Africa) moved to work in mines and agriculture in South Africa itself (Bundy 1979; Burawoy 1976; First 1982).[4]

Industrial countries account for about 40 per cent of labour flows, up from 36.5 per cent in 1965. In Latin America, for instance, much migration takes place within Central America: Nicaraguans to Costa Rica, Salvadorians to Guatemala and Guatemalans to Mexico. And in the Andean region Colombians migrate to Venezuela and Ecuadorians and Peruvians to Argentina. In the Southern Cone, Brazil has at least a million migrants from Argentina, Uruguay, Chile and Paraguay. There are also large migration flows *within* Brazil. Since the mid-1980s there

Table 3.2 World population and migrant stocks by continent, 2000

	Total population (millions)	Migrant stocks (millions)	Percentage of population
Asia	3672.3	49.7	1.4
Africa	793.6	16.2	2.1
Europe	727.3	56.1	7.7
Latin America/Caribbean	518.8	5.9	1.1
Northern America	313.1	40.8	13.0
Oceania	30.5	5.8	19.1
Global	6056.7	174.7	2.9

Source: IOM (2003: 29).

has been a reversal of European and Asian migration into Venezuela and the Southern Cone countries, and an increase in intra-regional movements of migrants searching for work in Costa Rica, Paraguay and Mexico. Many Argentines have left debt and economic crisis to search for work in neighbouring countries, and many who went to find work in Argentina in the 1990s have left. Economic uncertainty in Brazil in the 1990s helped motivate more than 300,000 to find work in Paraguay. About 2 million Colombians live in Venezuela, having escaped local conflict, and about 2.2 million Peruvians live abroad.

Another region that has attracted migrants for work is the Middle East. The oil sector, construction and domestic labour have depended in varying degrees upon foreign workers since the early 1970s. Foreign workers comprise 25 per cent of workers in Saudi Arabia, 65 per cent in Kuwait, 67 per cent in Qatar and 70 per cent in the United Arab Emirates. Migrants in the Middle East come from Bangladesh, Sri Lanka, the Philippines and Thailand, and also from the Near East, Egypt and Sudan (IOM 2003: 34). Although there appears to be a 're-nationalization' project in many Middle East states, as preference is given in skilled work to nationals, non-state employers prefer immigrant labour for the greater flexibility it offers and the greater leverage employers can exercise over foreigners.

In Asia, China's diaspora population has continued to grow, reaching perhaps as many as 50 million, and the improved skill base of Indian workers has made them attractive for other Asian countries. Most migrants in Asia come from the Philippines, Bangladesh and Indonesia. Seven million of the Philippines population of 85 million work outside their country of origin and have received considerable state encouragement to do so. Many countries in Asia attract labour from neighbouring states because of a demographic transition: the movement from labour surplus to deficit. These include Thailand, Singapore, South Korea and Japan. The major flows are from Indonesia and the Philippines to Malaysia, Singapore and the Gulf, and from Cambodia, Laos, Viet Nam and Myanmar to Thailand (IOM 2003: 35).

Although the United States and EU member countries are perceived to be the prime 'target' for economic migrants, it gives a false representation of international labour movements to imply that these are the only destinations for labour migrants. Since 1985 Asia and Pacific countries have become centres for a burgeoning migration business. Economic reform and many local wars in Africa have promoted migration between African states and have also increased the numbers of migrants in the Maghreb in transition to Europe (Baldwin-Edwards 2006).

In Latin America and the Middle East economic, political and environmental crises have generated labour mobility. Of significance for

Table 3.3 Labour migration in Africa

Country/region of origin	Destination	Types of work
Sub-Saharan Africa	Europe and Libya	Mixed: construction, agriculture, domestic service
Algeria, Morocco, Tunisia, Egypt, Nigeria, Chad, Democratic Republic of Congo	Europe	Mixed: skilled, unskilled, refugees
Burkina Faso, Niger, Mali	Côte d'Ivoire, Ghana, Nigeria, Senegal	Construction, agriculture, domestic service
Liberia, Sierra-Leone, Chad, Togoland, Mauritania, Guinea Bissau	Guinea, Côte d'Ivoire	Refugees, informal sector
DRC, Rwanda, Burundi, Uganda and return migration	Equatorial Guinea, Gabon, Cameroon, Tanzania, SA, Europe	Skilled workers, doctors and teachers, refugees
Up to 1999: Malawi, Lesotho, Swaziland, Mozambique	SA, Zimbabwe, Zambia, Botswana	Mining, agriculture, domestic service
Post-1999: Zimbabwe	SA, Tanzania, Botswana	Refugees, informal sector

the types of migration flows that have characterized the 1990s has been a reduction in the importance of colonial relationships that shaped destination countries for migrants. For example, there has been a reduction in numbers of migrants from Algeria to France, Turkey to Germany and the Commonwealth to the UK. But there was perhaps too much invested by commentators in this somewhat stylized view of the historical pattern of labour migration. The conventional view in the UK, for instance, has been one that focused on the significance of New Commonwealth, or non-white, immigration after the Second World War. Immigrants from the Caribbean and then Bangladesh were first welcomed to fill gaps in the labour market in health provision and transport and construction, but as economic decline replaced growth, racial conflict led to immigration controls. By 1971 the influx of immigrants from the New Commonwealth had dramatically slowed and UK immigration policy had 'settled' to issues of no more non-white immigration and the declared importance of racial integration (Glover et al 2001: 7).

However, this is perhaps only a partial explanation of the reasons behind migration. For one thing much of the 'policy' of immigration was not led solely by market forces. And the need for labour and also labour migration was not uni-directional into the UK. There was return migration and also emigration of British nationals from the UK in the 1980s and 1990s. Immigration did not dramatically halt after 1971. In short there was substantial net emigration throughout the 1950s, 1960s and 1970s. UK policy makers after the Second World War were nevertheless mindful of the need to cope with what was seen to be a shortfall of labour in 1946 of 1.3 million (Cohen 1987).

Reliance upon immigrant labour was not inevitable and neither was it driven solely by the market. The UK could have continued to rely on a more evenly and permanently incorporated female labour force that had become so important during the Second World War. Alternatively, it could have relied upon intensifying the rate of exploitation; make the British working class work harder by lengthening the working day or accelerating the automation of factory production. What the UK relied upon was a mix of intensifying the exploitation of the British working class *and* immigrant labour.

Dependence upon a foreign labour force had many advantages. Particularly in the early days of incorporation, it was a labour force that was cheaper, sometimes less aware of its rights, and because it was seen largely to be temporary, there were savings on the costs of renewing and reproducing it. Family wages were not necessary if the workers' dependants were not resident in the UK. It was also cheaper to renew the physical energies of single men than provide the costs of supporting them and their families. There was also a likelihood, as racist prejudice became more evident, that a labour market segmented along racial cleavages might reduce working-class solidarity and collective actions against the interests of capital. As Cohen has noted: 'Whenever the balance of advantage tilts to the side of organized labour, capitalists move from seeking to subordinate labour to seeking subordinate labourers' (1987: 252).

Trends in migration into the UK and EU did change in the 1990s. Net migration into the UK increased and this has been explained in terms of the impacts of globalization: a strong UK labour market, and improved transport networks that reduced transaction costs and helped to improve information flows between migrants seeking job opportunities. In the 1990s within the EU, all countries became countries of net migration as the historically labour-exporting poorer countries of southern Europe became net labour receivers.[5] Portugal for example received migrants from Cape Verde and Brazil, and Greece from the Balkans and Near East. While France attracted the greater number of migrants from the Maghreb and its former colonies, not least as the Democratic Republic of Congo imploded, most of the EU was affected by two processes: the conflict in Bosnia and Kosovo, and the increase in asylum seekers. In 2002 the EU population increased by more than a million, of which 680,000 were international migrants – slightly fewer than in 1999. Net migration was highest in the UK, Italy and Germany. These three countries accounted for more than 60 per cent of the total net migration to the EU (Eurostat 2002: 1).

In absolute terms the destination country with the largest number of economic migrants is the United States. In 2000, 28.4 million foreign-born people, excluding undocumented workers, lived in the United States; about 10 per cent of the population (IOM 2005: 84). The United States has about 850,000 legal permanent entrants each year and 1.5 million entries with temporary visas (IOM 2003: 31; Martin 2003: 18). Immigration reforms in 1965 increased the level of migration to the United States as country quotas were lifted and replaced with priority for family reunions and skills seen to be necessary to enhance the economy. Reforms in 1990 placed an emphasis upon greater diversity of migrants, lessening the focus on family reunions; 70 per cent of immigrants are people with families already in the United States. Only between 7 per cent and 9 per cent were refugees or asylum seekers. In 2000 there were about 30 million non-migrant visitors to the United States who were tourists, workers or students (Martin 2003: 20).

Asylum seeking and forced migration

For governments in EU and North America, the greatest threat posed by labour, apart from the hyped security consideration, is the concern of challenges to national sovereignty and racial harmony. Challenges to these are seen to emanate from mushrooming asylum claims. Between 1980 and 1989 the United Nations Humanitarian Committee for Refugees (UNHCR) recorded 2.2 million applications for political asylum, but for the period 1990–99 there were more than 6 million claims. Yet in the period 1992–2001 only 12 per cent of claims were granted refugee status by the 16 countries of the Inter-governmental Consultations on Asylum, Refugee and Migration Policies in Europe, North America and Australia. The EU in 2000 granted asylum to less than 20 per cent of those applying for it, although most that had been denied their applied status were not returned home.

The failure to return asylum seekers led to tightening entry controls on people that sought refugee status. Governments and agencies claimed that applications were made by people who had no legitimate claim to escape persecution: they were merely economic migrants without the skills that would make them attractive to employers. And the idea of 'bogus' asylum seekers, the threat they posed, and the threat from migrants who offended, were sentenced, and were not deported from the UK after serving a sentence cost the Home Secretary Charles Clarke his job. Clarke was sacked in May 2006 for failing to keep tabs on criminals who were immigrants. But at the heart of that crisis was a fear in government that anti-immigration rhetoric, by the press and fascist parties like the British National Party, could have longer-term negative consequences for the re-election of a UK Labour government. Rather than address the importance of migration for the UK economy, it became convenient and politically expedient for Blair's administration to appear to pander to racist bigotry.

The increase in asylum applications, 9/11 and the 'war on terror' have accelerated the securitization of labour migration issues. A paradox is that governments in the EU and United States have tried to placate domestic opposition to asylum seekers by tightening border controls. In doing this, however, the United States does not seem to have heeded lessons from its own recent past. In fact, the US immigration service budget increased threefold in 1980–2000, during which time the number of illegals entering the United States to find work also tripled from 3 million to 9 million (Sutcliffe 2003: 267). The reality is that as states try to show their toughness on immigration, defending what politicians identify as the security and wellbeing of national citizens, smugglers and traffickers of human beings intensify their efforts to defeat detection.

Only a tiny proportion of the world's 175 million migrants are those that cause fear of swamping in developed countries by asylum seekers and migrants without bona fide immigration documents. Their significance, however, and the debate about them can be best characterized by the cases of Europe and the United States. These cases highlight the securitization of labour issues and also, as we see later, the way in which governments manage labour influx, particularly for skilled labour needs, while criminalizing the needs of unskilled workers.

The United States and 'illegals'

Most immigrants into the United States come from Mexico and Asia. These movements have at different times been subjected to attempts at 'regularization', including in 2006 rhetoric by President G.W. Bush of an amnesty for illegals already resident in the United States. That rhetoric was sidelined, however, by prioritization of US homeland security rhetoric and foreign policy concerns with Iraq and Iran. But they were kept on the policy agenda by immigrant workers themselves who brought much of the United States to a standstill in large-scale strikes and demonstrations early 2006.

There are about 12 million foreigners in the United States who do not have either immigration or work papers. Half of these are Mexican and most gain illegal entry along Mexico's 3,200 km border with the United States. Since 9/11 security issues have dominated US immigration issues, ruining any chance of building on the North American Free Trade Agreement (NAFTA) to promote a freer movement of labour between the two countries. Fanciful as that suggestion might have been, the demise of any relaxation in border controls between the United States and Mexico reduced the refugee inflow into the United States more generally after 2001. The number of refugees admitted to the United States fell from 68,426 in 2001 to 28,455 in 2003, the lowest level of arrivals of refugees for five years: 47,000 for example were admitted in 2000–01.

The attack on 9/11 scuppered a US–Mexico agreement on Mexico's economic migrants. Early in 2001 the two leaders agreed to place migration among major bilateral issues, to promote the legal status of Mexicans living in the United States who did not have permission to reside. US policy makers have become so concerned with the 'threat' of migrants into the United States that they have considered ending the right of birth citizenship for 'illegal aliens' (Kyle and Dale 2001: 51).

Since 9/11, securitization of US borders has clearly focused on controlling the influx of people while not inhibiting the movements of commodities. Thus the US–Canada Smart Border Declaration of 2001 declared the importance of promoting regional security and secured movement of people and goods. And the US–Mexico Border Partnership Agreement of 2002 sought to establish 'smarter' borders: improved supervision of legal immigrants but above all the safe passage of goods and services. Improved information sharing of migrant data between Canada and the United States and Mexico and the United States has stigmatized labour seeking work, its mobility and freedom of movement.

The United States has increased surveillance of people seeking to visit the United States by requiring interviews with consular officials for visa applicants. The emphasis has been on applicants from Arab countries and from Muslim countries. An electronic database in 2003 began tracking student visitors. New technology was introduced at US ports to monitor, photographically record and fingerprint visitors, and a new National Security Entry–Exit Registration System required foreigners from designated areas, again mostly from Arab and Muslim countries, to be subject to 'special registration'. Enhanced security concerns in the United States have intensified the monitoring of people that accompanied the USA Patriot Act of 2001, which gave wide-ranging powers to the state to watch, arrest and deport people suspected of being terrorists.

There has always been a keen debate and often an antagonistic relationship in the United States between the employers of 'illegals', especially capitalist farmers and the hirers of unskilled labour, and the US state. It is not a simple relationship. US politicians representing large farm areas have often colluded with the hiring of illegals because of the benefit to their constituents. Mid-West politicians, for example, have been fearful for some years of a clampdown on meatpackers who hire illegals because it harmed hog and cattle farmers. Disruption to meatpacking increased the supply of livestock that could not be slaughtered, lowering the price of meat.

Yet the United States has increasingly prioritized security issues and the need to reduce the number of undocumented workers while seeking to safeguard labour inflow in areas of scarce skills. The challenge for the United States has been to deliver on its security agenda while not alienating constituents who depend upon undocumented workers. US state agencies in fact trebled the number of border guards with Mexico before 9/11, leading on average to the death of one migrant every day as they tried to make more inhospitable and hazardous crossings into the United States. Washington seems to have managed to escape a lot of the criticism from capitalists regarding the state policy on illegals because state agencies have focused on the criminalization of smugglers and traffickers. In doing that the state has distinguished between the 'industry' of the immigrant and the 'evil' of gangsters that transport or facilitate the movement of undocumented workers.

In the United States, the industry most dependent on undocumented workers is the food sector. There have been many examples in recent years of that dependency. This included in 2001 the prosecution of the biggest food processor for conspiring to smuggle illegals to work in its plants (*New York Times* 21 December 2001). Such was the consternation in the United States at the prosecution of Tyson Foods that commentators noted the US food industry would be severely disrupted if restrictions on the numbers of migrants into the sectors were reduced and if wage rates were increased.[6] The economic gain to the meatpackers from employing illegal labour from Mexico and Guatemala was easy to see. In the mid-1980s packers got US$18 an hour compared with the rate of just US$6 per hour paid to illegals in 2001. About 25 per cent of packers in the mid-West are illegals according to the US Department of Agriculture.

The *New York Times* noted in several articles in the early 2000s that the meat packing industry, but also farm employers, had profited significantly by paying low wages, intensifying the pace of work and hiring people who were prepared to work in hazardous conditions. The companies took advantage of illegal labour because workers always had the threat hanging over them of being sent home. The high turnover of staff ensured that the employers' costs were kept to a minimum as workers did not qualify for holidays or insurance. Foreign labour worked especially in fruit and vegetables. In California, 10 million immigrants comprise 30 per cent of the states' population and a third of its workforce. Foreign labour milks cows in Wisconsin and Oregon, and processes and packs potatoes in Idaho. As the President of the Potato Growers of Idaho noted in December 2001: 'Immigrant labour, whether it's legal or illegal, is critical. Most Mexicans here [in the United States] will have papers but the farmers won't have any. There is real good counterfeit stuff out there' (New York Times 21 December 2001).

The US Department of Agriculture estimated at the start of 2000 that 40 per cent of the million farm labourers in the United States were illegals. And even as the US government was trying to control the flow of Mexican labour, deporting as many as 150,000 a year, it is important to note that Mexicans abroad sent only 15 per cent of their income home, spending 85 per cent of it locally. The Mexican community contributes US$82.1 billion a year to the US GDP (IOM 2003: 148).

Europe and 'illegals'

Western Europe had 3.8 million foreign citizens in 1950, 11 million in 1971 and 20.5 million by 2000; an additional 8 million were foreign born. The main recipients of labour inflows, in absolute terms were Germany and France. Table 3.4 details the figures of migration flow for Western Europe.

By the end of the 1990s asylum seekers and undocumented workers were perceived by EU politicians to be a major challenge to immigration policy. Calls for a common EU policy were voiced at a special meeting in Tampere (Finland) in October 1999 to develop partnership with countries of origin to help manage migration and to develop a common European asylum system. This latter was to be based on the Geneva Convention and to respect the rights of migrants. Yet this declared policy, linked with an agreement in Cotonou (Benin) in June 2000 that supported partnership between the EU and African, Caribbean and Pacific (ACP) countries to help reduce migration by dealing with local sustainable development and poverty eradication in poor southern countries, has been repeatedly challenged.

The EU Commission noted in November 2000 that, notwithstanding the need for a common EU policy on migration issues, each state needed to exercise its own policy shaped by national priorities. These national concerns spilled over into a diplomatic row between Britain and France in 2001–02. The UK government insisted that France close the Red Cross

Table 3.4 Net migration flows in Western Europe, 1960–2000

	Average annual net migration balance			Cumulative net flow 1960–1990		1990–2000		1960–2000	
	1960–1990	1990–2000	1960–2000	in 000s	as % of population	in 000s	as % of population	in 000s	as % of population
Austria	1.3	3.6	1.9	308	4.0	294	3.6	602	7.5
Belgium	0.9	1.5	1.0	247	2.5	153	1.5	400	3.9
Denmark	0.6	2.5	1.1	97	1.9	129	2.4	226	4.2
Finland	-1.0	1.3	-0.5	-140	-2.8	64	1.2	-76	-1.5
France	2.1	1.0	1.8	3,270	5.8	585	1.0	3,855	6.5
Germany	2.1	4.4	2.6	4,857	6.1	3,638	4.4	8,495	10.4
Greece	-0.1	4.2	1.0	27	0.3	442	4.2	469	4.4
Iceland	-1.4	-0.4	-1.1	-9	-3.5	-1	-0.4	-10	-3.5
Ireland	-3.0	2.4	-1.6	-285	-8.1	91	2.4	-194	-5.1
Italy	-0.6	2.0	0.0	-904	-1.6	1,177	2	273	0.5
Luxembourg	5.4	10.0	6.5	58	15.2	42	9.7	100	22.8
Netherlands	1.5	2.3	1.7	644	4.3	360	2.3	1,004	6.3
Norway	0.8	2.0	1.1	98	2.3	88	2	186	4.2
Portugal	-4.6	0.3	-3.4	-1,197	-12.1	35	0.4	-1,162	-11.6
Spain	-0.3	0.9	0.0	-286	-0.7	358	0.9	72	0.2
Sweden	1.9	2.2	2.0	476	5.6	194	2.2	670	7.6
Switzerland	3.0	3.3	3.1	569	8.3	235	3.3	804	11.2
UK	0.1	1.5	0.4	114	0.2	827	1.4	941	1.6

Source: IOM (2003: 240).

refugee centre in Sangatte. The centre, next to the Channel Tunnel, presented an easy opportunity, the UK complained, for inmates from the 2,000 strong camp to jump onto trains bound for the UK. The UK had 22,370 asylum applications in 1993 and 71,365 in 2001, down from 80,315 in 2000. Most applications came from Afghanistan, Iraq and Sri Lanka. About 28 per cent of applicants receive either refugee status or exceptional leave to stay. But the UK provides very limited housing and other assistance, especially for refugees and people seeking asylum.

UK government policy seems to be based on the assumption that most of the claims for asylum are 'bogus': improved humanitarian assistance might encourage more claimants. A consequence of that misconceived idea has been the failure to provide adequately for the basic human needs of people seeking asylum, and a growth in destitution for individuals and families who managed to escape to the UK only to be treated inhumanely there.

The 1999 Immigration and Asylum Act, and with it the creation of the national Asylum Support Service, was intended to speed up decisions about the status of applicants and to encourage dispersal of applicants out of London. The UK government spent £747 million in 2000/01 for asylum support although only £6 million was spent on legal aid to applicants. Immigration officials removed 8,925 applicants who lost their bid for refugee status (Martin 2003: 66). In September 2006, the UK Home Secretary forcibly repatriated Iraqi asylum seekers whose cases were still pending in the High Court, one of many UK government actions that were contrary to the Geneva Convention.

In 2000, 36 per cent of EU foreign residents (just over 8 million people) were in Germany, forming 10 per cent of its population. Infamous for its policy of guest workers, especially from Turkey, Germany refused citizenship until 2000 to babies born to foreigners in Germany. Like the UK and other EU countries, however, Germany began in 2000 to seriously address what were real contradictions in its immigration policies. While spending US$3.5 billion a year on immigration enforcement, limiting the 250,000 foreigners who moved to the country each year, not counting an additional 100,000 asylum seekers and a similar number of ethnic Germans, an influential committee of parliamentarians argued the need for an *additional* 50,000 professional immigrants. This demand led to the introduction of a somewhat watered down 'green card' granted to workers with skills needed to boost the ailing national economy (*Economist* 2 November 2002).

Western politicians have been faced with a conundrum, and one that they have grappled with unsuccessfully: how to secure the borders to the EU to prevent immigration, and how to allow immigration from workers with skills that the EU's ageing population cannot offer. While progress seems to have been made with security through the Schengen protocols, an effective strategy to promote immigration to renew the labour capabilities in Europe remains poor. Politicians will not grasp the nettle of immigration and argue the need for the human right to work, security and mobility of labour. Instead they pander to the racist objections to migration and the needs to preserve national sovereignty.

Order and value: labour demands and state responses

There is a major tension within the EU and the United States regarding how to deal with the increased pressures that migrant labour, in its many different forms, presents the developed capitalist world. This is a tension between delivering domestic political and social order (assuming as many wrongly do that immigration is a source of disorder) as well as maintaining the sovereignty of international borders on the one hand, and on the other ensuring a supply of labour domestically that can satisfy the needs of local and international capital.

In addition to creating conditions for capital accumulation, reproducing supplies of labour and maintaining order, states in capitalist society have three broader functions (Hay 1996). As the embodiment of 'nation' they establish the boundaries around which inclusion and exclusion are made, and in particular they establish what is meant at any given time by the term *citizenship*. The state as *territory* establishes the geopolitical area within which administrative sovereignty is established, border patrols are maintained and foreigners are defined. And the state as *institution* embodies the apparatuses and practices of the bureaucracy and the types of intervention the state makes.

The contemporary capitalist state is often perceived by its office holders as being in crisis, partly because of the persistent fear of a challenge to its sovereignty from migration. Many of the reforms that have been put in place or discussed since the new millennium, and also before, regarding the control of labour inflows can be seen as a response to the false representation of the challenge that labour migration has posed. The internationalization of labour may lag behind the internationalization of capital, but the struggles that are effectively international class struggles (fought by migrant labour to access employment and other security in capitalist economies, among other things) can only be properly understood if seen as a central feature underpinning capitalism. Migration will not go away. But it is insufficient to only recognize that the twentieth century was 'the age of migration' (Castles and Miller 2003). Migration as I have indicated has always been part of the growth of capitalism. It is necessary to go beyond the counting of migrants and asylum seekers to try to understand how the contemporary phase of migration is located as part of the character of contemporary capitalism.

Migration is just one dimension of an international struggle with capital. As Bracking (2003) has noted, migrant labour might indicate mobility but it also confirms an international hierarchy between states. Dominant neoliberal formulations are wrongheaded to assert migration will diminish if poverty in the Global South also falls. There simply 'is not a close correlation between poverty and successful migration' (Sutcliffe 2003: 273).

State controlling labour?

There is a conflict between the concern of governments to satisfy the perceived needs of its national constituents – or at least the most powerful elements of these – and a universal ethic that values the importance of securing the safety and wellbeing of all people (Weiner 1995: x). The perception of an international crisis of migration has five dimensions, although the notion of 'crisis' is seldom questioned (Weiner 1995). These are:

- the problems of controlling entry
- absorbing the arrivals
- the international relations between states necessary to reduce the threat of conflict between states resulting from refugee flows
- crises within international regimes and institutions to deal with increased flow of labour
- the moral concerns about how states might be able to ration who is allowed in and who is not.

One dimension to the crisis for Northern states is thus how to resolve a conflict between supporting a priority of global human rights (although just for whom this is a priority is unclear) against national interests and those of established citizens in the receiving countries (Weiner 1995: 18). This perceived crisis has been somewhat confused by the debate in Europe regarding EU enlargement and a fear that poor East Europeans will rush into the West. There is also a concern that the demographic profile in Europe, Japan and the United States, where many are experiencing below-replacement fertility rates, actually requires *accelerated* inflows of labour.

One migration myth received much exposure after the accession of ten new states that joined the EU in 2004. The myth was that there would be a flood of East Europeans into the West. Despite long lead times on the freedom of movement of labour from countries like Poland, Hungary and the Czech Republic, EU officials and the tabloid

European press feared social and economic damage from a tidal wave of labour into the older EU member states. Yet even Germany, which has the highest absolute number of foreigners – nearly 10 per cent of the total population – had only about 1 per cent from the new candidate countries. In the UK, where the foreign resident population is only 3.4 per cent, candidate country representation among foreign residents is only 0.1 per cent (*Guardian* 10 December 2002; Papapanagos and Vickerman 2003; cf. Dustmann et al 2003). And the type of workers likely to migrate to the older EU states, usually on a temporary rather than permanent basis, are those that clearly add a net benefit to the receiving countries. They are usually younger and mobile educated males who add to the proposed need to enhance flexible labour markets, working where indigenous workers will not, in jobs seen as too demeaning and which are poorly paid. It also seems that remittances from European migrants in Europe are a high proportion of net earnings – 80 per cent for Polish workers in Germany – which are then spent on investment rather than just on consumption goods in the migrants' home countries.

The other fear that stokes the paradox for developed states regarding migration policy is the idea that population in Europe may have peaked in 1997, and similarly in Japan and the United States, although not until 2050 in the latter. There is thus a real need to ensure the inflow of labour of working age to take up the slack not provided by domestic labour. As one establishment journal indicated at the end of 2002, the choice for Europe's old may be between 'being cared for by legal migrants or illegal ones' (*Economist* 2002: 13).

There is certainly a fear of depopulation in many Spanish villages which has led to strategies to attract migrants to work in agriculture, construction and services. The Spanish Association of Towns against Depopulation, formed in 2000, searched for married couples under 40 years of age without college education but with work permits and at least two children under 12 years of age to sign contracts to work for five years. In return they were offered work at US$690–965 a month, and free health and education services (*International Herald Tribune* 29 July 2003).

The UN estimates that replacement migration for developed countries from the South is very high (UN 2000). A report used three different replacement scenarios for 2000–50. The first related to the size of the total population, the second to the size of the working-age population (15–64) and the third the potential support ratio, those in the range 15–64 against those over 64. The scenario is based on a repopulation policy rather than guest worker system. In the first scenario 15 countries of the EU need 47 million migrants, in scenario two 79 million and 674 million in scenario three. This final scenario would translate into net migration of 14 million if the consequences of demographic ageing were to be offset; that is, the balance between working age and retirement remained constant from 2000 to 2050.

This report has many flaws. It operates, for example, with a very static view of migration. Another gap is that it seems to avoid the recognition that demographic ageing is universal (Fargues 2003: 3). The immigrants set to work in the EU will themselves age and need to be replaced and cared for in old age. And as it has been noted elsewhere, the demography of the sending countries is also changing. In other words, by 2030 the fertility rates in the traditional sending countries like Brazil, Mexico, Egypt and the Philippines will fall below replacement levels (*Economist* 2 November: 13).

The migration debate in the developed countries, moreover, objectifies Southern poor countries. There is little dialogue with 'sending' countries and migration is itself defined in the first instance as a 'problem'. As one commentator (Sassen 1999) has asked, why do receiving countries not treat immigrants as partners? Different historical moments have reflected how Western states have seen immigrants as necessary and important to the receiving economy but never as full and equal partners. The West's response to both the increase in migration and asylum seekers and the increase in numbers of origin countries has mostly been to increase border patrols. Tightening the borders has merely accelerated the ruthlessness of traffickers.

It might have been more helpful for Northern states to identify today's refugees and immigrants as the 'new settlers' (Sassen 1999: 6), but this challenges Western governments to rethink notions of identity and historical notions of belonging: something they are unable and unwilling to do. They are unwilling to do it because of the fear of an electoral backlash against perceived increased numbers of 'foreigners' – a collective noun for migrants and asylum seekers – and they are unable to do it because they seem to universally have a view that migration is an issue of law and order. Where it is seen as a case of economic necessity to reduce pressures on domestic labour markets, a more pragmatic policy view is taken. That has increasingly involved the issuing of temporary work visas that might be extended if a case for so doing can be made by employers.

I have indicated that the contemporary monologue about migration can only be properly understood in its historical context. Migration increased with the onset of industrial capitalism, and especially of manufacture and technological developments that improved mobility of labour in the nineteenth century. Increases in levels of productivity, driven by colonial conquest and transformation in Europe, also loosened people's attachment to the countryside (Sassen 1999: 35). But capitalist transformation also meant that additional hands to work, either refugees or labour migrants, were not always welcomed. Two moments capture the emergence of an antagonistic relationship between states and foreigners. The first emerged during the West's conquest of the Ottoman Empire and the second with the advent of the First World War.

The Great War strengthened the interstate system, and the 'foreigner' became defined as not belonging to national society and without citizenship rights. 'The coupling of state sovereignty and nationalism with border control made the "foreigner" an outsider' (Sassen 1999: 78). Hannah Arendt (1958) long ago highlighted the link that emerged with the development of the nation state with citizenship linked to birth. The mushrooming of refugees and migrant labourers that emerged after the First World War challenged that link and also threatened conflict between nation states. In this sense 'the emergent inter state system was the key to the creation of the stateless person, the identification of refugees as such, and their regulation or control' (Sassen 1999: 84; Hayter 2004).

The contemporary dilemma regarding how to deal with migrants for receiving states is illustrated by the shifts in policy direction that EU and US governments have made. On the one hand, states want adequate flows of both skilled and unskilled labour, but on the other states want to manage and control those flows.

Control of labour is everything, and emerges when factors other than law and order, racial prejudice or unemployment of local labour surfaces in the national psyche. A recent assessment of four major immigration countries, the United States, New Zealand, Australia and Canada, noted a focus on family immigration and humanitarian immigration while always expanding economic migration (IOM 2003: 154). Economic migration for these traditional immigration countries, and also the UK and Germany, has particularly emphasized a search for well-educated foreigners. Competition for this category has hardened as skill shortages, notably in high tech and information and communications technology sectors, have grown. Western skills shortage has emphasized the importance of capturing the abilities of people from the South that benefit capitalist development in the North. In policy terms this has led many Western states to reform immigration regimes to expand provision for long-term and temporary visa holders.

The United States admitted in the financial year 2000 543,950 foreign workers; 25 per cent of the net growth of US employment. Two-thirds of these were professionals on visas allowing them to stay for six years. They would be eligible for an employment–economic immigration visa if they became sponsored by an employer who could show that there was no qualified US resident to fill the vacant job (Martin 2003: 20). These foreign workers were on H-1B visas and they highlight a potential conflict between the US state and US employers. The latter, notably finance or high-tech capitalists, want a global search for the best workers to fill US jobs.

During the dot.com boom in the 1990s, so called 'body shops' emerged to find and help US employers access foreign labour; this led to criticism of exploitation of labour that was more willing to work longer hours in poor conditions. A result of the struggle between employers and government and pressure groups wanting to maintain US standards of employment was a limit on the number any firm could employ under the category of H-1B admissions – no more than 15 per cent – and an agreement that US workers could not be made redundant to accommodate the foreigners (Martin 2003: 22).[7]

The UK has also stepped up its policing of asylum and immigration while simultaneously providing new opportunities for guest worker programmes. These temporary schemes have targeted the needs of employers who require people with professional skills where shortages in the labour market are most felt. The government agency, Work Permits UK, receives applications for visas from UK employers who want to hire non-EU foreigners. About 150,000 applications are made each year by foreign professionals, about 90 per cent of which are approved. These include jobs as doctors and nurses as well as engineers. Under the Highly Skilled Migrant Programme foreign professionals are admitted, without limit, for 12 months as long as they reach a 75-point target on a 100-point scale. Points are awarded for educational qualifications and experience.

Far fewer unskilled workers are admitted: only about 40,000 young people from the Commonwealth on working holidays for up to two years, and these from Australia, New Zealand and South Africa. The UK government announced that it would like to recruit more from the black Commonwealth and from Eastern Europe. 'New Labour' was repeatedly forced by increased racial tension at the end of the 1990s to both defend the importance of 'Britishness', whatever that meant, and argue the need for a more robust immigration regime that would encourage foreigners in professional occupations and keep out of the UK 'bogus' asylum seekers and economic migrants. Admission of immigrants with professional qualifications was defended because of the need to keep up with European competitors in science and technology. It was also noted that the UK's foreign-born population paid £2.6 billion per annum more in government revenue than they received in state benefits, although the tabloid press mentioned little of that (Gott and Johnston 2002).

The intensification of a policy to allow only those immigrants with skills that were important to support the economic interests of UK capitalism led to an expansion of searches for 'illegals' at ports of entry and the fining of carriers of illegals.[8] It also led to attempts to minimize the numbers of asylum claims by locating UK immigration officials overseas to monitor the papers of travellers to the UK. In 2000 46,600 foreigners were refused entry at UK ports and more than 50,000 foreigners were given notice that they were to be deported. This was almost twice the number in 1999, and 81 per cent of these were asylum seekers (Martin 2003: 70).

Since January 2003 more draconian measures have been taken to identify the ubiquitous 'bogus asylum seeker'. Legislation insisted that immigrants claimed asylum immediately on entry to the UK, and those who did not were left without benefits of any kind, creating large-scale homelessness and abject misery during an appeal process for people who had tried to escape persecution elsewhere.

The UK, as well as trying to stop undocumented workers entering, like the United States, toughened penalties against employers of illegals. Fines can be levied up to £5,000 for each illegal, but despite the rhetoric of clampdown there seemed to be only low-key prosecutions; only 23 employers were charged in 1999.

Western governments are intent on trying to legalize workers that they wants for economic development and competitive advantage and to regulate the influx of unskilled workers and asylum seekers As the *Economist* noted, 'Legal immigration is easier to regulate than illegal, and more likely to bring benefits in the long term' (2 Nov 2002: 15), yet the strategy it has argued for, and the strategy increasingly in place in the UK and elsewhere, becomes a mechanism of cherry picking the most skilled immigrants. It also provides a racist platform to recruit workers only from similarly developed countries. For example, why should Canadians, *The Economist* has argued, seek to limit migration from Australia or New Zealand? Immigration of people from similarly developed countries is likely, they assert, to reduce racial tension. But how then are those who want to migrate in the Global South to be discouraged from so doing, and why should they be so discouraged if the promise of globalization is to facilitate a free market in labour as well as capital?

Labour mobility and international inequality

I have stressed that capitalist states have been unable to resolve the contradiction of ensuring the stable supply of labour with the ideological and often racist opposition to labour flows – the latter appearing in times of economic crisis when long-established migrant communities who have worked for decades alongside indigenous communities become threatened. The possibility of migrants and their communities being threatened lies with the emergence of the category of refugees and migrant labourers being reframed as 'foreigners' and thus having unequal access to state provision and protection.

With the emergence of late capitalism and the aftermath of the First

World War, Western states were quick to put to work invited foreigners. A major challenge in the contemporary period is the Western states' ability to stem the flow of labour that is seen to challenge the ability of employers to valorize capital. This challenge has led policy makers in the UK and elsewhere to read important questions regarding migration in a particular way. That is, to look at the issue of Western state sovereignty and order and at how sending countries might be helped in their development to reduce the impetus for migrants to move to Europe. This is another version of the questions regarding the causes and consequences of migration:

- How beneficial is it to the sending and the receiving country?
- What happens to the countries that lose the skills of those who migrate?
- How much income is actually remitted to offset the social and economic costs of sending countries?
- How much is retained in the receiving countries to minimize state costs of hosting migrants?

These questions, however, are dominated by neoliberal concerns of the motivation of individuals to migrate and a focus on the 'factors' of production (Lewis 1955; Todaro 1969). Land, capital and labour and natural resources are presented in an *a priori* manner, as static givens that have no context, no historical trajectory, and no class intermediaries to struggle over how they might be allocated and what might be done with them. In short, much migration theory fails to account for the development strategies of countries from where migration might begin. This individualization of choice is the favourite organizing principle for neoclassical economics, which reduces debate to costs and benefits without recognition of the way in which migration is itself part of a wider internationalization of capital (Amin 1995: 31; cf. Hermele 1997).

Although it is important to assess who migrates and why, the analysis of these calculations should not be devoid of an assessment, first and foremost, of *who does not migrate* and why there is not the exodus from poverty in the South to the North that neoclassical economics suggests is integral to poor people's decision making. It is important to explore migration as one of several strategies of the poor and the not so poor, and also of the rich to improve their livelihoods. As Kothari notes:

> Migration is best understood as a cause and consequence of chronic poverty for those who move as well as for those who stay behind and consequently, key to understanding the role of migration in chronic poverty is the relationship between 'mobility' and

'immobility' and more generally the interconnectedness of people and places.

(Kothari 2002: 4)

While this leads Kothari to understand the role of migration in creating conditions for the persistence or opportunity to escape chronic poverty by exploring processes of 'exclusion', I have suggested here, and it is highlighted elsewhere in this book, that exclusion emerges historically in the South not simply because of the decisions taken by the poor, their ability to make rational choices or not, and what they actually decide upon, but also, and often in a defining way, because of the active undermining of the South by the North. We need to be careful not to allow the label 'exclusion' to prevent an understanding of the ways in which poverty is created and reproduced.

This view of an unevenly integrated world where capitalist development in the North has impoverished the South and continues to do so has been criticized from within the debate about migration. In theorizing diaspora there has been a questioning of teleological views of the world, of nationality, geographical boundaries and 'spaces', and how movements of peoples actually help shape new hegemonic power relations (Braziel and Mannur 2003). In this debate there seems little room for 'centre–periphery' analysis of the world, as global flows of people and money take place at the disjuncture of different 'landscapes'; new borders and boundaries that need new language to explain the tension between homogenization and heterogenization of international economic and social processes (Appadurai 2003: 29).

The concern to move forward in the analysis of diaspora is noteworthy (Zack-Williams and Mohan 2002), but the evident additional focus on cultural determinants of boundaries that might transcend nation states neglects the importance of structuring explanations of the modern world in terms of the repeated struggles between capital and labour. As Massey noted, just as there are no purely spatial processes, neither are there any non-spatial social processes. It is clearly the case that developments in capitalism have included changes in types of labour process and search for new forms of labour supply.'Yet it is not labour process that determines location but the search after profit and fluctuating conflict between capital and labour (Massey 1984). Three processes have shaped that struggle: the role of remittances, the increased role of trafficking and Southern people's livelihood struggles.

The counter to capitalism's struggle for labour has been an increase in the level of remittance sent home by labour migrants. Remittances are now a greater source of foreign exchange for developing country than all combined forms of foreign aid. Table 3.5 lists the top 20 countries receiving remittances. Officially, remittances for all countries according to the IMF in 1999 amounted to US$63 billion but if unofficial channels are considered the figure is closer to US$100 billion (IOM 2003: 310). And while remittances were until the 1980s largely sent from Europe, by 1991 Asia had become the largest source for remittance income.

Superficially this income provides an enormous subsidy for Southern states, but it only does so if it can be managed and directed to socially useful production. As Bracking (2003) has noted, while remittances might well enhance the incomes of families that can access them, their unofficial character helps elites to externalize funds bypassing state regulation.

Remittances are a two-edged sword. They represent a strategy of resistance by people in the South. Bracking has shown how in Zimbabwe remittance income enlarges the informal sector that can challenge the authoritarian state. Yet she has also argued that remittance income can fail to enter official channels, thereby denying improvements in welfare provision. It may be mostly accessed by ruling political elites who undermine any social contract that might, albeit tenuously, exist between states and citizens (Bracking 2003).

Whether remittances contribute positively to national and local incomes depends on many factors and should not be assumed from the statistics of remittances in national statistics (Taylor 1999). Issues of importance include the mechanisms and control over remittance income, the use to which remittances are put and the control over the remittances. Those decisions take place at the national economic policy level and in the household of the migrant worker as well as at many different mediating points between these.

Table 3.5 Top 20 receiving countries of migrants' remittances, 2000

Country	Remittances (US$000)	Country	Remittances (US$000)
India	11,585,699	Dominican Republic	1,688,999
Mexico	6,572,599	Greece	1,613,100
Turkey	4,560,000	Colombia	1,553,900
Egypt	3,747,000	Ecuador	1,316,700
Spain	3,414,414	Yemen	1,255,206
Portugal	3,131,162	Indonesia	1,190,000
Morocco	2,160,999	Sri Lanka	1,142,329
Bangladesh	1,948,999	Brazil	1,112,999
Jordan	1,845,133	Pakistan	982,899
El Salvador	1,750,770	Jamaica	789,299

Source: IOM (2003: 311).

Remittances can become part of an essential strategy both for survival and for accumulation. As we have noted above, the accumulation strategy is not solely that of the migrant and his/her family. Foreign exchange does provide opportunities for survival, for purchases of farm equipment, education and clothing needs as well as house building. It must not be forgotten, however, that the physical and social cost to the migrant for access to remittance income is very harsh.

Migrants in Egypt, for example, who are not just the *tarahil* or seasonal migrants within Egypt, but those who from desperation of rural poverty move to Cairo or Giza City, do so living on the absolute margin of life. Unskilled and uneducated workers generally exchange rural poverty for urban squalor, moving to try to become night watchmen or day labourers on building sites, without health and safety provision, and nowhere to sleep except the building site or the lobby of the building where they may become the doorman. And those who do manage to escape, for example, to Saudi Arabia become controlled by *Kafeel*. These 'managers' determine what the migrant does and where he/she can do it. The migrant is unable to move cities without written permission from the *Kafeel*, who effectively control indentured labourers.

One such migrant who farmed half an acre near Giza worked for eight years in Saudi as an agricultural labourer. A broker in his village had helped him move overland via Nuweiba in Egypt's Sinai to Saudi. But his life in Saudi centred around broken promises and the control by a new foreman. He had paid EGP (Egyptian pounds) 2,500 to get to Saudi and had, over eight years managed to accumulate only enough to buy two water buffalo and to rent one additional acre of new land (albeit without the security of any written contract). His remittances also paid for the laying of a concrete floor in his father's house, but all his other earnings had been used for his living costs in Saudi and to help buy clothes and education for his children in Egypt. Agreements over his wages in Saudi had never been honoured, he always received less than he had been promised, contracts were never honoured and the *Kafeel* took 25 per cent of all his earnings (interviews, Cairo: August 2003).

This chapter has highlighted the many contradictory relationships between migrant labour and capitalism. The most glaring is the way in which economic globalization bypasses liberalization of markets for labour. Although the movement of people for work and as the essential ingredient for the valorization of capital has been a key element in the development of capitalism, states and political regimes have repeatedly elevated concerns of national sovereignty over the full integration of foreign labour.

Despite the attraction of work and payments for labour by employers that are much less than payments for indigenous labour, and despite the cheapness of that labour force's reproduction for states that invest in welfare and education, foreigners are denied access to full political and national rights in the countries where they work. We have noted that this is not without conflict between capitalists that have different labour needs. But we have noted too that the securitization of international political economy has served the interests of states to persecute a more aggressive strategy against workers who have originated from outside their national borders. But if economic internationalization of capital has revealed one important aspect of labour migrancy, it is that Northern government attempts to secure greater national sovereignty by regulating and excluding labour are misplaced.

Assumptions about labour migration are now being challenged, and one point of debate is whether it is possible or desirable to distinguish between places of migrant settlement and return (Castles 1999: 12). It is also important to examine ways in which opposition to the free movement of labour has emerged not only from capitalists that seek to continue the use of cheap and expendable labour, but from strategies by migrants themselves to find employment and challenge restrictions on their mobility.

At a time when issues of global governance are being raised, albeit in a muted manner, it is time that the Global South was part of a wider debate regarding Northern capitalist demands for labour. Part of that debate might include the role that Southern labour has played and continues to play in the creation of Northern capitalist wealth. It would need to also address the possibilities of reducing the barriers of entry to migrants in Europe and the United States, but in the contemporary security climate such a change seems utopian. It is clear however that while the consequences for migrants of seeking work outside their country of origin are often calamitous, even when they find work, people will continue to seek to move location. It is a genuine and legitimate strategy to try to reduce inequality between people in the North and the South.

4 Land, poverty and politics

Land, dispossession and accumulation

This chapter examines the debates regarding rural poverty, land reform and development in the Global South. Struggles within the Global South have often been centred on conflicts of unequal land holdings and reform. Contemporary debate regarding rural poverty emphasizes the continuing significance of unequal land holdings that keep the landless and near-landless in poverty (IFAD 2001; Ghimire 2001; Barraclough 1999). It is a debate that focuses on the efficacy of the small farmer. And it has a lot of merit in that it centres on those families and households that are vulnerable to shifts in markets and climate, and from which many of the migrants emerge that we looked at in Chapter 3.

Whether rural people's vulnerability should lead policy towards redistributive land reform is contentious. There are many different pressures on farmers and the landless that go beyond issues of access to land, and it is uncertain whether improvement in land holdings alone would resolve these (Bryceson 2002). I return in Chapter 6 to the debate regarding whether redistributive land reform is now largely irrelevant for reducing rural poverty, especially in the context of pressures from globalization (Bernstein 2003).

Here I shift discussion regarding the policies of land reform as a mechanism to reduce poverty towards the importance of the way land continues to be a political and politicized issue and how it is also used as a mechanism for accumulation. In doing this I raise the issue of accumulation by dispossession: the way in which struggles over land are used by dominant classes to promote primitive accumulation (Perelman 2000; Harvey 2003).

There are two dimensions to capitalist accumulation. One relates to relations between the capitalist and wage worker and the structures of property rights; commodity exchange and ideology that mystifies exploitation and class rule and presents it as a normal state of affairs where equality of opportunity prevails. The other is the relationship between capitalist centres and non-capitalist economies: in short, imperialism (Luxemburg 1968; Bond and Desai 2006). For Marx:

> primitive accumulation [was] the historical process of divorcing the producer from the means of production. It appears as primitive,

because it forms the pre-historic stage of capital and of the mode of production corresponding with it.

(Marx 1974: 668)

While Marx's work implied a short-term character to primitive accumulation, a necessary forerunner to capitalist development, Rosa Luxemburg and more recently other activists have indicated that much of contemporary relations between imperialist states and former colonies, and also within developing countries, is shaped by continued patterns of primitive accumulation (Bond 2006). As Harvey has noted, primitive or original capitalist accumulation included a wide range of processes:

> commodification and privatization of land and the forceful expulsion of peasant populations, conversion of various forms of property rights ... into exclusive private property rights, suppression of rights to the commons; commodification of labour power and the suppression of alternative, indigenous, forms of production and consumption.

(Harvey 2003: 74)

These processes also include, as I show elsewhere in this book, strategies of plunder and resource extraction, coercive labour regimes and forms of financial control. All these processes and patterns of capitalist development have continued beyond the formative stages of capitalist development. They have continued into the contemporary era and are shaping the character of capitalism in the Global South.

If capitalism was born from the theft and robbery, the slaughter and mayhem that it created in the seizure of assets from the Global South, it has continued with accumulation by dispossession in the contemporary period. Plunder of Africa's resources, for example, has continued with mining and mineral wealth extraction, as we see in Chapter 5. Land has also been central to the ways in which the poor and near-landless have been treated. In Egypt, for example, we shall see that the acceleration of poverty that has ensued has directly added to the wealth of landlords, thus increasing social differentiation in Egypt's countryside. Dispossession in Zimbabwe's history has also benefited the white settler elite, but the recent accelerated processes of land transfer, especially since 2000, while rewarding many near-landless and landless from the overcrowded and colonial inheritance of communal areas, have also enriched the political class of the ZANU PF elite.

Central to my case studies is the persistent politicization of land, the role of violence that accompanies it and which is often state orchestrated, as the status quo is challenged in Zimbabwe's case by the state itself. The politicization of land has brought into focus two further issues. The first is the nature of property rights in the twenty-first century. As redistributive land reform has been pushed off the agenda by international financial institutions (IFIs) and governments alike, it has been replaced with concerns to embolden rights in land, to privatize it, thereby celebrating security to land holders with titles but diminishing those without. And this has been done not only in the name of celebrating capitalist rights to property but traditional customary rights too; this has sometimes euphemistically been called 'new wave land reform'. That leads to the second important consequence of the politicization of land: continued and often accelerated rural poverty and de-peasantization. Here it is crucial to see poverty in relational terms that enable us to see how poverty and wealth are two sides of the same coin as struggles over land lead to winners and losers.

Rural wealth creation is dependent upon the impoverishment of less wealthy farmers. Social differentiation appears as the resolution of a core agrarian question, namely how will the countryside modernize? Yet the mechanism for that modernization – the form that it takes, the processes that accompany the dispossession of smallholders and the increased economic strength and political power of larger landowners – is a site of immense contestation rather than inevitability. Somewhat paradoxically, this contestation has a serious consequence for the advocates of small farmer interests. For if the countryside is characterized by conflicting interests that generate and reproduce poverty (as a result of there being winners and losers in the struggles over local resources), what point is there of devising poverty reduction strategies that redistribute land knowing future social and economic processes will always undermine the poor and lead to continued and accentuated rural inequality? If struggles over land are important sites for class struggle, then strategies for rural development must recognize that and provide a structure to promote their democratic resolution.

I support what might be called a modified view of the small farmer approach. That recognizes the 'inherently unstable' nature of small farmer or peasant forms of production (Woodhouse 2002: 5; Byres 1996) as well as the complexity and conflictual nature of rural society. It is important to stress that the wealth of the rich, larger landholders is predicated upon the poverty of the poor, but this does not mean *ipso facto* that support for smallholders should be jettisoned in some fatalistic and predetermined manner, or that there will never be any movement of the poor from poverty to improved conditions of existence in the countryside (cf. Dyer 1997 with Mitchell 2002 and Bush 2002b). Instead, it is necessary in supporting strategies for poverty reduction to provide safety nets and a policy framework of support for the rural poor. But these are not the piecemeal nets of old that are reluctantly exacted from states ignorant of, and uninterested in, the peasant livelihood. New support must recognize rural class conflicts and the inequalities they generate. It must also capture the dynamism of social transformation that does not penalize poverty by allowing the rich to be the predators of the poor.

Agricultural modernization needs to be sequenced with economic development more widely. Employment opportunities for the rural poor, whether in the towns or the countryside, must be real rather than simply projections of policy makers' imagination. This inevitably means a crucial role for the state in delivering land reform. Commenting on a review of land reform experience in developing countries, Barraclough has noted that 'in each case, the state's role in land reform was crucial. It sometimes promoted reform, sometimes prevented it, sometimes reversed it and sometimes diverted it to benefit groups other than the rural poor' (Barraclough 1999: 33). The state can thus act in contradictory ways, but the restrictions placed on it by popular protest are crucial to defending the rights of landless and poor. The poor need powerful allies, domestically and internationally to ensure the delivery of policies for greater rural equality.

An additional theme in the debate about land reform is its location in the context of development more generally. Since 1945 the modernization of land and tenure has been at the core of what is understood as 'development' or 'modernity'. Put simply, strategies to improve rural wealth creation and all that this has meant for urban development (notably the production of cheap food for workers and town dwellers) have been the bedrock of national wealth creation.

The dominant view expressed from the Global South and from Northern industrial countries after 1945 was that rural wealth creation and national economic development required land reform. The favoured policy initiative was to distribute unequal land holdings to reduce rural inequality and promote greater productivity and efficiency. Since the late 1970s, however, there has been a reduced emphasis on redistributive land reform. It has been replaced almost universally with a policy to liberalize rural markets and empower large landowners.

I shall examine some of the reasons behind the policy shift and some of the consequences of it. I shall suggest the need to challenge the institution of property rights and to consider what these might mean in the contemporary period. These themes raise a more general question; does the twenty-first century still hold the possibility for land reform in the way in which early epochs may have done? Even a most persuasive advocate of the position that the emergence of globalization in the

1970s has brought peasant farmers under the 'dull compulsion of economic forces' stresses the importance of the ensuing fragmentation of labour and the possibilities for struggles against state policy by poor farmers, landless workers and other social forces (Bernstein 2003).

Agrarian reform: from poverty reduction to the modernization of poverty

Three-quarters of the world's 1.2 billion absolutely poor, those who consume less than a dollar a day, live in rural areas (IFAD 2001). Although dependence upon agriculture for a living is challenged by processes of agrarianization/de-agrarianization (changes in the size of rural populations dependent upon agriculture because of shifts in the size of the sector) and peasantization/de-peasantization (changes in the number of rural producers engaged in a peasant labour process) (Bryceson 2000: 3; 2003), the rural poor have often been sidelined in debates about poverty and the important contribution they might make to economic growth and development.

Despite overwhelming evidence of rural-based poverty, official development assistance to agriculture has declined from around 20 per cent in the late 1980s to about 12 per cent at the start of the twenty-first century (IFAD 2001: iv). Food yields and outputs in the 1990s fell compared with increases in the 1970s and 1980s, and a consequence of this decline has been an increase rather than a diminution of rural poverty levels.

There are many reasons for the changing fortunes of peasants, defined here to encompass:

- those engaged in an agricultural livelihood that combines self-provisioning with production for exchange
- the importance of family labour for production
- subordination to extractive class forces, whether local, national or international
- residence in village communities that are often isolated from urban centres and efficient transport and communication networks (Bryceson 2000: 2; see also Shanin 1976; cf. Bernstein 1994, 2001).

Peasants confront many dynamic processes that challenge their status and livelihoods. This has added to the definitional slipperiness of the category 'peasant' because they almost universally have multi-occupational roles; they might be more accurately defined as worker-peasants, as at one moment many work for wages locally or in town, and at other times they work their own land or that of neighbours, again for cash or sometimes for sharecropping. Two of the biggest challenges to rural dwellers, however, have been an inequality in land holdings and the consequences of what effectively has been a persistent urban bias in development.

Declaring the importance of improving peasant access to resources, particularly land, has been a recurrent theme in international forums since the late 1970s. The Peasants' Charter, as it has become known, or more formally the World Conference on Agrarian Reform and Rural Development, declared in 1979 that the rural poor needed improved access to land and water. Better access to resources needed to be matched with improved service provision and participation in the design and implementation of rural development programmes: in other words a democratization of rural society.

These declarations were reinforced by follow-up meetings of the International Fund for Agricultural Development (IFAD) on hunger in 1995 and the World Food Summits of 1996 and 2000. As one commentator noted, 'Empowering the poor through secure access to resources is the foundation of rural poverty alleviation' (Moore 2001: 3). The rural poor have few assets, and the weak asset base ensures what has recently been labelled an 'interlocking logjam' that makes it difficult for them to move out of poverty (IFAD 2001: 24).

The 'logjam' effect is evident because of different but interlinked and reinforcing dimensions to rural poverty. Illiteracy, especially female illiteracy, makes movement out of poverty difficult. Low levels of productivity result from poor access to work, land and improved techniques for production. And where rural employment opportunities are uncertain or non-existent, access to land remains the most important bulwark against impoverishment and destitution. Among the interlocking factors sustaining rural poverty is limited land access. Most rural poor are landless or near-landless farmers whose vulnerability is heightened by economic or environmental crisis, and the burden usually falls harder on women than on men. In particular, households headed by women are discriminated against in terms of access to important farming inputs, including land and credit.

The need to improve access to land as a mechanism to reduce rural poverty has been largely eclipsed by a second major factor causing the persistence of rural poverty, which has been labelled 'urban bias' (Lipton 1977). This refers to the ways in which the countryside seems to be repeatedly short-changed in the national distribution of income and wealth creation. In summary, urban areas seem to have benefited disproportionately compared with rural areas from strategies for economic growth, allocation of resources and the impact of poverty reduction strategies. While the concept of urban bias has been criticized, it captures the policy outcome of government relations with the countryside. However, the extent to which this is an intentional outcome or the product of a range of competing pressures that are local and international is often obscure. For example, international pressure may undermine prices paid for agricultural products or returns to rural infrastructural development. Yet as we shall see, even where there are strong landowning interests, as in Egypt, there is collusion with urban-based industrial concerns, and often landowners are the same individuals who own and control powerful political and urban-based economic interests.

Since 2000, in Zimbabwe (and the military's costly intervention in Congo), Mugabe's generals and other party members have been rewarded with farms and land. Urban bias here is more than simply a spatial concept that distinguishes town from village. It goes beyond an account of urban–rural distribution of budgets to indicate the class interests of policy makers and their backers: a strategy to promote accumulation by dispossession.

The power of urban interests has often undermined strategies for improving agricultural budgets; this demonstrates the importance of agricultural growth for poverty reduction, and the need to promote institutional reforms that would empower rural dwellers to control more of their lives and voice grievances to local and national elites. Urban entrepreneurial classes have different interests from those of the rural poor. This is evident over such issues as the pricing of food and farming inputs, when it is the interest of the urban classes to have cheap food, ensuring less upward pressure on wage bills and cheaper inputs to agro-industries, among other things (Maxwell and Slater 2003 15; Irz et al 2001).

The form that agricultural growth might take and the interests linked to the strategy adopted to promote it are immense arenas of political and economic conflict. Urban-based classes usually succeed in the struggles over food prices. They have not done so, however, over the emergence of markets in parallel to formal conduits for moving commodities, nor over what it is that small-scale farmers produce.[1] Marginalization of the rural poor ensures that agro, industrial and financial capitalist interests benefit from policy formulated in urban centres for dominant classes that are not entirely urban based. Yet because of the migrant labour feature of most peasant communities (where at least one member of each family works in town), the actual division between an urban proletariat and migrants is often blurred. In these circumstances policies for agricultural and industrial development need to capture the erosion of any separation between workers and peasants.

Most fundamentally of all, the failure of governments to promote an effective rural development strategy entails a refusal to recognize possible development implications for alleviating rural poverty. Planners continue to ignore the view that 'a dollar of rural income, compared with a dollar of urban income, has three to four times the effect on poverty alleviation' (Timmer 1995: 461).

In summary, the rural poor are unable to escape from their poverty not because they are less productive or have insufficient skills (Deininger 1999: 652) but because of a number of political and economic processes that continue to marginalize their effective participation in strategies to reduce their poverty. Not the least of these is the unequal distribution of assets, especially land. The continued marginality of the rural poor can lead to a number of often contradictory policy initiatives. Should strategies to reduce rural poverty, for instance, where that is understood to mean landlessness or near-landlessness, lead to calls for land redistribution? Alternatively, should such a characterization of poverty be addressed by concentration on urban job creation and industrialization (which might in the early stages be labour intensive) which might provide employment and opportunity for the rural poor more effectively than their continued link to land, albeit under conditions of great inequality?

A brief review of the historical experience of land reform as a vehicle for reducing rural poverty indicates areas of success. Such a review is also revealing of the pressures that ultimately eclipse a major strategy for the redistribution of national resources, and the ways in which agrarian reform becomes replaced by agendas of privatization and liberalization of land markets.

Land reform

Land reform refers to:

> a significant change in agrarian structure, resulting in increased access to land by the rural poor, as well as a secured tenure for those who actually work on the land. It also includes access to agricultural inputs, markets, services and other needed assistance as a vehicle for promoting the modernization of agriculture.
>
> (Ghimire 2001: 7)

Land reform was important to economic development strategies in the post-war period. From China and Chile to the Philippines and Viet Nam, distributive land reform was central to the need to produce cheap food for increasing populations and foreign exchange from export revenue (Barraclough 1999; Dorner 1972; Ghimire 2001). Land reform was politically important for revolutionary regimes to inhibit the economic power of large landowning classes. Land reform was necessary on grounds of both equity and efficiency, although it did not

Table 4.1 Summary of reasons for redistributive land reform

Economic reasons	• Increased efficiency of small farms compared with large farms· • Improve incentive structure by providing more secure tenure rules • Improve supply of capital and labour from countryside to town only when real jobs in town exist for rural migrants
Political reasons	• Reduce possibility for political unrest from landless and near landless • Diminish power of landowners
Social reasons	• Sustain rural communities by reducing tendency for rural–urban migration

always meet these desired goals (Deininger 1999: 651; Lipton 1993: 643; Barraclough 2001; Thiesenhusen 1995; Sobhan 1993).

Land reform in the period of redistribution (1950s–70s) invariably involved the state compulsorily taking over land of the biggest landlords, who were usually compensated for their loss.

Driven by newly independent governments intent on reducing poverty and injustice and promoting rural development, the reform of land tenure was possibly the most important plank in the strategy of most new states, whether the reform was driven by the market or government fiat. Land reforms depended notably on the ability of the peasantry and the state to deliver on promises of reform by reducing the economic and political strength of dominant landowning classes.

Land reform was contentious. This was the case even if compensation for land loss was made, because of the political implications that resulted from changing property relations. In almost all cases of reform after the Second World War, land reform led to hard-fought political battles between landowners and the newly empowered landholders. That is the case whether the agenda of reform was initiated from the grassroots, movements of peasants and farmers, or by a military regime. But the litmus test of success also involves more than just a shift in the balance of landownership and control, although that is important enough. It also requires that the wellbeing of peasants improves, compared with a pre-reform period. Linked to that is the need for the land newly taken over to be at least as productive as before reform, and for a new pricing regime not to penalize initiative and peasant opportunity to raise the levels of marketable surpluses: much reform land had been an under-utilized resource in the hands of its previous owners.

Success in raising productivity depended on a broader range of macroeconomic policies, where agricultural development was seen as inextricably linked with wider processes of development that recognized important linkages between town and country. Land reform, in short, had to have a twin impact for it to be successful. It had to reduce poverty and it had to improve productivity. It also had to contribute to development more generally. It had to encourage the improved contribution of capital and labour to non-agricultural sectors. The almost universal case across the developing world after 1945 has been the failure of the agricultural sector to hold labour until it was absorbed by other sectors (Dorner 1972: 17).

Land reform was central to the development projects of many Third World states after the Second World War and in this, at least until the early 1970s, the international political and financial institutions were often, although not always, supportive. As early as 1951, for example, a United Nations report on land recognized that many existing land tenure systems inhibited economic development. The United States also encouraged limited land reform, if only to release political steam from the kettle of rural dissatisfaction.

South America in particular was seen by the United States in the late 1950s and early 1960s as a hotbed of unrest. In 1961, following the Cuban revolution, the Kennedy administration promoted the Alliance for Progress. Set up by the Organization of American States, the Alliance encouraged moderate land reform and the removal of the worst excesses of the *latifundia* estate system. Washington in fact, had encouraged land reform in Puerto Rico as early as the 1940s, but the United States helped in the overthrow of the Arbenz government in Guatemala in 1954 after a radical reform distributed to 100,000 *campesino* families more than 2 million acres of land that belonged to the US United Fruit Company.

Despite the slowing of US support, and in particular the reluctance of the Brazilian military after seizing power in 1964 to promote even limited reform, radical movements and governments elsewhere drove land reform. It was central to the first peasant revolution of the twentieth century in Mexico between 1910 and 1914, to Bolshevik Russia after 1917, China after 1948, and later to Chile under Frei (1967–73), Nicaragua (1979), El Salvador (1980) and Ethiopia (1973). Land reform was also central to post-colonial reconstruction in Algeria and Tunisia and in trying to break the back of the Pasha class of landowners in Egypt in the mid-1950s. In southern Africa in Mozambique, Zimbabwe, South Africa and Namibia, liberation movements were organized around the struggle to redress the unequal racial distribution of land.

Unsurprisingly the most extensive land reforms were initiated by revolutionary regimes. The beneficiaries were more numerous in Cuba, Bolivia and Mexico than in Panama, Colombia, Ecuador,

Honduras and Costa Rica. Notwithstanding the evidence for reform the actual consequences of land redistribution was uneven. Households directly benefiting from redistribution of land, as a total of agricultural households varied from a high of 90 per cent in China and 75 per cent in South Korea to just 8 per cent in the Philippines and 2 per cent in Morocco.

Each reform was unique in the way that it was enacted and in its consequences. One effect evident across different cases in North Africa and the Near East, but elsewhere too, was a dramatic impact on poverty reduction. Following the reforms in Egypt (1952, 1961), Iran (1962, 1967), Iraq (1958, 1971), Morocco (1956, 1963, 1973) and Tunisia (1956, 1958, 1964), infant mortality, fell by an average of 33 per cent and life expectancy rose by 10 per cent (El Ghonemy 1999: 11). These important improvements in wellbeing were due to a range of factors that included improvements in irrigation and remittances, but land reform was a major driver in shifting the balance of forces toward the poor and especially the rural poor.

Yet the benefits of land reform were smaller, and the beneficiaries fewer, than they might have been. The scale of land distribution was still limited; ceilings on land ownership were often set very high, thereby reducing the availability of land for redistribution and sustaining the power of large landowners. High oil revenues from the fourfold increase in petroleum prices in 1973 and 1979 were not used for agricultural development, a feature of oil-led growth characterized as 'Dutch disease'.[2]

In short, investment in agriculture by governments in the Near East in terms of the share of total investment fell from the late 1970s, leading many countries to become heavily dependent upon food imports (El Ghonemy 1999: 12; King 1977; Rihan and Nasr 2001).

Elsewhere, in Bolivia for instance, where large estates were taken over by tenants more than half the rural poor gained improved access to land. Food production increased but a lot of this was not marketed, as peasant households increased domestic consumption. Output might have been higher if there had been state support for agriculture more generally (Barraclough 1999: 15).

Return to the market

A decline in support for redistributive land reform was driven by the dominance of the Washington consensus in the 1980s, and with it the modernization of poverty. The lost development decade of the 1980s was a product of conservative and reactionary governments in the United States, UK and Germany which drove deflationary domestic policy and aggressive adjustment policies in the Third World. They were aided by the collapse of the former Soviet Union and Eastern European countries, as the South no longer had support or an alternative economic strategy to emulate.

The IFI agenda was focused on linking debt relief in the Third World with tough conditionality for internal economic reform in the South. That reform was to liberalize markets and open trade. It included the need to liberalize markets in land and agricultural production, input provision and marketing.

The resistance to liberalization was uneven, stronger in the Near East, for instance than it was in South America. Egypt, Algeria, Morocco and Tunisia held out longer against the World Bank and IMF than most countries in South America, but they were brought increasingly to heel as unsustainable foreign debt and agriculture, together with rotten infrastructure and corrupt regimes, forced them to recognize they could not withstand isolation from the global pressures for reform.

Although resistance to reform was very evident in Egypt, Sudan, Algeria and Tunisia, from both corrupt regimes and labour movements that tried to defend living standards as structural adjustment demanded the removal of subsidies, governments were forced to address issues of the liberalization of earlier land reforms of the 1950s and 1960s. Privatization of state and collectivised agriculture took place in Morocco, and in Algeria state farms were broken up and tenure was reformed, promoting family farms (Taleb 1998).

In Nicaragua during the period of the Sandinistas up to the 1990s, 40 per cent of total cultivated land was distributed to poor farmers and new frontiers were cleared for the land-hungry, yet these gains to promote poverty alleviation were reversed in the following decade. As many as 2000 out of 5362 large holdings were returned to previous owners, and others that had been dispossessed by the revolutionary regime received compensation for their losses. And state support for farming, including networks of agricultural co-operatives, was withdrawn (Thiesenhusen 1995: 131–6).

In Bolivia, gains from land reform in the 1950s gave way to consolidation in lowland areas, where in the early 1990s as much as 85 per cent of productive land was held by 3200 large landowning families (Ghimire 2001: 47). Legislation in 1996 created conditions for complete private titling and land sales of agrarian reform land, but privatization at all levels has been challenged since mid-2006 with the election of President Evo Morales and the strength of his Movement to Socialism.

In Peru the positive impacts of land reform during 1969–75, which had improved land access to rural poor, were challenged in the 1980s by declining government support for agriculture, the dismantling of rural co-operatives and challenges to indigenous rights to land by the commercialization of agriculture, logging and mining concessions (Ghimire 2001; Barraclough and Eguren 2001).

Pressure to move from redistributive land reform towards market-driven formulae came from both forces of globalization and the collapse of the post-war ideology of developmentalism (Bernstein 2003). The idea of development in many ways embodied the intensification of commodity production, including agrarian modes of production in the modernization of agriculture. After the 1970s, for Bernstein, the agrarian question for the South – the issue of the ways in which agriculture would be modernized, the social differentiation that it would create – had been resolved for international capital. This was due, among other things, to the increased productivity of agriculture in the North. Put simply, the classic agrarian question of the need for cheap food in the South in the transition to capitalism was resolved with the availability of cheap food in the North: thus 'the agrarian question for capital on a world stage is resolved' (Bernstein 2003: 20).

Struggling over land

Egypt: from redistribution to privatization

The government of Egypt (GoE) has reneged on the significant set of redistributive land reforms of the 1950s and 1960s. The Egyptian case highlights the power of a landowning parliament and an authoritarian regime to implement a change in tenancy laws that directly rewards large landowners.[3] It is a example of where rural violence and the abuse of human rights seem to have become structured into the fabric of political life. It is also a country where most discourse notes the limited amount of arable land, about 5 per cent, and population pressure on a thin strip of land along the Nile valley, implying natural resource scarcity as a reason for economic crises (Kaplan 1997; cf. Mitchell 2002).

Egypt also has an important broader geostrategic role as the biggest country in the Middle East. It is a staunch ally of the United States, and in 2007 was 17 years into an economic reform and structural adjustment programme. That was predated in 1987 by the liberalization of agriculture. Rural transformation promoted by President Mubarak has been characterized by rural violence, the politicization of land and crude neoliberal characterizations of the shortcomings of small-scale farms and farmers.

Nasser's land reforms of 1952 and 1961 redistributed about a seventh of Egypt's cultivable land from large landowners to smallholders, tenants and the landless. Before the seizure of power by the Free Officers in 1952, 0.1 per cent of total landowners owned 20 per cent of the cultivated land and 3 million *fellahin* (peasant farmers) owned less than 1 *feddan* (0.42 hectares or just over an acre). These near-landless comprised about 75 per cent of landowners but only held 13 per cent of the total cultivable land. Nasser's reforms were intended to distribute land to the landless or near-landless. It was a strategy to raise rural incomes and improve agricultural productivity. Nasser also wanted to erase any political opposition to the Free Officers from the Pasha class of large landowners who were the backbone of the old regime. After the reforms, the number of people owning less than 20 *feddans* increased by 13 per cent and the land they owned by 74 per cent. The largest estates of more than 200 *feddans* disappeared. While disparities remained between landholders, rural incomes improved and so too did nutrition and rural infrastructure provision. For the first time tenant farmers were given rights to land in perpetuity and rents were capped. There were also ceilings on land holding of 100 *feddans*, although families could still hold up to 300 *feddan*, and the amount a landlord could rent out was limited to 50 *feddan* (King 1977: 382–3). There were almost 2 million beneficiaries of the reforms.

Nasser's reforms also included reform of agricultural credit co-operatives previously dominated by landlords. New co-operatives were to be run by the government and became an arena of control of rural producers, determining cropping patterns, supplying all inputs and providing credit and marketing structures. Nasser also improved the supply of rural health services and subsidies. Yet ceilings on land holdings remained high, not effectively diminishing the power of landlords. The peasantry were effectively demobilized as part of a social contract whereby the state delivered a certain number of protections for the *fellahin* against the vagaries of the market and big landlords, while the peasantry agreed not to mobilize independently against the authoritarian and unrepresentative state.

Unlike the reforms in Latin America, rural development in Egypt could have received a major boost from the increase in oil revenue that accrued to the state in the 1970s. But instead of funding more radical rural development and redistribution, oil revenue led to de-investment in Egypt and more generally across the Arab world. Investment in agriculture slumped in the 1970s and 1980s as regimes imported food and consumer goods rather than produce them nationally.

Gross investment in agriculture between 1980 and 1992 fell in Egypt from 31 per cent to 23 per cent, in Algeria from 37 per cent to 28 per cent, in Morocco from 23 per cent to 22 per cent, in Sudan 12 per cent to 10 per cent and in Tunisia from 28 per cent to 26 per cent (El-Ghonemy 1999: 12). The 'boom' years of oil-led growth, of economic open-door policy (*infitah*), were also years of the states' neglect of agriculture.

The 1970s in Egypt were important in rolling back Nasser's legacy.

President Sadat tried to reverse the gains made by smallholders and tenants and he bolstered the economic and political strength of large landholders, paving the way for Law 96 of 1992.

Economic reform in agriculture

Agriculture in Egypt accounts for about 19 per cent of the country's GDP – 39 per cent if industrial activity linked to agriculture is included – at least 36 per cent of employment and an estimated 22 per cent of commodity exports. Half of Egypt's population of 65 million live in rural areas (www.usaid.gov/eg/proj-agr.htm). Using a three-year cotton rotation cycle, in the Delta and in lower Egypt cultivated land is divided into three parts: clover or short berseem is planted in winter as a fodder; cotton is planted as the summer crop after two cuttings of fodder have been taken. The second portion of land may be used to grow long berseem and the third wheat. In summer these pieces of land might then grow maize, rice or sorghum. Alternatively a two-year crop rotation cycle may be employed which divides land into two parcels. The first may grow short berseem in winter and cotton in the summer months while the second may be divided into two, growing a legume in winter and wheat in the other. In summer these crops are usually followed by maize, rice or sorghum.

Regional variations to this pattern of crop rotation include the cultivation in summer of rice in the northern part of the Delta followed by winter cereals and legumes, and in the southern part of the Delta and middle Egypt, maize in the summer, and in the winter, wheat and legumes. In southern Egypt sorghum is usually the main summer crop and in Upper Egypt sugarcane dominates all seasons as the cash crop that replaces cotton.

Pricing policy reform has shaped agricultural reform more generally, and has ignored the importance of, among other things, looking at non-price policy determinants of farmer decision making that relate to households, resource access, markets, labour access and credit (Hopkins 1993). With the concern to 'get the prices right', the IFIs have used economic reform in Egypt to promote market liberalization and this has increasingly been focused on issues of land tenure and tenant–landlord relations.

The economic reform of Egypt's agricultural sector began in the mid-1980s. Reforms targeted market liberalization, input provision and the promotion of the export of horticultural production (USAID 1998a, 1998b; USAID and GoE 1995; http://www.usaid.gov/eg/proj-agr.htm; and for a detailed critique Bush 1999).

The United States Agency for International Development (USAID) has been in the driving seat of Egypt's agricultural reform programme. It has had two big programmes: the Agricultural Production and

Credit Project, running between 1986 and 1996, which cost US$289 million; and the Agricultural Policy and Reform Program (APRP). The APRP is part of US assistance to Egypt, which is set to decline from US$775 million in 1999 to US$410 million by 2009.

USAID has focused on changing farm-gate pricing policy and the promotion of what effectively is a US farm-type model of extensive capital-intensive agriculture. The withdrawal of the government of Egypt from economic activity has been central to USAID policy and to revoking the heritage of the Nasser period. USAID has noted: 'Due to state intervention, agriculture sector growth during the early to mid-1980s was very poor with value of production growing at less than 1 per cent per year' (www.usaid.gov/eg/proj-agr.htm).

Reformers have declared agricultural reform successful because of increases in the real value of crop production in the 1980s, increases in farm incomes and wheat production, and expansion of the cultivated area (Faris and Khan 1993; Fletcher 1996; FAO 2000: 3). Yet a number of critical failures remain (Bush 1999; Mitchell 1998, 1999). Apart from the dubious nature of the statistical basis for the success declared by the IFIs, it continues to be the case that the agencies and the GoE draw on data from the early reform period, namely after 1987 up to the early 1990s, rather than subsequently. Early improvements have not been sustained. It is also very doubtful that they were due to economic liberalization (Mitchell 1998). Agricultural exports remain in the doldrums and Egypt's infrastructure is unable to deliver high-quality horticultural produce to ports for speedy despatch to export markets.

Agricultural reform, and economic reform more generally, has failed to create employment or reduce poverty. Between 1990 and 1995 agriculture lost about 700,000 jobs (Fergany 2002; *Al Ahram Weekly* 19–25 December 1996). As we saw in Chapter 1, the GoE statistical service, using the poverty-line criterion defined by the cost of a minimum basket of nutrition, noted that that the numbers of poor more than doubled in Egypt between 1990 and 1996, from 21 per cent to 44 per cent of the population. But if the measure of US$1 per person per day is used, and we assume very economically that EGP(Egyptian pounds) 500 is necessary per month for a family of five, more than 80 per cent of Egyptians are poor. Even USAID has noted that 'Egypt has not succeeded in reducing poverty,' but its strategy to do so is to incorporate the country more into the world economy and to promote public–private partnerships (www.usaid.gov/country/ane/eg/).

The violence of tenure reform

Law 96 of 1992 repealed Nasser's agrarian reform law, revoked rights that tenants had to land in perpetuity and applied market rates to rental values. There are about 1 million tenants who support 9 million family members, and as many as 90 per cent of these rent five *feddan* or less. During a five-year transitional period, contracts to land could still be inherited but the rent was increased from 7 to at least 22 times the land tax.[4] The transition period had provision for landowners to sell their land and evict tenants, but compensation of 40 times the land tax was payable to tenants for each year remaining on the contract up to 1997. Landlords could take back their land after 1 October 1997 or charge a market-based rent. Rents sometimes rose by as much as 400 per cent and although it seems prices had stabilized by 2001, the increases in rent had disastrous consequences for rural poverty. Landlords after October 1997 had power to summarily dispossess households of land that had sometimes been farmed by the same family since the 1950s. Annual contracts should have been issued by landlords but seldom were, and therefore landlords had increased flexibility to eject farmers when they wanted to.

There have been two particularly disturbing features of the consequences of Law 96. The first of these has been the impact on poverty levels among tenants, especially female-headed households and children. The second has been heightened tensions between owners and tenants that caused high levels of rural violence and contributed to the politicization of land. Farmers were shocked by the severity of the implications of Law 96, and many of them simply did not believe that the law would be enacted. The GoE had done little to publicize the consequences of the act and recruited the Grand Sheikh of Al Azhar to issue a statement that the law was consistent with Islamic principles, namely the sanctity of private property. Opponents of the law were deemed to be outside troublemakers. Not the least among these were statements from the radical Islamic group *Gamaa el islamia* that was active in the early 1990s, especially in Upper Egypt where implementation of the law was particularly severe. The Gamaa did not see any legislation that impacted adversely on the poverty of the poor as being Islamic and they opposed it.

For the IFIs, Law 96 was part of the ongoing liberalization of the Egyptian economy. For the GoE it served to both deliver an aspect of liberalization to the IFIs that was easy and did not penalize power holders, and it also reconfirmed the power of landholding groups, thereby sustaining the legitimacy of the regime with a class that was also involved in urban and industrial entrepreneurial activity (Mitchell 1999; Sfakianakis 2002).

One of the understated aims of aims of Law 96 was to create a land market. Security of tenure for landowners, rather than tenants, was thought necessary among policy makers to raise rural investments and to ensure the easier transfer of land between owners. Before 1992 land sales were dependent upon agreement with tenants, who also had to be compensated for the sale of land on which they had tenancy agreements. After 1997 the landlords could do what they liked in terms of exchanging land but this has not expanded the land market. On the contrary, much land that has changed hands has been within landowning families.

USAID sees the difficulty of expanding the market for land as a result of difficulties in proving ownership. Thus it has logically began to show concern with the development of titling. Proof of ownership, it has argued, as well as a diminution of Islamic inheritance laws (blamed for the parcelling of land within households), is necessary to boost incentives of security of tenure. Titles are also seen as necessary to boost farmer access to credit (USAID Cairo, interview April 2000). In focusing on land markets USAID's policy makers failed to do their homework. They failed to examine local mechanisms for land transfers as well as new thinking within the IFIs themselves regarding the importance of local knowledge (Adams 2000; Deininger and Binswanger 1999: see also Toulmin and Quan 2000). They have more seriously, however, failed to grasp the importance of issues relating to security of access to land and the poverty of the landless and near-landless. It is also clear that Law 96 and the way in which it was implemented politicized the issue of land in Egypt more than in any way previously.

Elsewhere I have called this the counter-revolution in Egypt's countryside (Bush 2002a). Tenants have lost rights of inheritance and security of tenure, and if they renewed contracts rents were unsustainably high. Dispossessions of land and houses that had been erected on tenanted land led to enormous economic hardship. In one such case a 49-year-old farmer in a Giza village, his 35-year-old wife and six children were removed from a piece of land that he farmed and on which he had built a small dwelling. After implementation of the land act he was evicted from both the land and his house. The landowner refused to offer compensation as the law required, and only allowed the family back to the dwelling at a much increased rent of EGP50 a month. This followed the family's mobilization of support from villagers to petition a change of heart from the landowner. The consequence of the increased rent was that the farmer became a seasonal worker for EGP6 a day.

The new land law changed poor people's livelihoods overnight. Female-headed households were particularly vulnerable to increases in rent that proved unsustainable, even though they may have previously been able to pay the rent and farm effectively. Studies of female-headed households especially reveal a dramatic drop into poverty and accelerated social differentiation (Bush 2002b). And rather than the tenancy reform serving to promote rural stability, security of tenure, and solidity in markets and land values, leading to proposed greater prosperity, the opposite has been the case. Rural landlessness and poverty have increased and labour relations may more accurately be described as characterized by a return to indentured and forced labour. Women have pulled their children from schools as costs have become prohibitive; they have been forced into wage labour as the alternative of family labour has diminished and the need for cash increased. Household debt has mushroomed and reliance upon family support has been stretched to a maximum.

The violence of escalating Egyptian rural poverty was matched by rural conflicts between landowners and tenants, and between tenants and police and security forces. Although the levels of overt conflict were less than was originally feared, ameliorated by the swamping of rural areas by security forces in 1997, there was nevertheless widespread violence. Although data accuracy is always problematic when the state refuses ease of access, the Land Centre for Human Rights in Cairo, for the period January 1998 to December 2000, recorded 119 deaths, 846 injuries and 1409 arrests related to Law 96 and land conflicts. Other authors have noted the way in which local anger at landlords was expressed with covert, subtle but nevertheless effective criticism of the wealthy in villages where local cohesion and sustainability was seen to be under threat (Tingay 2004).

Economic reform has helped to deliver the interests of large land-holders (Saad 2002) who are closely linked to the state, and where necessary this was done at the barrel of a gun and by threatening and torturing farmers who were brave enough to challenge the law. The reforms were driven by a very crude view of the need to modernize Egypt's countryside, to ensure that Egypt's farmers understand and can take advantage of the benefits of the declared new market economy. It has been based on an assumption of small farmer inefficiency, something that flies in the face of research on Egypt's *fellahin* that is ignored or dismissed by the IFIs working in Egypt (Dyer 1997).

Early evidence suggests that a strategy to reward larger landowners has been effective and it has penalized smallholders who have a myriad of simultaneous relations to the land, as owners, tenants, labourers, sharecroppers and so on. Compared with 1990, the category of fully owned holdings of land rose by a full 20 per cent, accounting for 18 per cent of the total landholding area. And the proportion of area accounted for by holdings of 5–50 *feddan* rose from 23 per cent to 39 per cent (GoE 1990, 2000).

The GoE has turned its back on Egypt's small farmers. The change has been accompanied by a rhetoric of redressing an imbalance between landowners and tenants. Erstwhile Prime Minister Atef Sidki noted, in closing the parliamentary debate confirming the law, that 'it is inconceivable that an owner would expel a tenant just because a law was issued' (Saad 2002: 103 citing Al Ahram 25 June 1992). Yet this is precisely what many owners did, and they had the support of the state and security forces that colluded with owners. The GoE in fact had set the tone for dispossessions in the parliamentary debates, as the lives of tenant farmers and smallholders more generally were repeatedly undermined (Saad 2002).

Zimbabwe: land and liberation

Control of land, and in particular the wresting of the country's finest arable land from Rhodesia's white settlers, was a major platform in the war of liberation that culminated in the Lancaster House agreement of 1979 and the subsequent independence election in April 1980. The second *Chimurenga* war began in 1966 and had major impacts from the start of the 1970s when it transformed rural life and threatened Ian Smith's Rhodesia, which had issued a Unilateral Declaration of Independence from Britain (Ranger 1985).[5] While there was not a definitive military victory, Joshua Nkomo's ZAPU and Robert Mugabe's ZANU – whose respective military wings, ZIPRA and ZANLA, waged a guerrilla struggle – placed the distribution of colonial land at the forefront of the fight for liberation. The tussle over land was crucial in generating the promise of independence and the incentive to support the liberation struggle from among the majority Black population. They eked out an existence in marginal tribal trust lands, after independence called Communal Areas (CAs).

Superficially, this case illustrates a stark contrast with the return to market formula for allocating land that Egypt's recent history has shown. The dramatic media attention that Mugabe's regime has generated highlights the breach of the rule of law and erosion of the sanctity of property rights for large-scale commercial farmers (LSCF) in favour of war veterans, hired thugs and the landless, who have received government support and police protection in their occupation of white farms. This strategy is legitimized by nationalists as a necessary and legitimate feature of restitution.

Yet upon closer scrutiny there are similarities in the way in which land has been politicized, and in particular how violence has been used to transform property rights in defence of strong political and economic forces that marginalize the very poor, intentionally or not – in Zimbabwe's case, farm workers. Political elites in Zimbabwe have used the rhetoric of redistributive land reform as a mechanism for poverty alleviation, growth and equity. Yet evidence indicates the rhetoric has been used to bolster ailing political support for a regime that has been unable to stem the tide of economic collapse. Seizure of LSCFs' land has also been used to reward politicians, party cadres, army generals and other government loyalists who have provided the necessary military back-up for a moribund regime. The finger of accusation and blame in the pilfering of farms and equipment has pointed at major cabinet ministers. Joseph Made, Christopher Mushowe and Didymus Mutasa, for example, have each been accused of 'looting' a once thriving vegetable farm, Kondozi, in Manicaland (*Guardian* 25 April 2006). I shall return later to this pattern of accumulation by ZANU PF officials.

As in Egypt, land issues have been projected to legitimize state authority and provide financial gain to the winners of economic transformation. Yet while the spoils of changes in property rights have accrued to state officials, the smallholders and the landless have remained the losers, albeit in the case of Zimbabwe many have been allocated or have themselves seized some land. That has not been the case for Zimbabwe's 250,000 plus farm workers, who have been abandoned and made redundant in the face of the 'progressive' forces of the country's war veterans (Rutherford 2001b).

Another series of questions link the two seemingly opposed cases: what is to be done with smallholder farmers, and how can land reform promote poverty alleviation? Will the overcrowded CAs become more fragmented as social differentiation drives both landlessness and the opportunity for larger farmers to benefit from the impoverishment of others? Will the recent 'fast track' resettlements help reduce CA land pressure as well as (eventually) generating agricultural surpluses for domestic food supplies and export revenue which has plummeted since 2000?

Mugabe's third *Chimurenga* was declared to resolve Zimbabwe's agrarian question once and for all by transforming the persistent racially skewed distribution of land. In doing so he sought to galvanize political support and salvage legitimacy, which had been undermined after he failed to win a constitutional referendum. And in 2006 he declared that white farmers could apply to return to some land but only as leaseholders. Was this a final capitulation to the recognition that fast-track reforms contributed to famine and food insecurity in Zimbabwe, or was it a culmination in the nationalist control of the country's resources which inevitably had challenging consequences, many of which were driven by external forces opposed to Mugabe and struggles for Zimbabwe's national sovereignty? Mugabe clearly used the land question as a mechanism to curry favour from ZANU PF's rural constituency during the violent election campaign of March 2002. That populist rhetoric is offset against allocations of the most productive land to party officials.

The land seizures have certainly aggravated a longer-term decline in Zimbabwe's national economy, and there is little yet to indicate that the reforms will ameliorate poverty levels in the short or medium term. The prevalence of poverty levels increased sharply in the 1990s and at the start of the twenty-first century. According to Zimbabwe's Central Statistical Office (quoted in Sachikonye 2003b: 5), 61 per cent of households were seen as poor in 1995 compared with 40 per cent in 1990. But poverty has fast escalated since then, and even since the 1999 Zimbabwe *Human Development Report*, which noted the proportion of poor (that is, households with income below the food poverty line set at Z$1180 for rural dwellers and Z$1511 for urban areas) was rising to 74 per cent (UNDP 1999).

Zimbabweans are categorized as 'very poor' by the Poverty Assessment Study Survey (PASS) of 1995 if their income is less than the total consumption poverty line, which was set at Z$1924 for the countryside and Z$2554 for towns. PASS estimated that 61 per cent of Zimbabweans were in households where the per capita income was insufficient to satisfy basic needs. Forty-five per cent lived below a food poverty line that meant they were not getting basic nutritional needs. Poverty, moreover, was more prevalent in the countryside than in the urban areas. Three-quarters of all households in rural areas were categorized as poor, compared with 39 per cent of urban households. Zimbabwe slipped on the UNDP Human Development Index from 121 in 1990 to 128 in 2000 (its score of 0.551 in 2000 was less than the score of 0.572 in 1980) (UNDP 2002c, 1993). By early 2006 4.3 million Zimbabwean's were receiving food aid, the life expectancy for women at 34 years was the lowest in the world (for men 37 years) and almost 4 million Zimbabweans had officially left the country, mostly to neighbouring countries to try to survive and find currency that could help family members at home. While Mugabe rallied supporters (marking 26 years of independence from Britain), saying his government was to focus on food security and foreign exchange generation, he ruled over 1000 per cent inflation and for a further year prevented FAO crop assessments that were intended to assess the extent of the country's humanitarian disaster.

Control of land has always been systemic to the way in which politics has been conducted in Zimbabwe. Zimbabwean politics since independence has been structured around the frustration at not being immediately able to transform the colonial inheritance of a racially skewed distribution of land. And the 1990s seemed to reflect an acceptance of the obstacles to land reform, not the least as politicians began to incrementally benefit from piecemeal acquisition of farms in the LSCF sector. Yet from 2000 there was a political *gestalt*. With the 'fast track' land seizures and resettlements, the nationalist revolution was possibly entering its final stage but the consequences for the economy – or perhaps the way the economy stumbled from crisis to crisis in the 1990s – jeopardized the success offered by the new impetus for reform.

Until 2000 LSCFs occupied the most fertile land. The sector accounted for 20 per cent of the GDP, 40 per cent of export earnings and one in every four jobs. Almost 2 million of the country's 14 million people relied on commercial farms for a livelihood, and more depended upon the strength of the agro-industry linked to it. In contrast, smaller-scale farming in the CAs provided livelihoods for about 1 million households, but while the CAs account for 46 per cent of the arable land, about 16.4 m hectares, the land is of poor quality and the areas are under-resourced in terms of access to markets, levels of inputs and ease of access for farmers to use oxen for ploughing. Table 4.2 highlights the distribution of land according to natural regions at the time of independence in 1980.

Many accounts of the historical past have focused on the racial allocation of land, which prejudiced any opportunity for black farmers to compete equally with white elites (Palmer 1977; Arrighi 1967; Weinrich 1975; Phimister 1988). A long list of laws during the white colonial and then UDI governments restricted the black population to the poorest and most marginal land, and discriminated against them in terms of access to inputs, marketing and farm-gate pricing. The Land Apportionment Act in 1930 established exclusive European areas which accounted for more than half of the total land area, while Africans were forced into native reserves which accounted for just 21 per cent. While the division was later adjusted to give equal African and European areas, restrictions on African settlement transformed their agriculture from shifting to settled cultivation. This accelerated soil erosion as the colonial government demarcated separate grazing and arable areas. The main reason for the divisions was to ensure a regular supply of

Table 4.2 Percentage distribution of land according to natural regions at the time of Zimbabwe's independence

Natural region	Large-scale commercial land	Communal areas	Small-scale commercial land	Other land	Total
I	63	18	1	18	100
II	74	21	4	1	100
III	44	39	7	10	100
IV	27	49	4	20	100
V	35	46	1	18	100
Total	40	42	4	15	100

Source: UNDP (2000: 31).

labour to white farms, mines and industry by the partial displacement of Africans from the countryside. Africans moreover were not allowed to compete on the same footing with white farmers in product markets; thus the Maize Control Act 1931 gave Europeans preference over Africans in local and export markets (Arrighi 1967; Stoneman 1981; Bush and Cliffe 1984).

The Native Land Husbandry Act 1951 placed the allocation of land in the reserves in the hands of government technocrats and encouraged the emergence of 'master farmers'. These were often village notables who were given titles to land, and the Act extended the accumulation of land in the native purchase areas by a potential African bourgeoisie. While persisting with views of the need to foster a conservative black farming elite, albeit one that remained disadvantaged compared with white farmers, the 1967 Tribal Trust Land Act returned the allocation of land to the chiefs and *kraal* heads.

In 1969 the Land Tenure Act ensured that 50 per cent of the country was reserved for white farmers only; this included the most productive land in the north and east, natural regions I and II. In contrast, the drier, more arid and less fertile lowland areas in the south and west, appropriate only for grazing, were reserved for the majority black population. By the early 1970s, 6000 LSCF had farms that on average were around 3000 hectares in size, though in the cases where there was irrigation, they were only 100–300 hectares. Ranches in the more arid ecological zones were up to 1 million hectares. The sector produced 90 per cent of marketed maize and cotton, and most of the export crops of tobacco, coffee, tea and sugar. This sector diminished in size and importance during the war years. It was often highly capitalized and one estimate is that only 3 per cent of the total land area was ever cultivated: between 20 and 40 per cent of the arable area (Stoneman and Cliffe 1989: 130).

Agrarian reform for the newly independent government in 1980 took the form of resettlement. It was initially a cautious strategy but, somewhat ironically, the pace and significance of the early period, until 1984, was greater than at any time until 2000. Robert Mugabe's ZANU PF was cautious about the pace of resettlement for two main reasons. The first was the felt need to learn from Mozambique's experience in 1974/5 and not promote a white exodus that would undermine the productive base of the white farm sector (Kibble and Vanlerberghe 2000: 19). And the second reason for caution was the effect of the Lancaster House Agreement. This had stipulated that for a period of ten years only land deemed to be 'under-utilized' could be expropriated, and this had to be bought in foreign currency. Other land transfers had to be on a willing-seller willing-buyer basis.

UK government defence of settler interests guaranteed that the

LSCF sector would remain unchallenged. The Commercial Farmers Union, representing settler interests, promoted instead the view that inequalities in land holdings should be addressed from within the CAs. The promotion of African agrarian capitalism was intended to be a safety valve to protect the interests of the white farming sector. Yet despite these concerns, the failure of the UK or US governments to deliver significant funding for the purchase of land ensured that the early period 1981–3 was, until 2001, the most successful in terms of resettlement.

In 1980, the government of Zimbabwe (GoZ) established a target of settling 18,000 households on 1.1 million hectares of land. By 1983 it had exceeded that target and acquired 3.3 million hectares. As Cliffe (2000: 38) stressed, 'most of the total of 3.8 m ha that was acquired by the 1990s was obtained in those early years.' In the period 1981–83, 25,000 households were settled. The GoZ Transitional Development Plan 1983–85 increased the target for resettlement to 162,000 households. Yet 'while almost 40,000 households had been resettled by 1985, the total reached by 1990 was only 48,000, and 71,000 by 1997' (Cliffe 2000: 38).

The lack of UK government and donor funding is often cited as the main reason behind why there was a shortfall in the numbers resettled because of the lack of funds to purchase land.[6] The willing-seller willing-buyer stipulation also meant that it was difficult to ensure new settlements were contiguous and that they would struggle to benefit from economies of scale (UNDP 2002b). Constraints on funds also hindered input and social provision such as school building and healthcare. There was no inhibition on productivity in the new schemes, however. Many authors have commented on the positive overall impact that resettlement had on agricultural production and

Table 4.3 Distribution of land in Zimbabwe, 2002

	1980		1997		2002	
	%	million ha	%	million ha	%	million ha
LSCF	39	15.5	28	12.1	–	1
CAs	42	16.4	43	16.4	–	–
Small-scale commercial	4	1.4	3	1.4	–	–
National parks/ urban	15	6.0	15	6.0	–	–
Resettlement areas	–	–	9	3.6	–	–
State farms	–	0.3	1	0.1	–	–

Sources: UNDP (2002b: 30) and author's calculation.

poverty alleviation. Resettled households were also identified as having a better ability to cope with drought and improve food security (Kinsey et al 1998; Hoogeveen and Kinsey 2001; Harts-Broekhuis and Huisman 2001; Kinsey 1999).

Resettlement went slower than was planned for several reasons. The most commonly cited of these are the constitutional and financial constraints already referred to and the absence of available land for purchase. Yet as Cliffe (2000: 39–40) noted, in the early years land was available, because it had been abandoned by settlers during the war, and although there were undoubtedly financial constraints on land purchase, coupled with fiscal pressures on the state made worse by drought in the early 1980s, it is more probable that the political pressures within the state itself disabled the important resettlement process. In many respects it is from these early years of independence that prospects for redistribution were dominated by the political failure to grasp the possibility for socialist reconstruction, and for agrarian reform within it, not least because the peasantry were increasingly disabled in their political voice and clout after the war for independence.[7]

Opposition to resettlement was mounted by Rhodesian MPs, the Commercial Farmers Union, and an aspirant black bourgeoisie who sought to capitalize on earlier settler regime assertions and a policy that favoured black 'master farmers' rather than land-hungry African 'cultivators'. Resettlement was eyed by the domestic bourgeoisie as the mechanism to promote primitive accumulation. The conflicting interests of the aspirant national bourgeoisie and landless ran alongside international community concern and settler interests within Zimbabwe that economic stability and export revenue should not be sacrificed on the altar of agrarian reform. It was asserted that the resettlement target of 162,000 would lead to environmental degradation. Despite these powerful lobbies, evidence indicated that resettlement worked. It supplied land (mostly) to the landless, and incomes and access to resources improved. However, it became increasingly evident that family wellbeing improved where smallholders had one or more family members with access to paid employment elsewhere (Harts-Broekhuis and Huisman 2001; Kinsey et al 1998).

Most of the 1990s saw an interlude in agrarian reform. The urgency for resettlement seemed to have expired, at least in terms of acquiring land for the landless poor. One of the themes of the late 1980s was that although about 22 per cent of land from the former LSCF sector was part of the 3.4 million hectares of resettlement, of the 71,000 resettled 500 were 'indigenous commercial farmers', 80 per cent of whom had bought land from their own funds (Sachikonye 2003b).

The GoZ did not feel, or was immune from, local pressure for agrarian reform in the 1990s. ZANU PF and Mugabe had easily won elections in 1990, 1995 and 1996. But there were two political and economic pressures that Mugabe seemed unable or unwilling to confront. The first was an economic and structural reform programme initiated in 1990 by the World Bank and IMF. Promoting orthodox conditionality, it reduced the GoZ room for manoeuvre in the agrarian sector by insisting on the reduction in storage of grain stocks and cuts in government financing of health and other public sector provision, which contributed to increasing levels of poverty and famine in the early 1990s (Bijlmakers et al 1998).

The second trend to emerge in the 1990s was an element in the ruling elite that wanted to buy land. It seems that 'The political and economic environment of liberalization was favourable to this aspiration, which found expression in lease of state land to cabinet ministers, parliamentarians, judges, senior army officers and civil servants' (Sachikonye 2003b). Individuals got state land at concessionary rates and it did not seem to matter whether they had experience of farming or not. Evidence of state cronyism gave donors an opportunity to tie any funding for land purchases (off the international agenda for many years) into a broader governance agenda. That angered the GoZ and provided a rationale for Mugabe to begin renewed rhetoric against the forces of imperialism.

Despite the lack of obvious pressure for reform the GoZ had initiated a Phase 2 for reform in 1999. It declared a new target to acquire 5 million hectares and settle 91,000 families. It seems that it was not thought that this level of land acquisition would jeopardize a strategic role for the LSCFs (UNDP 2002b: 7). The declared GoZ intention with this second phase was to reduce poverty and to increase the value of agriculture as a proportion of GDP by promoting small-scale commercial farmers. Donors, however, refused to help finance the 24-month inception phase which intended to redistribute as much land as possible by improving mechanisms for redistribution and maximizing initiatives by non-state actions.[8] Just 4697 families were settled on 145,000 hectares.

'Fast track' to chaos, or rural transformation and poverty alleviation?

The context for what became the most radical pattern of land acquisition, seizure and restitution was one of frustration with the international donor community, fears of imperial tampering with governance and agrarian reform, and desperate GoZ attempts to reconnect to its alienated rural support base. The failure to get donor support for the second phase of the Land Reform and Resettlement Programme led to the declaration in July 2000 that the government would redistribute 9 million hectares to 160,000 poor beneficiaries and 51,000 small to medium indigenous farmers. The approach broke with market strategies to acquire land. It put the GoZ centre stage in amending the constitution to legalize land seizures that were driven by government-inspired 'war veterans' (UNDP 2002b: 7–8).

The forerunner to the declaration of the fast track programme was the 16th Constitutional Amendment in April 2000, which allowed the government to take land without compensation. Land invasions organized by the 'war vets' began in earnest in the same month, spreading throughout the country. By the end of 2002 the land reform had gone much further. It had transferred 11 million hectares, most of which was prime arable land, from 4000 LSCFs to 300,000 small-scale farmers. As many as 54,000 black commercial farmers were also selected to get land. In 1980 the LSCF sector had 15.5 million hectares; by 2002 it had 1 million. This was a momentous shift in their fortunes but also in the character and shape of Zimbabwe's agricultural sector. Why did it take place when it did, and what has been the possible impact on poverty?

According to Sachikonye (2003a), the fast-track programme was a product of renewed grassroots agitation, lack of progress with donor support and the GoZ's defeat in the February 2000 referendum on constitutional reform. The fast-track programme has been characterized by violence, occupations and land seizures by groups composed of war veterans, peasants, and ZANU PF cadres and state security forces. While occupation of white commercial farmland was common in the early years of independence, squatters then were usually co-opted into resettlement programmes (Kibble and Vanlerberghe 2000: 21). After 2000 the occupations were violent and mostly coordinated by the GoZ, and certainly sanctioned after 2001 by the judiciary as the GoZ replaced judges and those in positions of maintaining law and (dis)order with party cronies. There was nevertheless another under-publicized dimension to land seizures. This was the way in which local government bureaucracy was challenged by groups of war veterans, youths and traditional authority to accelerate and shape the ways in which decisions were to be made about new settlers on the government list of 1471 farms slated for occupation (Moyo and Yaris 2007).

For obvious imperialist interests, the UK government and other donors opposed the occupation of white farms and the listing of farms for seizure. They objected to assertions of Zimbabwe's sovereignty and the state's challenge to property rights. The Abuja agreement in September 2001, after a meeting convened by the Commonwealth, agreed that land reform would be linked to governance reform. The GoZ took the opportunity to gain some time in its relations with the international community by agreeing to meet concerns about transparency on the 'listing' of farms, but this was short lived (UNDP 2002b: 17). The EU imposed sanctions, including restriction on the travel of the Prime Minister and his cabinet, although it did not prevent Mugabe visiting France for a Franco-African summit in early 2003.

It may still be premature to draw conclusions about long-term consequences for the agricultural sector of the fast track resettlement programme. Yet by 2006 there were disastrous social and economic consequences for farm workers, and a decline in the country's general macroeconomic performance. Two resettlement models were a component of fast track. The first was the A1 scheme to include village or self-contained farms, and was intended for small-scale farmers from densely populated CAs. Under the village scheme settlers were provided with three hectares of arable land and communal grazing, and each village was to be provided with minimum social services. A self-contained farm was to include contiguous land for cropping and livestock. The A1 scheme has been criticized for the lack of transparency involved in the processes that determined who was eligible for settlement, and lack of access for the Mashonaland provinces to this programme (Sachikonye 2003a). And while there was GoZ rhetoric about the importance of poverty reduction and gender rights, there was little official delivery of a policy framework able to deliver policy promises. Even the dramatic increase in resettlement resulting from fast tracking is unlikely to significantly alter the levels of rural population density.

The second, A2, model targets small-scale commercial farmers with experience in agriculture. These are allocated land on 99-year leases with a purchase option. This was declared as a strategy to 'deracialize the commercial farms'. A2 has attracted much criticism too for the way in which GoZ politicians, bureaucrats and military have been allocated land; most have little or no farming experience. Apart from continuing a naïve distinction, a carry-over from the colonial period, between small-scale 'cultivators' and commercial farmers, the strategy in both the A1 and A2 models has been to generate regime legitimacy rather than address the country's agrarian questions of rural poverty.

The other dimension of the process of land reform, however, is the way in which struggles over land policy, land seizure and the legitimacy of government action promoting a policy of restitution have developed. When histories of the struggles emerge, it might be that the under-reported rural contestation of how resettlements occurred indicates that a radical transformation of social relations of production was possible, and was evident in some locations, and that this was the outcome of conflicting class conflict within and outside the state.

For example, Moyo and Yaris have noted that while the war veterans' movement, the Zimbabwe National Liberation War Veterans

Association (ZNLWVA), emerged from the ruling party it did not act at the behest of ZANU PF. Representing 200,000 people across the country, the organization expressed many varied interests. It had a broad constituency ranging from the landless to those in positions of authority in security or business. Moyo and Yaros have noted that while the movement is usually seen as representing the interests of the state and its officials, 'the majority is part of the rural and urban poor' (Moyo and Yaros 2007, forthcoming; cf. Raftopoulos and Phimister 2004; Moore 2004). It might be that conflicts between the ZNLWVA and ZANU PF can be resolved in the long-term interests of the poor and landless and not solely in the short-term interests of Zimbabwe's crony capitalists linked directly to the state.

That resolution may be some time away. During the persistent drought of 2002–06 and the aftermath of GoZ military adventurism in Congo and sanctions from the international community, the fast-track strategy seems to have been a grievous failure. It has been disastrous in relation to food production and in generating revenue from export crops. Zimbabwe's formal economy shrank by 50 per cent in 2000–06, unemployment is at least 80 per cent, and there have been large-scale migrations that have made the parallel economy beyond the state more significant than the economy within its reach (Bracking 2003).

One group that has clearly lost out to the fast-track experience, apart from those white farmers still awaiting claims for compensation, are the farm workers that worked in the LSCF sector. Farm workers employed in the white farming sector numbered between 250,000 and 300,000. By 2002 their numbers were down to 180,000–200,000. Some of these workers may have access to land within or beyond the farm where they work (although this is a small fraction of the total), and a quarter of these workers are migrants from neighbouring countries, Malawi, Mozambique and Zambia. These may have Zimbabwean nationality or ID papers. Many farm workers have long attachments to the farms, where some have worked for up to 40 years. Many lost their jobs following the land seizures by war veterans, and much of the rural violence has been directed against farm workers. This has been a combined product of xenophobia because of their foreign origin and the belief that they were supporters of the opposition MDC (Amanor-Wilks 1995; Rutherford 2001a, 2001b).

Although the farm workers have had trade union representation with the General Agricultural and Plantation Workers' Union of Zimbabwe (GAPWUZ), it has been very difficult to provide effective representation. Farm workers are traditionally rather isolated on white farms where the owners resisted unionization and where organization was costly (Kibble and Vanlerberghe 2000: 26). Farm workers are in general very poor and there is a high level of HIV/AIDs infection, especially among women. Their lack of access to off-farm land makes self-provisioning safety netting difficult; there are high levels of illiteracy and poor working conditions. Only 59 per cent of children attend primary school, compared with 79 per cent for CAs and 89 per cent of urban children (Kibble and Vanlerberghe 2000: 23). Fewer than 5 per cent of the 300,000 farm workers have received land in the land reform programme, with at least 150,000 being laid off or chased from their employment.

It is also unclear how the balance between the commercial sector and the foreign exchange that it generated and the small-scale sector (which is important for marketed food too and not just self-provisioning) can be mediated by a regime that since 2000 seems to have used the allocation of prime agricultural land to create crony support for the ruling party through the use of public goods for private use and opportunity for capital accumulation. The speed of the fast track may have curbed the power of the old (local) settler interests once and for all, but it has also undermined local food security, export revenue opportunities and international legitimacy.

The power of international capital can be confronted more easily if there is a political agenda that strongly underpins government in an organic rather than authoritarian way. Two major errors stand out in Zimbabwe's recent agrarian history and prevent that. The first has been a failure to grasp the importance of sequencing the seizure of the LSCF. The argument regarding the need to balance access to the largely underutilized LSCF farmland and to allocate it to small-scale farmers was won politically through the use of terror, but the manner of the seizures since 2000 left the GoZ open to the easy jibe from the international community that it ignored the rule of law and abused human rights.

Mugabe was unable, and unwilling, to mount a concerted political agenda that contextualized the third *Chimurenga* as part of the unfinished nationalist revolution. Although his rhetoric was steeped in anti-imperialism it was accompanied by a belief that *ipso facto* it was legitimate because of the colonial legacy of settler theft of African land. Yet the blanket appropriation of white farms assumed that they were all financed by 'old settler capital', when many had in fact been bought since 1980. Those purchases may have taken advantage of the old racial division of land, but they would have only been allowed with a certificate indicating that there had been 'no present interest in the land'. This added to Mugabe's problems as the owners here were eligible for compensation, although just from where – with Zimbabwe's parlous finances – is unclear.

Persistent although limited settler ownership of African land would have had greater leverage with Zimbabweans, and with donors, if it had been based on a sequenced argument of principle that followed from years of difficulty with the colonial settlement, which prevented an independent agrarian strategy to ease poverty and promote national development. It would also have had greater resonance in Zimbabwe if early resettlement had not been ditched until political support for the regime was needed following mounting opposition; if a strategy for development in the more arid but ethnically unsupportive west of the country had been evident; and if Mugabe had not allowed his regimes to degenerate into plunder of national – and in the case of Congo, regional – assets.

This leads to the second indictment of the Mugabe regime, which is one that has been levelled at post-liberation regimes in southern Africa and elsewhere, although just where the balance of criticism lies between regimes, local and international political and economic forces varies (Saul 2003a, 2001). Simply put, the political infrastructure of liberation was too quickly dismantled and mass peasant movements demobilized too soon after independence.

It is the supreme contradiction, of post-liberation regimes that the mechanism that had ensured military and political success, namely the radicalization of peasant movements (Cliffe 1986), is controlled and then effectively snuffed out by new states intent of creating political legitimacy. Building a new legitimacy seems to take priority over building and positively transforming liberation ideology and practices. The social and political forces that created conditions for national liberation are jettisoned, perhaps in the fear that their persistent renewal would not tolerate emerging political leaderships that promote unacceptable government.

An effective antidote to the degeneration of the state in these circumstances would have been strong village and peasant organizations that had representation at the heart of government and that exorcized the power of the Commercial Farmers Union, among others. These forces could have been crucial in the transformation of an agrarian sector that built on local needs as well as national economic priorities and which went beyond cronyism. There is some hope that the movements of war veterans and the structure of land committees that they have overseen, which involve representation from traditional power holders, security and provisional authority, might yet prove to be a catalyst for radical social transformation.

The difficulties confronting autonomous action to support the rural poor and drive a genuinely redistributive programme of land reform are enormous. It is one thing for the war veterans to ensure that some allocation of the listed farms is delivered to the poor and needy. It is quite another to prevent the ruling party from ensuring that the political elite repeatedly use their positions of power to capture land for primitive accumulation. Evidence confirming the ways in which the ruling elite have seized land for their own financial gain jeopardizes the possibility of autonomous rural social movements.

In one case, for instance, the Masvingo Farm Machinery Committee swooped on farms in Mwenezi and seized tractors, trailers and other equipment. The Assistant Commissioner of that committee, a Mrs Ndanga, apparently had armed support to prevent opposition to her activities. She proceeded to auction the equipment, using local police stations as her showroom and auction hall (SW Radio Africa 2005).

Zimbabwe's resources seem to be viewed 'as non-cash payment for status' (Bracking 2006). Senior ZANU PF politicians and military have grabbed prime land along the Zambezi Water Project in Matabeleland. Among the officials who have either looked into seizing the land for themselves or who have already acquired it are ZANU PF chairman and parliamentary speaker John Nkomo, Obert Mpofu, Minister for Industry and Commerce, Thoko Mathuthu, governors of Matabeleland North, the Metropolitan Governor of Bulawayo and many others (*Financial Gazette* 2005).[9]

The failure to entrench early patterns of resettlement in the 1980s around meeting the needs of the landless did not move far enough beyond the old dualisms of colonial patterns of landholdings. These dualisms were encapsulated in the debate over a trade-off between either developing the CAs to promote capitalist agriculture through titling on the one hand, or promoting greater top-down state-directed people and land transfers, perhaps towards state farms, on the other.

Mugabe has superseded those debates with state-directed land invasions. These invasions have tried to take the sting out of the failure to meet rural aspirations while giving the gloss to the view that they have been driven by a people's movement. I have already expressed caveats regarding the possibilities that the war veterans have not been entirely dictated to by government, and that there may well be elements of a strong social movement to hold the GoZ to account in delivering meaningful land reform that will indeed redress long-term inequality. Nonetheless the ruling party (despite factional competition within it) still seems to be in the driving seat regarding land seizures. And party cadres are using reform to promote primitive accumulation.

ZANU PF's failure to implement a coherent and coordinated strategy that would have gone further than merely seeking to relieve land pressure in the CAs ruined an opportunity to go beyond another old dualism of the colonial legacy, namely white settler farms versus poor African CAs. The GoZ failed to grasp the need to bridge and show an organic relationship between the two sectors and the people that work in them; not least the continued importance of labour migrancy among 'peasants' who depend upon wage work as well as agricultural production (Cliffe 1988: 22–4). The transformation of the

CAs depended upon the transformation of the LSCFs and vice versa, and the transformation of both needed to be promoted democratically and with the participation of the economic and social interests linked to them.

The regime, however, in its desperation to cling to power resorted to a crude numbers game to relieve land hunger. But there seems little evidence that it was even very concerned with that outcome as food insecurity mounted. The regime has also failed to understand that the alleviation of poverty, a central aim within the theme of resettlement, required more than simply redistribution of land. The immediate causes of poverty, according to one account, lie in unemployment, low wages, drought, poor-quality land and shortage of land. In addition, there is the need for proper support mechanisms for agriculture (including credit that does not deter borrowing by the poor), subsidized inputs, and help with marketing and distribution of output as well as irrigation provision (Bowyer-Bower 2000: 99–100). Zimbabwe's economic crisis impedes this provision but it would be easier to envisage it being delivered if those most in need were positioned economically to generate the wealth necessary for its provision, and politically to access it.

5 Wealth and poverty: mining and the curse of resources?

This chapter examines the persistence of poverty in mineral-rich countries in Africa. I focus on cases in Africa because that is where mineral dependency is greatest and where recent discoveries of oil and increased global demand for petroleum have intensified imperialist interest. Struggles over oil and mineral wealth – within producer countries and between producer countries and extractive corporations and Western states – highlight processes of Africa's uneven incorporation into the world economy, which is marked by violent accumulation by dispossession of the continent's assets. I explore the debate about the 'curse of resources', which has been understood to mean that countries with an abundance of natural resources like copper and oil have tended to do less well economically than countries labelled resource-poor. I look at this in the context of the waves of optimism and pessimism for poverty reduction and economic development for the continent since the Second World War.

The early new millennium is a good time to address the debate about resources. This is not the least because 2006 witnessed yet another wave of optimism regarding possibilities for resources-led growth in Africa. Oil prices of US$75 and the highest metal prices for 20 years led the IMF to note the positive signals for projected economic growth in 2006: around 5.8 per cent in sub-Saharan Africa. Higher prices for metals, including a fivefold increase in the price of copper from US$1500 a tonne in 2002 to US$7700 a tonne in 2006, improved Zambia's economic growth by 2 percentage points (Larry Elliott, *Guardian* 10 May 2006). We shall see that this optimism is misplaced. It is nevertheless in keeping with Western deception that resources can and will, if only carefully managed, reward companies, satisfy Western consumers and deliver growth to producer states. Yet when world market prices for commodities increase, so too does the renewed scramble for the continent's resources, more aggressively coveted by imperialist powers with the declaration of 'war on terror' and 'legitimate needs' of the West to secure access to the world's resources.

In looking at the debate on the resource curse and how it relates to the prevalence of poverty in Africa, we need to be careful not to simplify the complex set of issues raised by an examination of the political economy of resources. We need for example to grasp the reasons why African elites have been unable to moderate the negative impact of trade regimes. They are regimes that penalize producers of raw materials by allocating to them only a small share of the final value added of their production (Watkins 2002). And while they are regimes that have tended to promote economic dependency they have also largely promoted political authoritarianism.

I focus on raw materials rather than more general resources such as skills, knowledge and other expertise.[1] I concentrate mainly on hard rock mining and oil production. And I sketch the argument that rentier politics has generated policies that have tied governments into the idea that rents from mining would continue and would promote development. Yet rents have seldom continued at projected levels or produced sustainable development. Rentier politics has generated state structures that embodied vested interests linked to mining and resource extraction. These interests became obstacles to policies for development that might more effectively have lessened mineral dependency. But state elites have not been unchallenged in their attempt to monopolize access to the rents from resources.

Despite the radical development rhetoric of many regimes in the 1970s where mineral exports formed a crucial part of government revenue, a politics of development complacency emerged in Africa. This complacency was brought into sharp relief by shifts in the terms of trade for minerals and the decline in world commodity prices. But this alone does not explain why African states failed to diversify, why rural development was neglected and why they were unable to control rents for national growth. The 1980s put paid to any realistic possibility of an alternative development strategy in the mineral economies, as it did to hopes of any sustained rates of economic growth in Africa (Arrighi 2002). The combination of structural adjustment, the lost development decade, recession in the developed world and the end of the Cold War ensured that many regimes based on 'spoils politics' entered the 1990s developing 'terminal spoils' (Allen 1999), where violence and the idea of state collapse became the dominant characterization of Africa.

I set the account of the main themes linked to Africa's involvement with mineral-led growth in the context of recent calls for an African renewal that have mining at the centre. I examine recent experiences of African mining and some of the consequences. Not the least of these have been conflict and complex political emergencies, and worsening poverty in resource-extracting regions of producer countries. I provide an overview of debates that Africa has suffered from a resource curse.

In Chapter 2, I showed how the concern with Africa's economic decline and trade relations remains important for commentators on African development. Yet this explanation for decline has obscured the role that *politics* within Africa has played in retaining development strategies that failed to deliver growth, development and equity. Resource dependence may generate a 'curse', but that is a symptom of the institutional and class basis of accumulation strategies that underpin crises and reproduce them. Exploring the strategies for development based on plunder of resources – and the dispossession of villagers under whose land minerals and oil lie – also helps explain links between violence and forms of resistance to the internationalization of capital driven by mining corporations. We look in more detail at strategies of resistance in Chapter 7. I will note here, however, that it is possible to see miners in small-scale operations who access mineral wealth and trade it beyond the limits of established official markets and state control, as engaging in strategies of opposition to plunder of resources by MNCs or state elites.

In sum this chapter stresses the need for a class-based analysis to highlight the importance of de-linking an *a priori* assumption that poor economic performance inevitably stems from resource dependency. I want instead to highlight the way in which dispossession of Africa's resources by imperialist states and the corporations of international capital serve to undermine the development that donors and policy makers assert is possible. And I want to show that the absence of democratic control over development policy and planning in African states serves both to dispossess people of economic wellbeing in mineral-producing areas and to uphold the economic interests of ruling elites.

The political economy of resources in Africa helps explain contemporary imperialism on the continent. Resource wealth has promoted local strategies of capital accumulation or more accurately primitive accumulation, which have created and sustained African elites, and it has also generated opposition to those elites and authoritarian politics. But Africa has also, despite what seems to have been its neglect by international capitalism, continued to be incorporated, albeit differentially, into the inexorable expansion of capitalism on a world scale.

Contemporary imperialism entails three processes. The first is the continuous and uneven export of capital from the developed capitalist heartland where mining company decisions are strategically located to parts of the underdeveloped world. The second is the impoverishing consequences of international business activity in the post-colonial world, which is dominated by unequal trade and the technological dominance of multinational corporations (MNCs) (Bracking and Harrison 2003: 6–7). The third dimension of contemporary imperialism locates the importance of the rule of capital within the context of the new military predominance of the United States.

A more open and aggressive US quest for global power explains why the Pentagon is keen to dominate not only the Middle East and central Asia's petroleum, but also reserves in West Africa from Angola to Senegal, and to promote military bases throughout the continent

(Ellis 2003; Bichler and Nitzan 2003; Abramovici 2004). US economic links with Africa are dominated by investment in oil, which accounts for 73 per cent of all US foreign direct investment (FDI) on the continent. Africa supplies 15 per cent by volume and 18 per cent by value of all crude oil imports into the United States. Of sub-Saharan African imports into the United States in 2001, energy products, notably oil, totalled US$14.3 billion and accounted for 67.8 per cent of imports from the region. Thus US imports from Africa are dominated by Nigeria (27 per cent), Angola (14 per cent), Algeria (11 per cent) and Gabon (8 per cent). South Africa is the only non-oil exporter of significance to the United States, accounting for 18 per cent. And US militarization of Africa is linked directly to the new oil fields on stream in Chad, the Republic of Congo and Equatorial Guinea. Although production will not come on stream in Sao Tome and Principe until 2012, 'oil signing bonuses' began in 2005 and the importance of these countries to the United States is already noted.

Unfulfilled optimism

Africa's development history since the Second World War has been dogged by swings of pessimism and optimism for growth and progress. African support for defeating fascism and Western capitalism's fastest-ever expansion in the 1950s led to a promise for independence. It also led to the possibility that African nationalist leaders could benefit from the new global prosperity if their country's modernization continued the historical pattern of remaining suppliers of primary commodities for Western capitalism. Primary commodities are raw or partially processed materials that will be transformed into finished goods. While there were notable exceptions – South Africa and to an extent, Kenya and Nigeria (where economic development managed more than simply an unreconstructed export-oriented dynamic) – most of the continent remained dependent upon raising export revenue from primary commodities, as indicated in Table 5.1. As a consequence, the continent was subject to fluctuating price changes over which states and producers have had little control. They have also had little influence in the finished product markets where raw material-based commodities accrue the highest value.

If the first wave of optimism for Africa's development prospects emerged after the Second World War, and the second briefly in the early 1970s, with the Group of 77 developing countries' call for a new international economic order, the contemporary trumpeting of Africa's renaissance has its roots in the end of the Cold War. As the Berlin Wall fell, commentators first considered the possibility that expenditures previously invested by the West in weapons of mass

Table 5.1 African export concentration ratios in the 1990s

Countries where one commodity accounts for over 70% of export earnings	Angola	(petroleum)
	Burundi	(coffee)
	Congo	(crude petroleum)
	Gabon	(crude petroleum)
	Guinea-Bissau	(cashew nuts)
	Libya	(crude petroleum)
	Nigeria	(crude petroleum)
	Sao Tome and Principe	(cocoa)
	Zambia	(copper)
Countries where two commodities account for over 70% of export earnings	Botswana	(diamonds and matte copper nickel)
	D.R. Congo	(coffee and diamonds)
	Equatorial Guinea	(petroleum and wood)
	Ghana	(gold and timber)
	Liberia	(iron ore and rubber)
	Mauritania	(fish and iron ore)
Countries where three commodities account for over 70% of export earnings	Guinea	(bauxite and aluminium, gold and coffee)
	Malawi	(tobacco, tea and sugar)
	Mali	(cotton products, live animals and gold)

Sources: African Development Bank (1997, Table 3.2); UNCTAD (1999, Table 19, pp. 87–9).

destruction would be directed towards the production of 'ploughshares'. This idea was short-lived. The first call for a 'Marshall Plan for Africa' (repeated by UK Chancellor Gordon Brown in December 2001 and again by UK Prime Minister Tony Blair in February and July 2002) went unanswered. Africa once more became a sink for promises unfulfilled.

As we saw in Chapter 2, a dominant paradigm promoting the optimism of Africa's development prospects has always had at its heart the view that increasing the continent's incorporation into the world economy will provide the platform for growth. Central to this has been the view that Africa's mineral and agricultural produce can generate access to scarce foreign exchange, improve employment opportunity and raise standards of living. This has received increased currency from three key sources: the UK government, international agencies and academic commentators.

The British contribution was initially driven by Prime Minister Blair. His 'Africa Partnership Initiative' and subsequent UK government documents have argued the need to help 'developing countries build the effective government systems needed to reform their economic management, make markets work better for poor people and meet the challenges of globalization' (HMG 2000: 23).

Effective government is seen as necessary to carry out basic functions and to be more responsive and democratic. The mechanism proposed by the UK government to enable effective government to develop in Africa relies on globalization working for the poor rather than the reality of the poor working for globalization. This is also the message in recent publications by international agencies. The World Bank has argued that Africa can 'claim' the new century if crucial progress is made on four fronts:

- improving governance and resolving conflict
- investing in people
- increasing competitiveness and diversifying economies
- reducing aid dependency and strengthening partnerships (World Bank 2000a).

This optimism is set against World Bank recognition that 'average income per capita is lower than [it was] at the end of the 1960s' (World Bank 2000a: 1). We have seen already the many dimensions of the world's poorest continent in Chapter 2. Among other things, trade relations that protect Northern markets but insist on liberalization in Africa make it impossible for international donor concerns with helping Africa's poor to be realized. And despite the hype of the possibility for resource-driven growth that re-emerged in earnest in 2006, the long-term decline in commodity prices reminds us of the difficulty of over-reliance on resources for economic growth.

In the short term the increased prices of metals and oil in 2006, driven by economic growth in China and speculation in futures markets, led to spectacular growth in Angola, the DRC and Zambia, among others. Between 2003 and 2005, for example, economic growth in the DRC was 6 per cent. Oil-driven growth in Angola led to expectations of 26 per cent growth in 2006 and projected 20 per cent growth in 2007. This was after 11 per cent in 2004 and 16 per cent in 2005 (Larry Elliot, *Guardian* 10 May 2006).

Seen outside any historical context, the growth figures seem extraordinary and they also seem to imply a tremendous opportunity for future sustained growth. Yet the context is crucial, and so too of course is what the revenue (as the outcome of growth) is used for in promoting sustainable and equitable growth. We shall look at the latter issue shortly. The historical context is that the industrial commodity price index from 1845 to April 2006 is marked by secular decline. Looked at in the context of the last 161 years, the increased price in

2006 more accurately reflects a breakdown in the trading of commodities. Taking 1845 as 100, the index for 2006 was down to 44. In this decline there were remarkable peaks but the decline, especially after 1945, is staggering. The World Bank's commodity price index shows a decline from the 1990 index of 100 for non-fuel commodities to a level of 85 in 1999. Other indices have all fallen from the 1990 index of 100 to 90 in 1999 for agriculture, 85 for raw materials, 71 for metals and minerals and 85 for food (World Bank 2000b: 324).

Improvements in the price of oil and metals have not been matched by increases in the world market prices for commodities like sugar, tobacco and cotton. Thus, while Angola may be reaping the benefits of high oil revenues, Malawi's dependence upon sugar and tobacco has seen its terms of trade fall by 20 per cent since 2000. Africa's cotton farmers have faced record low price levels. They fell 30 per cent during 2004, and the euro price fell by almost 40 per cent (IMF 2005: 14). The impact of this reduction in price for Benin, Burkina Faso, Mali and Togo (where cotton exports account for up to 8 per cent of GDP, and cotton production for 30 per cent of employment) is calamitous for finding investment to reduce poverty.

The vulnerability of producers and the variability between commodities have not deterred commentators on international development being optimistic about increasing the continent's incorporation into the world economy. Yet this ignores the systemic character of Africa's crisis while stressing the mantra of the need for the continent to embrace globalization. Despite a view that peace has broken out in Africa after the decade of conflict and terror in the 1990s, it remains evident that resource-led growth central to many of the models on offer seems possible only if secured by military protection in countries where donors perceive enduring problems of governance.[2] While the World Bank has noted that export diversification is possible if governments improve efficiency by reducing high transaction costs, devaluing exchange rates and promoting labour-intensive industries, they note ominously that 'Africa's industrialization is likely to be closely linked to natural resource endowments' (World Bank 2000b: 214).

This argument has been spelt out in the IMF 'in-house' journal (McPhail 2000). Although it is conceded that projects in extractive industries can have serious environmental impacts and be socially disruptive, if people are resettled for instance, it is also noted that they can 'make a significant contribution to the economic development of host countries' by ensuring that careful planning takes place. The confidence placed in natural resource projects is captured by the claim that:

> they generate sizeable revenues, create jobs and business opportunities, and often bring new roads and access to water and power to

the isolated rural areas in which they are typically located, they have the potential to stimulate economic growth, reduce poverty, and raise living standards.

(McPhail 2000: 45–6)

Additionally, it is argued that resource extraction projects bring best international practice in project planning and implementation to build administrative and institutional capacity in the host state (McPhail 2000: 45–6).

There is nothing new in this list of declared positive attributes that might accompany mineral-led growth. They mirror the broader themes linked to the perceived advantages of FDI that are encouraged by IFIs as an essential part of development possibilities in Africa. Mining capital is seen to foster market expansion and employment growth, cheapen the cost of local exploration and be generally economically progressive. It is meant to encourage local capital formation and a culture of market activity. Yet the counter to this is that mines still tend to be self-contained 'enclaves'. Because mines are located beside mineral deposits there is a problem in generalizing the proposed benefits of mineral exploration and production. Mines remain capital-intensive, with wages forming only a small part of overall costs. And while workers in mines may be relatively highly paid compared with other local workers, much of the higher wages is spent on imported consumer durables rather than adding to local savings. Trade union organization is generally discouraged.

Mining companies (excluding oil) are not the largest in the world. One estimate is that the ten largest companies have a combined value less than half that of Microsoft (Danielson and Lagos 2001). They are nevertheless powerful global actors. More than US$18 billion was spent on mergers and acquisitions in the metals mining and refining industry worldwide in 1997; a 50 per cent increase over 1996. And during the first quarter of 1998 deals worth more than US$15 billion were made.

Mining companies wield enormous influence in Africa, where reliance upon minerals as a source of revenue is high and where the assets of the mining companies can be greater than the GNP of the country where they operate. Fifty per cent of world nickel production is controlled by three companies and 65 per cent of tin output is controlled by just three corporations. The ten largest companies control around 70 per cent of the production of bauxite, copper and tin. The profits of Rio Tinto rose by 118 per cent to $5 billion (£2.7 billion) in 2005, and the enormous profits of BP and Shell in the oil sector dwarfed returns to oil-producing countries.

Mining MNCs often argue that the concessions they require from host states to enable them to operate are necessary because of the uncertainty of mineral exploration. Their costs are estimated against unknown futures, namely the time to get resources out of the ground, the quality of the deposit, the probability of future discovery and future price levels, as well as future demand for the resource they are mining. But because the mining houses are international companies, they are also concerned with a *global* strategy rather than the local concerns of the country where they may be *temporarily* based.

Mining companies thus make decisions to maximize their international strategic concerns and have a view of the *world* as well as one of any particular African state. Of the 25 largest companies, 19 are based in the industrialized world and just six in developing countries; none are headquartered in sub-Saharan Africa (two are based in the state of Morocco). The international reach of companies and the way in which decisions about national investments are shaped by global strategy is illustrated by the way the aluminium industry is organized.

The refining of bauxite into aluminium might be viewed as an African success story. Unlike the decline in African production of refined copper, the production of aluminium has steadily increased since 1975. Most of this increased production, however, is based in South Africa. In 1996, it represented 3 per cent of world production (Africa's total is 5 per cent). But this increase in South African aluminium was sourced by *imported* Australian rather than African bauxite. Gencor's smelter in Natal is used as part of the company's *global* strategy, which relies on Natal's cheap energy and South Africa's proximity to markets in Japan, Europe and the United States (Ericsson and Tegen 1999: 10–11; Campbell and Ericsson 1996). Gencor's strategy is not decided on the basis of South African, local or regional development needs.

It is not only the UK government and the IFIs that have been optimistic about a mining revival. Academic commentators too have offered a favourable view of Africa's development prospects for the twenty-first century. The optimism of the contemporary period has been created, it seems, by the adaptability of African communities to global change, famine and civil strife. African states have apparently created conditions for 'renaissance' by competing with each other for inward investment, market opportunity and the development of regional organizations.[3]

The history of Africa's primary commodity experience shows that commentators are misplaced when talking about the possibility of resource-based and labour-intensive industrialization, the benefits of the global market and political liberalization: Africa's experience with resource dependency is not a good one. A 'resource curse', an inverse relationship between resource endowment and economic growth, has summarized Africa's history of reliance on primary commodities for economic growth and poverty reduction. But this characterization of the impact of minerals and mining cannot be viewed as the inevitable outcome of resource abundance. Instead, a resource curse is better understood as the consequence of the way in which class and social forces have been shaped, and in turn shape state development policy. That policy has often become structured by the politics of spoils, corruption, war and ethnic conflict, but it is not in any *a priori* way necessarily linked to resource endowment.

One level of analytical entry into this complex relationship between domestic interests and international actors, and into the way this relationship is mediated by struggles around access to the state, is recent work on sectoral analysis. Shafer has argued that 'a state's capacity to get ahead depends on the attributes of the leading sector through which it is tied to the international economy: light manufacturing, mineral extraction, peasant cash crop production, or industrial plantation crop production'(Shafer 1994: 2). He has argued that the shape of different sectors determines international market structures, and these then provide different opportunities and challenges, as well as rewards to state actors. The role of different sectors also shapes the ability of states to be restructured.

This approach goes some way to help explain why and how resource export dependency can shape and is shaped by rentier politics. It may be that 'sectoral characteristics shape like minded individuals' capacity for collective action' (Shafer 1994: 9). This entry point for analysis should not, however, become an excuse for a preoccupation with the efficiency of African institutions or a deterministic explanation that particular types of politics follow *ipso facto* from resource availability. Instead, political struggles are fashioned around the concerns of dominant economic classes, strategies for accumulation that will ensure the reproduction of capital and the reproduction of political domination that satisfies those sometimes competing economic interests. We can now glimpse how some of those economic and political conflicts have worked out in Africa by tracing the continent's recent experience with mining, and later by examining the possible links between resources and conflict.

African mining

Much of Africa has had a long history of mining, and it remains a continent with some of the richest world reserves, with obvious potential for economic growth. In the late 1990s the continent could boast 13 per cent of the world's production of bauxite, 4 per cent of its copper and 27 per cent of gold production. Yet in all cases this is less than Africa's world share of production in 1985, when the continent accounted for

15 per cent of bauxite production, 16 per cent of copper and 67 per cent of gold production (Ericsson and Tegen 1999; Coakley et al 1998). By the late 1990s production increases for minerals were taking place less in Africa and more in Latin America and Asia. As Ericsson and Tegen have noted:

> In general, African absolute production figures are going down and the relative figures are going down even more dramatically, due to an increase of total global production. ... The decline started in the decade between 1975 and 1985 but has accelerated since 1985.
>
> (Ericsson and Tegen 1999: 9)

Copper production in Africa fell from almost 1500 kt in 1975 to a little more than 600 kt in 1996; iron ore fell from 64 Mt to 44 Mt and gold from 746 Mt to 622 Mt. That decline in production becomes more significant if South Africa is removed from the figures. If we do that, copper production in 1996 was just a third of its level in 1975 and iron ore a quarter. Increases in production from 2004 to early 2006 were threatened by the dramatic and swift fall in metal prices in May 2006 as future markets and traders feared what they perceived to be inflationary pressures and weaknesses in the US dollar. The bubble of demand had burst, and the long-term consequences of repeated fluctuations in world market prices returned to haunt producer countries.

Despite the secular decline in the industrial commodity price index African mineral producers have repeatedly been told to no longer 'sit on their natural mineral wealth, like rather inefficient dragons, confident that their riches will be there tomorrow' ('African Mining', *Financial Times* 19 March 2001). Much advice to African governments in the twenty-first-century has been to help facilitate the extraction of minerals and petroleum as quickly as possible to boost economic growth. One review noted that:

> Mining in sub-Saharan Africa is entering a new era. ... It is mining rather than other business sectors that currently has most to offer most African countries. This is because Africa has a greater potential comparative advantage in the mining of metals and minerals than it does in probably any other sector
>
> (*Engineering and Mining Journal* 1998: 32)

However, this potential is fraught with difficulties. Among these is armed conflict and difficulties related to the impact of HIV/AIDS, which as we noted in Chapter 2 impacts on immediately available African labour and opportunities for future training needs. This has an effect of deterring long-term private investment, as investors are fearful of the consequences of a dwindling labour force and the possibility that costs of welfare may well be borne by mining companies as states claw profit from a vulnerable industry.

Although many mining surveys have stressed the importance of improved investment in Africa, actual investment is uneven and so too is the distribution of mining resources and interest in particular raw materials. Strategic minerals like cobalt, vanadium and manganese and also zirconium and titanium are dominated by South Africa and Zimbabwe, while coltan (columbite–tantalite) is part of the booty for warring parties in the DRC (Campling 2001). These resources are used in lucrative aerospace and military programmes, microchips and telecommunications.

While South Africa dominates Africa's share of gold production, it is being chased by Ghana, where gold production increased by 300 per cent from 1975 to 1996. In global terms, South African dominance as the leading world producer of gold is under threat, for while it accounted for about 75 per cent of world production in 1975, by 1996 it only accounted for 25 per cent (Ericsson and Tegen 1999: 16, 25).

The South African De Beers company mines half of the world's diamonds in Namibia, Botswana and South Africa itself, and may face increased competition if peace is sustained in Angola and Sierra Leone.[4] De Beers controlled almost 80 per cent of the global diamond market, worth more than US$50 billion at the end of the 1990s. It is now being challenged by Russia, which is the world's largest producer of rough diamonds and is also involved in prospecting in Namibia and exploring for undersea diamonds.

Despite the decline in African production as a proportion of global production, there remains optimism about the potential for the mining sector as a driver for economic development on the continent. But where there has been growth, it has certainly enriched Western investors and MNCs and left host economies limited revenue to reduce local poverty and promote national economic growth. A country's incorporation into the world economy will be on the terms of corporate finance rather than local needs, and that reinforces the negative trajectory of the continent's uneven integration into the world economy.

After the Second World War and until the mid-1960s, the continent's largely foreign-owned mines provided minerals for the booming world economy. When it became clear in the 1970s that the benefits from that boom were not accruing to Africa, nationalist regimes tried to control and expropriate foreign MNCs. The mining sector was seen by nationalist politicians in Zambia and Zaire, for instance, as a vehicle for promoting economic growth (and personal wealth) and the strategy of taxing foreign companies served to enhance regime legitimacy (Shafer 1994). By the early 1980s it was apparent not only that this strategy for economic growth had failed to deliver its promise but that internationally the sector was in crisis. Reflecting on this downturn in 1984, the US magazine *Business Week* ran the headline 'Death of Mining'.

Crisis in the sector was only partly related to developing countries' strategies of nationalization. US companies felt mounting competitive pressure from European and Japanese companies, old plant and technology in the United States needed replacing, and many of the early rich mineral deposits were nearing the end of their lives. Additionally, global recession and the fall in demand for minerals led companies like RTZ, Phelps Dodge and Anglo American to diversify, rationalize internal structures, force wage cuts on workers and modernize plant.

Nationalizations in Africa pushed mining companies to seek alternative sources of minerals in Latin America and boost exploration in the United States and Australia. The collapse of mineral prices, neglect of plant and machinery, and poor management and technical skills left many African mineral producers unable to generate crucial sources of foreign exchange – a situation exacerbated by the lack of access to final product markets for African producers. The contradiction was that the mining sector, as the principal means to generate foreign exchange, required a rapid injection of foreign exchange to help its renewal and to ensure new investment in exploration and production. This was not forthcoming. And because African governments had taken responsibility for the mining sector through policies of nationalization, they became responsible for lay-offs, redundancies and falls in living standards when this perceived milch cow for development buckled (Lanning 1979; Shafer 1994).

Africa's mining sector collapsed in the 1980s. Nationalized companies, apart from those in South Africa, failed to invest in exploration and development. The sector's collapse was made worse by the inflation of African public sectors that accompanied and was driven by the promise of growth in rents from mining. The growth in the public sector generated opportunities for corruption, particularly the use of public office for private gain (Szeftel 2000). One response to this crisis was the emergence and increased importance of small-scale mining that was not always directly linked to the state. While on the one hand the state in Africa tried in the early 1990s to re-engage with mining MNCs that had begun to employ smaller-scale exploration and production companies, on the other hand, poor Africans increased or began mining activity as a coping strategy and a means to carve out a new livelihood.[5]

The crisis of African mining accelerated IFI pressure to privatize the resource sectors. The 1990s witnessed privatization of gold mines in

Ghana and the break-up of the big state-owned copper companies of ZCCM in Zambia and Gecamines in Congo. Nationalization in previous decades may not have been managed well and the constraints on Zambia, for example, were great. Among these was the domestic management of nationalization and attempts to try to harness collective strategies internationally to control MNCs in the 1960s and 1970s.[6] The assumption that privatization would guarantee profitability and improve performance was, however, disingenuous.

In early 2002 Zambian mining seemed to have all but completely collapsed as Anglo American announced its intention to leave the copper belt (the average copper price of US$0.88 a pound in September 2000 had fallen to less than US$0.60 in November 2001, a 15-year low). By leaving the copper belt Anglo American jeopardized two-thirds of national copper production, constituting half of the country's foreign exchange earnings and providing at least 11,000 jobs. Zambia's state copper company, Zambia Consolidated Copper Mines Ltd (ZCCM), had been privatized in March 2000; it had accounted for 10 per cent of GDP and 75 per cent of all foreign exchange earnings. The government had not only lost control of its most valuable source of revenue and strategic asset, but was engaged in a challenging process of privatization. It was a process, moreover, that did not reduce opportunities for corruption by state officials, but instead enhanced them (Craig 2000).

Undoubtedly the increase in copper price after 2002 had positive benefits for Zambia's economic growth, expected to be around 6 per cent in 2006–07, but rationalization in the copper belt after the national company's privatization by Canadian corporations aggravated labour discontent and added little to infrastructural development.

Ghana is often hailed by donors as one of Africa's 'success' stories, despite a mere 2.5 per cent of growth per capita in 2002–03 (World Bank 2004: 256).[7] Central to the characterization that Ghana has recovered from years of misrule by Flt Lieutenant Jerry Rawlings is the regeneration of Ghana's gold mining sector (Addy 1998).[8] In the mid-1990s, at a time of increased interest in Ghana's mining sector by international agencies and after Rawling's acceptance of structural adjustment in 1983, many concessions on favourable terms were offered to overseas investors in the mining sector. In 2000 gold accounted for 95 per cent of Ghana's mineral exports, and the 13 companies that mined it were predominantly South African, including Anglo American and Goldfields. Other companies were headquartered in Australia, Canada and China.

Ghana is the largest gold producer in West Africa with 70 tonnes registered in 2003. Small-scale miners recorded 222,762 ounces. Mining was boosted in the 1990s by more than US$2 billion in foreign investment. The twelve major gold-producing companies are foreign owned;

among others, Lonrho and Anglo American own Anglo Gold Ashanti with mines in Obuasi, Anyanfuri and Bibiani. The small junior partners in prospecting include BHP Minerals, Golden Star Resources, Gencor and Cluff Mining.

Investments in the gold sector have increased the value of minerals as a percentage of national exports from 20.3 per cent in 1983 to 45.48 per cent in 1995. Minerals have now replaced cocoa as the country's main source of foreign exchange, but only 10 per cent of the value of gold is retained in Ghana (Awudi 2002: 5) and the mineral still only contributes less than 2 per cent to the country's GDP. One commentator has noted that the Bank of Ghana 'estimates that more than 71 per cent of the value of the country's mineral exports is held in offshore accounts and the retained 29 per cent is perceived as an overestimate' (Hilson 2004: 10). Agriculture on the other hand accounts for more than 60 per cent of employment and in 2003 accounted for 35 per cent of GDP (World Bank 2004: 260).

The capital-intensive nature of surface mines, which have largely replaced deep-shaft mining, has meant the sector employs only about 20,000 workers; about twice that number are employed in small-scale mining (Awudi 2002). The remaining state sector has been retrenched, sacking 50 per cent of its workforce, who have retreated to the informal sector. Indeed the government of Ghana's economic reform programme, instigated by the World Bank and IMF in 1983, pursued not only a shift in the macroeconomic climate relating to devaluation and cutbacks in state spending, but also an aggressive reform of the country's regulatory framework.

In the 1990s, specifically with the Mining Act of 1998, Ghana dramatically reformed investment laws, beginning in 1986 with the Mineral and Mining Law, which relaxed regulations related to mining exploration and production, company taxation and allocation of concessions. The sector saw deregulation of profit repatriation and cheap asset transfers, and reductions in corporation tax from 55 per cent in 1975 to 45 per cent in 1986 and to 35 per cent in 1994 (Awudi 2002: 2). The tremendous increase in foreign investment and foreign control of Ghana's mines did not translate into a boost to the country's national growth or improved livelihoods of miners or villagers who lived in the vicinity of the mines.

Encroachment on and destruction of Ghana's forests has been one of the biggest concerns for activists and opponents of widespread opencast mining. The average area of a surface mine operating in Ghana is about 58 square miles. Companies have been given 30-year leases to operate. And perhaps only 2 million hectares remain from about 8.5 million hectares of forest. The extension of mining leases in forest reserves has also reduced Ghana's biodiversity. For example, 70 per cent of the Tarkwa area has been lost to surface mining concessions. These have denuded rich vegetation, displaced small-scale miners and led to the drying up of rivers. Between 1990 and 1998 14 communities, accounting for 30,000 people, were displaced from the Tarkwa area alone (Awudi 2002: 7).

The expansion of gold mining has led to the displacement of local communities and destruction of local agriculture, with particularly dire consequences for women whose loss of livelihoods has been difficult to replace. According to one source: 'Mining-related diseases and environmental degradation are rampant. As traditional sources of livelihoods are eroded, people, particularly women and children, are falling into extreme poverty' (*Drillbits & Tailings* 2000; see also Coakley 1998).

Spillages and leakages of hazardous waste, cyanide and other chemical pollutants have contaminated rivers and waterways, with mining companies reluctant to accept responsibility. Nine villages, for example, were affected by a spill of cyanide in June 1996 from Teberebe Goldfields in Tarkwa. Ghana Goldfield Ltd in Tarkwa spilt cyanide into the River Asuman and Humi River in October 2001, leading to villagers suffering from skin rashes and impacts on livelihoods following death of fish and bird life. The social impact on Ghanaian villages in close proximity to mines has resulted in poor health of the inhabitants: blasting has increased air and water-borne pollution, and processing has produced toxic chemicals, including cyanide, arsenic and sulphur dioxide. The mining area of the western region has the highest level of vector-borne diseases such as malaria, schistosmiasis and onchocerciasis. It has an above national average incidence of TB and acute conjunctivitis. Skin disease is caused by people's exposure to toxic chemicals, and arsenic dermatitis causes mental-health disorders. Sexually transmitted infections like HIV and syphilis have a high incidence related to high levels of migration and transition populations. Social impacts in addition to population growth, displacements and prostitution include high levels of violence and increased drug use (*Drillbits & Tailings* 2000; interviews, Tarkwa, November–December 2006).

The Ghanaian case highlights the social consequences of the regeneration of gold mining by foreign-controlled companies and inadequate state regulation. Another important assessment of just how successful African mining recovery has been, or where the potential for using the sector to harness economic growth lies, can be found in the area of refining or beneficiation. It is here where important value added from the mineral sector is based. Beneficiation refers to at least one stage of refining raw materials or ores towards a finished metal. And while there seems to have been some progress in this regard the figures are misleading.

Many of the resources refined in Africa are imported rather than produced locally. This is the result of mining corporations determining supply and demand for commodities on the basis of their global strategy rather than local African need. In 1975, 66 per cent of African-produced copper underwent beneficiation in the producing region. This figure rose to 79 per cent in 1996. For bauxite/aluminium the figures were 12 per cent and 28 per cent respectively. Yet a lot of West Africa's bauxite was not smelted in the region but exported, sometimes as aluminium oxide (partly smelted bauxite), and as we noted above, much of South Africa's bauxite was imported from another continent. Although there may have been increases in the smelting of copper, for example, this has occurred at a time of falling production (Ericsson and Tegen 1999: 12).

Cursing resources?

Ghana's experience with mining and the ability of transnational corporations to dictate global strategy rather than promote local development has confirmed what many politicians in the Global South have frequently called a curse accompanying resource wealth. The founder of OPEC, Juan Pablo Pérez Alfonso, described oil as 'the devil's excrement' and Zambia's erstwhile President Kenneth Kaunda noted the 'curse of being born with a copper spoon in our mouths' (Quoted in Ross 1999: 297). And while the proportion of developing country exports accounted for by primary commodities fell between 1970 and 1993 from 80.4 per cent to 34.2 per cent, in part due to the boom of manufacturing sited there, three-quarters of the states in sub-Sahara Africa still accrue half their export revenue from primary commodities (Ross 1999: 298).

The idea of a resource curse relates to the relative economic, political and social underachievement of countries with resource wealth compared with those that do not have natural resource endowments. Where resources account for a high proportion of export revenue there tend to be poorer rates of growth and higher levels of poverty. According to the World Bank: 'Data on real per capita GDP show that developing countries with few natural resources grew 2–3 times faster between 1960 and 1990 than natural resource-abundant countries' (World Bank 2003: 149). The only African country with a high dependency on minerals that has sustained relatively high levels of growth, and is therefore the exception to the rule, is Botswana.[9]

There are at least five main reasons why countries with resource dependency seem to do less well than those without resources (Ross 1999; Auty 1993, 1995; Clark 1997; Mahdavy 1970; Yates 1996). They are:

- a fall in the terms of trade for primary commodities
- the instability of international commodity markets
- weak or non-existent linkage between resource and non-resource areas (both spatial and sectoral)
- impoverishment of rural livelihoods
- 'Dutch disease' (an appreciation of a country's exchange rate following an increase in exports accompanying resource exploration, an effect that is often paralleled by the movement of investment away from non-resource sectors as labour moves to be employed in mining enclaves).

Even as commentators were welcoming the 30 per cent improvement in Africa's overall terms of trade in 2000–04, the short-term hike in commodity prices had already, in Zambia for instance, raised the real exchange rate and so worsened trading conditions for non-commodity exporters. The accompanying neglect or adverse impact on the agricultural sector following the hike in the value of the *kwacha*, Zambia's currency, made exports more expensive.

The five broad areas discussed above contribute to the failure to sustain high levels of revenue generated from raw material exports or to spread them evenly. The causes of this debilitating consequence for resource-driven growth need to be set alongside the balance of class and social forces within a particular country, and the allegiances of dominant economic interests. It is only then that it becomes possible to get a sense of two crucial common tendencies. The first is the failure of the state to promote a diversified development strategy that is independent of external rents rather than local productive activity. The second is to apply nuanced and historically grounded theoretical frameworks to understand the way in which so-called 'state collapse', warlordism and tyranny has been linked with Africa's resource-rich countries.

Rentier politics

One concept that has been used to highlight the development dilemmas of resource-dependent economies is the 'rentier state'. This term has been used to characterize states in the Middle East that are dependent upon oil revenue for government expenditure. It has also been used in the African context to understand the political consequences of oil rent dependency in Gabon, and it might be applied to countries like Nigeria, Angola and – for minerals more generally and timber – Liberia and Sierra Leone (Yates 1996).

A rentier state is one that receives regular and substantial amounts of external rent. The requirement to raise revenue from local productive activity and taxation becomes less important in those circum-stances. The middle class may also forgo the trappings of liberal democracy and representation if it can acquire wealth more directly through access to the state and the distribution of the benefits of mining, mineral sales, contracts, exploration rights and so on.

The idea of a rentier state has been analytically important. It has helped characterize authoritarian politics and the spread of corruption in the Middle East and Africa. Spoils politics in the circumstances of underdevelopment, and where a resource is available for exploitation, is not an affirmation of primordial loyalty. Instead it results from lack of opportunities for capital accumulation beyond the state. There are simply fewer chances that a bourgeoisie involved in productive capital will emerge, perhaps in manufacturing. This is because it is far easier for dominant classes to secure access to ready-made wealth in the form of rent, and for the state in those circumstance to become increasingly autonomous from society at large.

One of the difficulties of the term rentier state, however, is that it has tended to mask social relationships that constitute the state. In trying to understand why economic growth and poverty reduction have not followed booms in resource prices or mineral production, it might be more accurate to talk about 'rentier politics'.

'Funnel states' distribute rent and in so doing create (sustain) a rentier politics mentality (Shafer 1994). Where states benefit from access to resources, they do so not because of any productive activity that the bourgeoisie has generated through a strategy of capital accu-mulation but because of a country's natural endowment. A consequence of this, evident in the 1970s optimism expressed by African elites who instigated the nationalization and expropriation of mining companies, is that political leaders became deluded. Many assumed an endless stream of rent from mineral development. Ineffec-tual government and planning became a character of regimes where access to rent was easy and a substitute for productive activity. It also became an avenue for the allocation of state contracts to reflect personal interests and spoils politics rather than merit or economic effi-ciency. This does not mean that resource-based industrialization is flawed or that access to rents from mining MNCs will automatically create corrupt political regimes. Nor does it mean that spoils politics, corruption and graft are automatic features of politics on the continent because Africans cannot manage their public affairs (Chabal and Daloz 1999; Zartman 1995). It is instead to stress that rentier politics can emerge where the balance of class forces shaping state policy pursues the 'easy' route of revenue generation from resource rents, often because there is little popular control over the state.

Rentier politics emerges more quickly where institutional barriers to corruption and political processes to inhibit it are weak, and where opportunity for capital accumulation is structured primarily through membership of or connection with the state elite and linkages with foreign capital. Nigeria's military regimes, particularly Abacha's, reflected a complex mix of local politics and the way the country was inserted in the world economy, generating conditions for military rule and authoritarian politics while constraining opportunity for capital accumulation that was not linked to membership of state elites or the oil sector.

Rentier politics goes some way to explain why it is that regimes are unable to take corrective action in the face of the consequences of rent dependency (Ross 1999). As a 'high-absorbing' oil exporter, with a large population in relation to its proven reserves, Nigeria has been under more pressure than low-absorbing oil exporters, or capital surplus exporters like Saudi Arabia and Libya, to invest and consume its oil revenue quickly. After its civil war and before the 1973 oil price hike, Nigeria's economy grew at close to 8 per cent a year. Agriculture accounted for 39 per cent of its GDP and it was self-sufficient in food, exporting groundnuts and palm products. Manufacturing only accounted for 6 per cent of GDP. With the fourfold price increase in petroleum in 1973 and 1979, Nigeria initially invested overseas, but that savings strategy did not last long. The country accumulated foreign debts of US$30 billion between 1979 and 1981. Investments in infrastructure, including road building and education, swallowed the windfall from oil price rises. After 1979 the country began a resource-based industrialization programme that included the building of a new capital in Abuja. It also involved attempts to develop a capital goods sector, but the programme was regionally distributed on the basis of meeting the interests of local elites rather than a coherent development strategy (Auty 1995: 193; Forrest 1993).

Nigeria's economic growth plummeted towards the end of the second oil boom in the late 1970s. The country's industrial structure failed to meet its development needs. The Abacha regime was characterized by political authoritarianism, wasteful expenditure, corruption, persistent subsidy of loss-making public companies in the interests of local patrons rather than collective need, oil price subsidies, the execution in 1995 of MOSOP[10] leader Ken Saro-Wiwa and eight other Ogoni activists, and the persistent harassment of communities in the Niger Delta oil-producing areas. Real GDP growth of about 2.6 per cent from 1996 to 2000 (petroleum accounted for about 90 per cent of export earnings) was offset by population growth of 2.4 per cent and inflation of 20 per cent (Amuzegar 1999: 233).

By 2003, the majority of Nigerians were poorer than they had been in 1970. Per capita income was US$320, with high levels of skewed income distribution: the top 20 per cent of Nigerians accounted for 55.5 per cent of income or consumption, and the bottom 20 per cent for just 4.4 per cent (World Bank 2004: 259). External debt remained large, accounting in 2002 for 64 per cent of GDP. Nigeria's dire economic condition led the *Financial Times* in its special country supplement in 2004 to note that 'No country provides a more graphic illustration of the curse of oil' (White and Peel 2004: 1).

Yet if Nigeria illustrates the implications of a resource curse, there was no inevitability about the country's decline. Nigeria's economic crisis represented a failure to manage resource booms, the inflation of a grossly inefficient public sector wherein rentier politics shaped the decisions about the allocation of resources, and a failure to sustain the extended reproduction of capital beyond the oil sector. It thus also reflected the undermining of non-resource economic sectors like agriculture and manufacturing. The failure to manage the distribution of resources accruing from the oil booms of the 1970s set in motion a political dynamic that confirmed the political domination of the state apparatus as the vehicle for distributing the largesse from oil rent.

The strength of the military gave it the necessary influence to defend its own corporate interests and those of the ascendant Nigerian capitalist class linked to oil. That ensured that there were no savings available to be used when the oil boom passed. There had been only ineffectual investment in production during the boom, and output from that investment after the fall in oil prices was limited and of poor quality. And there was little indication that Nigeria had learnt any lessons about how to avoid all these pitfalls after 2000 when oil prices improved significantly.

The 1970s and 1980s might be viewed through the lens of too much pressure by the ruling elites for immediate consumption, and for this consumption to retain the balance of power between southern and northern-based elites that had ruled Nigeria since independence. And here the fact that Nigeria was a strategic ally of the United States in Africa and a major supplier of its petroleum is significant for the failure to condemn repression and authoritarianism in Nigeria during the worst excesses of the military. Nigeria supplies 7–9 per cent of US oil imports. It is the fifth largest source of imported oil into the United States (www.state.gov/r/pa/ei/bgn/2836.htm), which took 38 per cent of its total exports in 2002. It is understandable why, despite occasional hand-wringing in Washington, the excesses of different military regimes did not disrupt the oil business. However, when the autonomy of the state and untrammelled corruption in the 1980s and 1990s threatened the stability of international capitalist interests of oil corporations, international collusion with Abuja became more problematic.

All three oil majors that operate in Nigeria (Shell, Exxon-Mobil and Chevron Texaco) have been implicated in allegations of repression and impoverishment of the oil-producing areas (Fleshman 2002; Milieudefensie 2000; Peel 2005). The Niger Delta Region (the states of Bayelsa, Delta and Rivers) accounts for 75 per cent of oil production and more than 50 per cent of government revenue (UK Parliament 2005: 5). Although many inhabitants of the Niger Delta supported the process of political liberalization at the election in 1999, there has been little improvement in their livelihoods, at least for those who have not been co-opted by the new federal government.

The Niger Delta has one of the highest levels of youth unemployment in Nigeria; 70 per cent of the region's inhabitants still have no safe potable water or access to electricity. And while the national average for access to a doctor is 1:40,000, it is 1:82,000 in the Delta and in some locations only 1:132,000. It is not surprising that the Niger Delta is a major source of political and military opposition to the impact that oil production has had on the people who live in oil-producing areas.

In 2004, the newly formed People's Volunteer Force of the Niger Delta, an armed group of Ijaws, declared 'a total war' against the Nigerian state. It accused the international oil companies Shell and Agip of collaborating 'with the Nigerian state in acts of genocide against our people' (Weston 2004: np; see also Ibeanu 2002; Human Rights Watch 1999b, 1999c).[11] Following Mobil's oil spill of 40,000 barrels in January 1998 (roughly equivalent to one-sixth of the *Exxon Valdez* spill in Alaska) and the resulting destruction of the local fishing industry, which led to thousands of claims for compensation, a fisher noted: 'Mobil is the only visible entity. They are making a lot of money here, and we've been left like monkeys out here in the swamp' (*Drillbits & Tailings* 1998).

The failure to ensure a broader distribution of the rents that have accrued to the Nigerian state is an important element in the politics of rentierism. Another has been the failure to ensure that reserves have been saved to compensate for resource depletion or shifts in market demand. In the 1970s when the price of copper fell, there were attempts to establish international stabilization funds and a cartel of copper producers. Neither was long-lasting or effective. The sums of money required and the international support for such a venture were not forthcoming. It is partly because of rentier politics that states have made no provision for future expenditure that was not dependent upon resource rents. The stream of revenue from resources is finite, depending on the quality, quantity and international demand for a resource. These are issues over which African states have little control, but they can make strategic decisions about the pace of depletion and the allocation of revenue that accrues from mining (Auty 1995: 200; Shafer 1994).

The limitations on that decision making are shaped, however, by the structures that emerge around the rentier state as policy and development programmes become increasingly dependent upon rent. And it is not only the flow of rents per se that becomes a feature of rentierism but the way institutional factors change state structures, the framework for decision making and 'prevailing notions of property rights'. All these affect the relative power of social classes and establish a broader context for understanding governance structures shaped by rents (Karl 2001: 7).

Fuelling conflict

If poor economic performance and rentier politics are linked in the Global South with reliance upon primary commodities, the most immediate contemporary concern for raw material producers has been a prevalence of war and civil conflict.[12] Put simply, resource endowment in Africa has been linked with war. Struggles over access to resources have often been seen as the cause of conflict over diamonds, rutile and bauxite in Sierra Leone; diamonds and oil in Angola; diamonds and coltan in the DRC; iron, diamonds, timber and rubber in Liberia; bananas and camels in Somalia (Le Billion 2000: 24). Although it is too simplistic to reduce conflicts to a 'single motivation', resource wars have been often characterized as resulting from resource scarcity (grievance) or resource abundance (greed) (Le Billion 2000: 22–3). The preoccupation of authors with the distributional struggles over resources, among other things, has tended to focus disproportionately on resource-rich countries and ones where resources are significant for Western state interests.

An alternative explanation for resource wars has viewed conflict resulting from what I have argued here is a rentier politics, namely when 'wealth depends on state or territorial control, [where] competing groups will resort to non-co-operation or violence to control revenues' (Le Billion 2000: 23; Reno 2000; Collier 2000b; de Soysa 2000). Access to resource rents is seen as a vehicle for keeping elites in power, and challenges to those rents will therefore be a cause for conflict. An example of this type of conflict is the bloody civil war in Liberia where Charles Taylor attempted to seize power in 1989 and, after he failed to do so, took over and controlled the timber and mining sectors outside the capital Monrovia. In the early 1990s Taylor supplied a third of France's tropical hardwood requirements via French companies (Duffield 2000: 84).

A key feature of Angola's long-running and now concluded civil war was the heavy reliance of the MPLA government upon oil rents from US oil majors, while the late Jonas Savimbi's UNITA rebels used diamond wealth in the captured territory to fund their continuation of military conflict. This is not to argue that mineral wealth necessarily destroys a country. Rather, it is the failure of wealth to be distributed widely and evenly that has generated grievances (Hodges 2001) in contexts where access to the state has been the determining factor in strategies for capital accumulation.

In the case of Angola, it is incontrovertible that loans to develop the oil industry were used by the Angolan government to purchase arms to continue its war against Savimbi. The control of diamond exports by UNITA, valued at US$300 million in 1999, helped sustain rebel access to arms and led among other things to the establishment of a highly developed parallel market in diamonds and other commodities. Before the 2002 ceasefire, Angolan government military gains in 2000 dramatically cut UNITA access to the diamond trade down to US$100 million, but that was still sufficient to fund a military operation (De Boeck 2001). We have noted already how oil fuelled militarization and conflict in Sudan; the discovery of oil in western Upper Nile led to government atrocities against local inhabitants, forced population movements and mass displacements, and to reported collusion between operating oil companies and the Islamist Khartoum-based regime (Verney 1999; Flint 2001; Brittain and Macalister 2001; Curtis 2001: 12).

In contrast to the view that resource wars simply relate to struggles of greed or grievance, or in a more reductionist vein that economic factors such as the demand to access mineral wealth are the *primary* cause of war (Collier 2000b), it is more useful to look behind issues of conflict to what has recently been called 'complex political emergencies' (Cliffe and Luckham 1999; Duffield 1998).

It is necessary, for example, to look at the interaction of *both* greed and grievance and at the characterization of political forces that shape the way in which political and economic power is exercised in countries beset with violence (Cliffe and Luckham 2000: 295). Examining conflict in this way does not reduce causes of conflict to resource endowment but asks questions that go beyond evidence of resource abundance or scarcity. It goes further too by not prioritizing an immediate need to understand the *cause* of conflict. Understanding conflict is not reduced to struggles over resources but to recognizing factors that shape the ways in which states and politics have been constructed. Central to these factors is an assessment of the competing interests of local classes and the consequences of the specific incorporation of different African countries in the world economy. It may also offer the advantage of looking at the possibly transformative features of conflict that effectively reduce the role of the state as a central actor.

War and violence may be the mechanisms by which new relations of legitimacy are forged between and within warring parties, and new networks of power, politics and economy emerge. This more nuanced attempt to understand the way in which violence and conflict have emerged, and what links conflict may or may not have with resource endowments, will also provide an insight into the proliferation of small-scale mining in Africa.

The expansion of small-scale mining is often seen solely as a state or business initiative to adapt to changes in market demands. Yet it might actually instead be a manifestation of resistance by miners and others to the global economy. Clearly here, as revealed in the case of Angola, there is a difference between what a state can do with a sector such as petroleum, where transborder activities are limited – although as we will see below in the Nigerian case, not impossible – compared with the activities that emerge around alluvial diamond or gold mining. Rather than always viewing conflict as a means to access resources, it might be more appropriate to see resource access as providing a mechanism to help resist liberalization and provide a means for the producers themselves to take control of local assets.

This is one possible explanation for the struggles of people in the Niger Delta against the oil companies and the government of Nigeria. Instead of seeing the attacks against oil installations by Ijaw youth and others as issues of law and order, they can be seen as struggles to access locally generated resources before they are piped out of the region. Terrible accidents have occurred when villagers in the oil-producing regions and other poor Nigerians not in producing areas tap into pipelines carrying crude. A pipeline blast in southern Nigeria in 1998 killed more than 1000 people; in September 2004 a pipeline exploded near Lagos as attempts were made to siphon oil; and 200 were killed in May 2006 in South Western Nigeria as villagers tried to capture oil east of Lagos (www.onlinenigeria.com accessed 15 May 2006). In May 2006 foreign workers were kidnapped in the centre of oil operations in Port Harcourt, and regular attacks on installations – on land and also at sea, when youths have secured oil platforms from oil companies – are part of the struggle between the dispossessed in oil-producing areas and the coalition of foreign firms and the national government.

These attacks are viewed by the government of Nigeria as acts of criminality. There has been a tremendous increase in recent years of collaboration between companies and the state in the promotion and recruitment of security agencies to defend oil installations. The Supernumerary Police (SPY), although hired and recruited by the state, work for and guard oil company installations and have added to the immense tension in oil-producing areas where the forces of law and (dis)order have mushroomed, leading to the dilution of state monopoly of arms. Instead of labelling acts of sabotage or theft of oil as criminality, it seems more accurate to view them as legitimate struggles against a state and corporations that fail to return revenue to oil-producing areas.[13]

On the other hand, however, the huge scale of oil 'bunkering' (a term adopted from one meaning to supply a ship with fuel) in massive barges is usually promoted by individuals and groups sometimes linked to government.[14] Before the oil reaches the terminals, gangs tap into the pipelines and fill barges with oil. Their contents are then delivered to offshore tankers. The quantities of this theft are enormous, and have led to an increased militarization of oil-producing areas as the government of Nigeria, helped by US advisers and military, tries to reduce the loss to the state and foreign companies. Shell admitted to losing an average of 100,000 barrels of oil a day to bunkering in 2003. But this figure seems an underestimate. A confidential report to Shell in that year stated that between 275,000 and 685,000 barrels a day were stolen, generating US$1.5–US$4 billion per annum to those who appropriated the oil. The US military estimate the figure as closer to 200,000, which on a US$65 barrel is US$13 million a day – far more than any savings the Nigerian government have managed to extract from donors on debt rescheduling (compare Donnelly 2005: 3; Peel 2005: 11).

Sustainable mining?

Donors and development agencies alike have indicated that resource-led growth in Africa, and elsewhere, offers an effective strategy for economic development and an opportunity to reduce poverty. The effective use of natural resources in development is seen to be dependent upon the ability of a state to encourage foreign direct investment, ensure responsible and transparent financial management and improve local governance. Convergence of interests underpins the view that resource-led growth is possible and desirable.

A major recent enquiry into the global mining industry, by an international environmental advocacy group, has argued that there are important areas of potential convergence for an agenda for change. Not departing far from World Bank views, the International Institute for Environment and Development (IIED) has promoted an upbeat characterization of the possibilities for collaboration between developing countries, international corporations and the international community (IIED 2002). Recognizing the continuing importance of the mining industry, and that any enquiry into its impact and future is controversial, IIED has argued that it remains possible to link the mineral sector with sustainable development. IIED noted:

> The challenge of the sustainable development framework is to see that the minerals sector as a whole contributes to the welfare and well-being of the current generation, without reducing the potential for future generations to do the same.
>
> (IIED 2002: 4)

This indeed is a challenge that, in the context of contemporary obstacles to development (and particularly in the way in which the politics of accumulation by dispossession is driven by imperialist states), suggests the sustainable development model will not work.

The development of a strategy around mechanisms of control and development with the industry itself, so mining companies can, among other things, review end-of-life plans at existing operations, ensure companies invest in sustainable development community plans, promote integrated materials management, product stewardship and so on, is laudable but flawed (IIED 2002: 35–6). 'The notion of a "sustainable" mining based development is an oxymoron' (Slack 2001: 2). There is only negligible space for state flexibility in benefiting from value added in finished product markets. And it is also improbable that African states will construct a development strategy that can guarantee streams of revenue from raw materials, never mind actually use the revenue in ways that will benefit the most poor in enclaves where minerals and oil is mined. While Nigeria in July 2005 improved the proportion of revenue accruing to its oil-producing states compared with non-oil-producing ones, the 'deal' fell far short of the 50 per cent demanded by the oil states (Peel 2005: 4).

Although there have been some improvements in revenue allocation, the use of revenue for development and poverty reduction remains mired in struggles over spoils and allocative mechanisms within states, and among powerful brokers within regional and federal government, as well as chiefs and the youth of oil-producing states who demand a radical shake up of federal finances and greater equity in the allocation of revenue. Much of recent discussion regarding the problems that MNCs generate for host countries centres on whether the negative consequences for development would be reduced if codes of conduct were adopted. Part of those codes relate to the need for greater transparency in dealings with oil companies and their relations with governments (Global Witness 2002).

Following the World Environment Summit in Johannesburg in 2002, UK Prime Minister Tony Blair helped facilitate the Extractive Industries Transparency Initiative (EITI) in 2003 (www.eitidev.forumone.com). The

EITI received a lot of publicity for its attempt to refocus the impact of mining companies away from just their environmental externalities towards the way in which they affect economic development. At the heart of the EITI is the idea that corporations and governments should 'publish what they pay'. Many large mining houses signed up to this initiative, Shell, BP, Exxon/Mobil, Chevron Texaco, Anglo American, Total and Rio Tinto. Additionally there has been much fanfare that institutional investors linked to managing $9 trillion of investment funds also signed up to the EITI. The payback for government, according to the UK's DfID, is that stable government will emerge from greater transparency.

In addition to the mining houses, many international NGOs also signed up to the idea of publishing the financial transactions between mining companies and governments. These included CAFOD, Save the Children and Global Witness. The NGOs were nevertheless somewhat critical that the emphasis in the relationship regarding publishing financial transactions has fallen heavily on governments and not companies.

Emphasis on government responsibility was reiterated by the UK Chancellor on a short trip to Nigeria in May 2006, accompanied by the rock singer Bono. Gordon Brown stressed that African corruption remained at the centre of the continent's continuing crises. The question of responsibility, openness and transparency is central to those who claim the possibility of holding companies and governments to greater account, and while the idea of openness is important it has only moderately been achieved.

Transparency, it seems, has become a mantra and a substitute for critical thinking about why and how some states in Africa have become mired in examples of corruption. Such was the dismay at the one-sided nature of transparency that focused on corruption rather than the roots of injustice and inequality, the agency Global Witness became publicly very critical of the EITI in 2005. The NGO was underwhelmed by the lack of progress in the UK government's own declared expectations of transparency, and by the inadequacy of systems of voluntary agreements rather than legal enforcement of a tough code of practice. Global Witness, among others, had become irritated at the absence of benchmarking of EITI, the failure to expect good practice between companies and governments, the absence of independent verification of data, paucity of access to financial data and lack of official auditing of company accounts.

The background to the EITI had shaped the voluntary nature of the code. In February 2001, BP had threatened to disclose its financial transactions with the Angolan oil company SONAGOL. In response SONAGOL threatened to rescind a US$5 billion contract. The publication of the detailed payments between BP and the Angolan government would have revealed widespread corruption and state embezzlement in Luanda. Yet the threat of losing a US$5 billion contract pushed BP and the UK Foreign Office into overdrive to secure the oil contract and to retain only a voluntary agreement between oil producers and the oil companies.

The EITI was a reaction to the challenge of 'publish what you pay'. Each major oil company became nervous about taking a lead in transparency after BP was threatened with the loss of an enormous contract. The erstwhile UK Secretary of State for International Development, Clare Short, apparently viewed the voluntary nature of EITI as a preliminary to mandatory systems, but Washington was never interested in compulsion. Exxon have only ever discussed voluntary codes, although even they have realized the tremendous power of the US$9 trillion investment fund that signed up to EITI.

The real power of geopolitics was realized, of course in the lead up to the US–UK invasion of Iraq. Angola was a member of the UN Security Council at that time and was challenged to improve governance before receiving further development assistance. Yet a visit to Luanda by the UK minister Valerie Amos encouraged Angola to vote in support of the Iraq invasion. In return it seems the Popular Movement for the Liberation of Angola (MPLA) officials would not be pressurized to reveal how much they individually benefited from contracts with oil companies, and no timeframe was put on political liberalization.

By 2006 there had been some progress in the establishment of different country committees and organizational back-up for EITI to operate, but there remained no example of prosecution of companies while accusations of government failures in Africa continued. There seemed also to be very little progress in the idea that the EITI would become a platform for civil society agencies and independent scrutiny of accounts. Certainly the Nigerian EITI was dominated by representatives from international business, IFIs and donors. Of the 28 members of the committee of the First Roundtable on the NEITI Audit Results, which met on 12 January 2006, only six were representatives of civil society. There was only one representative from the Rivers State Assembly and apparently none from the youth organizations or other representatives that struggle daily against the excesses of oil companies and state officials. The meeting was chaired by the British Ambassador, Richard Gozney (www.NEITI.org accessed 25 May 2006).

Debating transparency, considering the creation of stabilization funds for commodities that are especially susceptible to changes in world market prices, and donor linkage of conditionality with governance and human rights in producing countries continue to be part of discussions of greater control of mineral-dependent states. Yet African states remain unable to control the international pricing of commodities, operating in a limbo between current prices and possible future shortfalls. In such a world planning is difficult and fraught with concerns as to how to meet different needs and expectations. There is no donor sympathy or money for a commodities fund that might provide a lifeline to producer countries in times of commodity price free fall. Mineral exports will continue to be a major part of Africa's (under)development and at different times the continent may even seem to benefit, albeit unevenly, from such a link. It is mistaken to assume that all sub-Saharan Africa's responses to the global mining industry will be the same, or that the constraints on a country like South Africa or Nigeria will be the same as they are for Ghana or Burkina Faso.

How well African people benefit from local resource endowments is dependent both upon the outcome of the prices paid to producing countries for primary commodities and the robustness of local social and class forces to ensure that mineral dependency does not generate rentier politics. But both these processes of establishing pricing mechanisms that are shaped locally, rather than internationally, and the creation of local class politics that are not driven by primitive accumulation and the dispossession of people in mineral economies of their wealth, remain subject to the vagaries of the global capitalist system and not just the capture or improved efficiency of the state in Africa.

6 Securing food and famine

Within a decade no man, woman or child will go to bed hungry.
(Henry Kissinger, World Food Conference, 1974)

We pledge our political will and our common and national commitment to achieving food security for all and to an ongoing effort to
eradicate hunger in all countries, with an immediate view to
reducing the number of undernourished people to half their present
level no later than 2015.
(World Food Summit Rome Declaration, 1996)

We will spare no effort to free our fellow men, women and
children from the abject and dehumanizing conditions of extreme
poverty.
(Millennium Declaration, 2001)

It is the biggest outrage of the twenty-first century that people die from
starvation and 852 million in the Global South are chronically or
acutely malnourished. It was already clear by 2005 that the first Millennium Development Goal to eradicate extreme poverty and hunger
would not be met. A selected target of that MDG was to halve, between
1990 and 2015, the proportion of people who suffer from hunger (UN
2005). It is also evident that the more ambitious World Food Summit
target, set in 1996, to halve the number of people who suffer from
hunger between 1990 and 2015 from 800 million to 400 million would
not be met either. Population growth has meant that to reach the UN
World Food Programme (WFP) target of 400 million 'the proportion of
the population who are undernourished would need to be reduced not
by half, but by two thirds' (FAO 2005: 6).

The failure to meet these targets is not surprising. It is one of the
many ironies when discussing famine and food insecurity that
hunger persists and recurs: most commentators fail to recognize that
famine is an integral part of late capitalism, or modernity (Edkins
2000). Laudable as it may be to seek to reduce global hunger, it is
offensive that the strategy the UN and other IFIs have thrown their
collective weight behind is only to *halve* hunger by 2015 and not to
eradicate it. Is that because there are no funds in the UN system to
eradicate hunger, or is it because there is no political will, either in
the UN or its most powerful member states, to stop people dying of
starvation?

I want to now explore why famine and food insecurity is an inevitable feature of late capitalism. Why it is impossible within the context of capitalism for food insecurity to be eradicated, and why the humbling of the world's poor (by maintaining them in a position of such precariousness) sustains Northern power and the power of Southern technocrats. I highlight policy makers' failure in order to demonstrate that technical agendas for improving food security fail.

Food not only has the most important use value necessary for the maintenance and social reproduction of life; it also, like any other commodity, has an exchange value: to be realized it must be bought and sold. Therefore capitalism, as we have already seen, commodifies land and labour, and in its internationalization has also commodified resources like water and forestry. The commodification of food has ensured that famine will not disappear. Capitalism does not place value on food production for self-provisioning. Global production of food far exceeds global demand for it, and the EU and United States pay their farmers to take fertile land out of food production. Indeed, the average availability of food across the world seems to be increasing, as indicated in Table 6.1. There is nevertheless a demand everywhere for sufficiently inexpensive food for purchase by a working labour force necessary to ensure the reproduction of capitalism. That is precarious in Southern social formations.

In the Global South combined and uneven development maintains a fragile balance between development of forces of production around industry, often in an enclave of mining or manufacture, or plantation especially for export. Here we will need to revisit a number of agrarian questions to explain why agriculture in the Global South is not transformed universally into capitalist agriculture. And we need to ask why the vulnerability of food producers creates the possibility for famine and why smallholder producers and pastoralists are among the first to

Table 6.1 Trends in the availability of food in developing regions

Region	kcal/person/day 1990–2	1999–1	Average annual (%) increase in kcal/person/day (1990–2001)
Developing countries	2,535	2,677	0.49
Asia & Pacific	2,522	2,702	0.61
Latin America & the Caribbean	2,707	2,842	0.47
Near East & North Africa	2,972	2,951	-0.17
Sub-Saharan Africa	2,185	2,255	0.45
Countries in transition	2,939*	2,886*	-0.23*

Source: *The State of Food Insecurity in the World 2004* (FAO 2004).
*Figures for countries in transition relate to the period 1993–95 and 1999–2001.

die. Finally we shall see how the issue of dispossession by accumulation, in the case of Sudan, reminds us of the ways in which contemporary capitalism reproduces itself in Africa.

The persistence of rural social relations of production that have been underdeveloped and disarticulated (a process closely linked to urban society) helps maintain industry but may also inhibit its widespread emergence. Food production is vulnerable to the market, to the ability of producers to gain income from often fragile ecosystems and of urban dwellers to purchase it. Purchasing power vulnerability places a high burden of responsibility on states in poor (and not so poor) countries to protect the weak and also to access income to purchase food locally or become dependent upon external assistance and food aid. But this analysis does not, contrary to the policy makers whose work I shall scrutinize below, mean that every effort must be made to integrate farmers, especially smallholding peasants, into the world market or to establish (new) secure systems of land tenure. The problem is not weak tenure or that producers are insufficiently integrated or are part of imperfect markets: the problem is the market itself and the commodification of everyday life.

The character of markets and commodification leads me to focus on two further issues. The first is to challenge the dominant technicist characterization of food crisis in Africa. Africa will be the focus because it is the only continent where hunger is increasing. It is also the continent where most famines have taken place since the Second World War. Technical solutions to social and political problems of food production, distribution and exchange remain central to IFI strategy for ameliorating food insecurity, and they form part of the shopping list of donors and African governments. Yet they also fail to anywhere address the second issue I shall explore, and this is the distribution of political and economic power that shapes the ways in which food insecurity leads to famine.

Why, we might ask, should famine and humanitarian assistance be used to simply reset the clock to circumstances of a pre-famine period when they were the conditions that were unable to prevent a food crisis and, in many of Sudan's famines and many more besides, were active in the creation of famine? Issues of political and economic power, of social control over food, are seldom addressed by IFIs, and the language of 'new partnerships' that have mushroomed since 2000, between donors and African leaders, has done little to reshape the way in which food insecurity can be reduced. This discussion will lead us back to criticism of promoting property rights as a panacea for food security.

I problematize the way in which famine and food security is discussed by the IFIs, and I do this by focusing on the new Comprehensive Africa

Agriculture Development Programme (CAADP) and NEPAD's idea of 'an agricultural-led development' (www.NEPAD.org). These are situated in the context of the work of FAO and the UN. I argue that three major silences in the donor world ensure that famine will continue to feature in Africa's underdevelopment:

- the failure to understand the character of international food regimes
- the failure to understand the importance of questions of class, rural transformation and capital accumulation
- issues of politics, power and rural violence.

Africa's food crisis

Hunger causes more than 18 million deaths a year worldwide: upwards of 35,000 a day. At least 60 per cent of these deaths in the Global South are among children under four years of age. Issues of food security and the recurrence of famine are at the core of debate about the future of Africa. Sub-Saharan Africa is the only place in the world where the

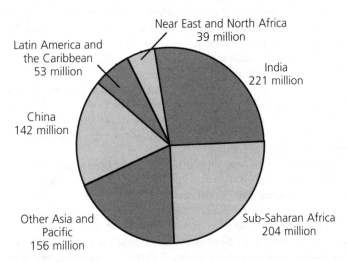

Total numbers of undernourished people in the major regions of the developing world. A further 37 million undernourished live in the industrialized countries and countries in transition.

Figure 6.1 Where are the hungry?

Source: *Where Are the Hungry* (FAO 2004).

numbers of malnourished continue to rise: there were at least 204 million in 2005. A reduction in the number of the world's hungry is seen by the protagonists of the MDGs to be central to the larger project of poverty reduction (UN Millennium Project 2005: 2). Hungry children do less well at school, poor nutrition for women undermines health and gender equality, and the poor are seen to use the environment less sustainably than if they were empowered 'custodians of land, waters, forests and biodiversity' (FAO 2005: 4). The number of underweight children in sub-Saharan Africa (SSA) rose from 29 million to 37 million between 1990 and 2003 (UN Millennium Project 2005: 8).

Hunger does not only take the acute form that is mostly seen in TV pictures of emaciated children. That starvation accounts for only about 10 per cent of the world's hungry. The *percentage* of those suffering chronic hunger, understood to mean people lacking food to meet daily needs, fell according to the UN for the period 2000–02 compared with 1990–92, except for Western Asia. The *number* of people going hungry, however, has increased since 1997. Increased population size and poor agricultural productivity have been identified as the most profound reasons for the setback for the MDGs (UN Millennium Project 2005: 6).

In early 2006, more than 40 million people in Africa were threatened with starvation. Of those, 20 million were in the Horn of Africa, Ethiopia, Somalia, Djibouti and Kenya, but there were millions more at risk in Eritrea, Sudan and Tanzania. This famine was seen by the WFP as a result of drought, and the conditions were described by the WFP's Executive Director as the worst he had seen. It was a major concern for the WFP that the amount of money needed to provide for local food purchases, as well as imported grain, was small compared with the enormity of the problem. Kenya, Somalia, Ethiopia and Djibouti needed, he estimated, US$311 million but only had US$89 million available. Perhaps more starkly he noted that 'We could eliminate hunger for children in Africa for £3bn' (*Guardian* 8 March 2006). Since 1973 there has been at least one major drought in the Horn of Africa every ten years: 1973–74, 1984–85, 1987, 1992–94, 1999–2000 and 2005–06. In Ethiopia the 1984 drought affected 8.7 million people, 1 million died and 1.5 million head of livestock died. The same drought affected 8.5 million people in Sudan, where at least 1 million people died as well as 7 million animals.

Africa's food crisis (the crisis for the chronically undernourished that receives far less attention than for the most acutely starved) is usually explained by a decline in food production per capita at a time when per capita economic growth has stagnated and food imports increased. Although food production in Africa kept pace with population growth immediately after the Second World War, the rate of increase declined significantly after 1960. The problem became particularly acute after

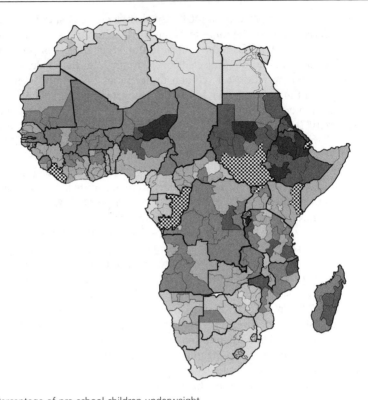

Percentage of pre-school children underweight

☐ 0–10%　　■10–19.9%　■20–29.9%　■30–39.9%　■40–49.9%　■> 50%　　　⊠no data

Map 6.1 Hunger hotspots in Africa: areas with more than 20 per cent underweight pre-school children

Source: CIESIN at Columbia University, available from www.ciesin.columbia.edu/povmap/..

1974. Among other locally specific reasons in famine-prone countries, such as drought, poor levels of agricultural investment and surplus extraction from the countryside to support urbanites, it was then that the vagaries of the international market in grain impacted heavily on food insecurity in Africa.

Two variables are used by the FAO to determine whether a country is food secure. The first is per capita availability of food for direct consumption and the second is the distribution of food within countries. Adequate nourishment is usually taken to be in the band of 2400–2500 calories a day. One of the difficulties with the FAO data is that it aggregates figures of calorific intake and hides the fact that at least 20 countries in SSA and South Asia have an average per capita food availability of less than 2000 calories a day.

Indeed, not just the lumping together of data but the quality of data is a major impediment to understanding the dynamics of Africa's food crisis. Data accuracy in sub-Saharan Africa is notoriously problematic. Phil Raikes noted that 'there are few countries in sub-Saharan Africa where the level of total food production is known to within plus or minus 20 per cent' (Raikes 1988: 18). Although there have been improvements in recent years, the underlying reasons why the data presented by agencies and governments needs to be treated with a health warning remain. First, most staple food production comes from small peasant farms and these are not covered by systematic crop reporting or registration. Second, where mechanisms for reporting exist they are usually related to large and medium-scale farms, whose contribution to total production is thus exaggerated (Raikes 1988: 19). Additionally, it remains difficult to get accurate data for area cultivated, and census data remains largely unreliable. Moreover, there is little opportunity for independent checking. Evidence used to calculate area cultivated and yield per hectare is usually gathered by an extension officer who uses a previous year's figure and then 'estimates' the proportion by which it has increased or decreased. An important issue here is that if it is difficult to estimate production apart from what is marketed, there will be no account of production used for self-provisioning. Small-scale farmers, moreover, can be cagey about actual levels of production for fear of taxation.

There seems to be a built-in downward bias on production figures. Yet all things being equal, increases in population require, and get, larger levels of production in most cases unless crises of fertility, land access or other entitlements to food are dramatically changed. Second, the use of marketed production as the means of estimating total production ignores the effect of the popular peasant strategy in the 1970s, 1980s and 1990s, when there was a downward pressure on farm gate prices that led producers to use more financially rewarding parallel markets instead of state marketing structures. Thus, marketed production figures underplay the importance of burgeoning illegal markets, smuggling, cross-border trade and barter trade (Duffield 2001). It might also be useful for governments and aid agencies to downplay production figures to encourage donor support.

Agency explanations for the food crisis

There is clear unanimity among a range of agencies and donors that explore the causes of starvation and strategies to combat it in Africa.

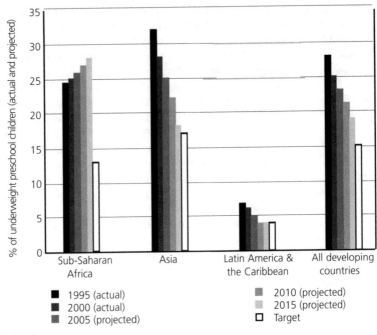

Figure 6.2 Hunger in sub-Saharan Africa compared with the rest of the world

Source: WHO (2003).

The agencies that I group together include the World Bank, WFP, UN Millennium Project, IFPRI, NEPAD and FAO. This grouping combines policy think tanks and international donors. I group them to demonstrate the way in which the hegemony of the proffered explanation to Africa's food crisis exerts enormous influence over African states. The strategy that follows from the diagnoses has been assimilated by African leaders and academics, and is a further illustration of the continent's subordination to the forces of international capital and the calls to incorporate Africa further into the 'global' trade regime.

The dominant characterization of food crisis has deterred explanations that involve any attack on the structures of power that create and perpetuate food insecurity. That omission is set against a backdrop of occasional rhetoric, notably by the FAO and UN, regarding the role that inequality and poverty in Africa, especially among the continent's farmers, plays in inhibiting an expansion of agricultural productivity. Here poverty becomes another trope of imperialism (Bond 2006).

Small differences exist between the agencies but there are many similarities also. Sympathy for the 'small farmer' is expressed by FAO and the UN, yet even that does not save poor farmers from criticism of their actions as *causing* environmental degradation (FAO 2005: 25). Moreover, while the increased evidence about urbanization raises issues of what type of strategy should be encouraged to ameliorate Africa's hunger, the strategy is not discussed in terms of whether it is essential to safeguard the livelihoods of smallholders against all other pressures:

- rural–urban linkages
- consequences of the predominance of labour-migrants or 'peasantariat' dependent upon income opportunities in both town and country
- sequencing of reform strategy.

Fundamentally, agency prescriptions for reform do not prioritize elements of a strategy and neither do they challenge the power structures in Africa, and between Africa and the developed world, that are at the core of Africa's food crises. Collectively it becomes apparent that trade replaces food security as the major driver for agency policy and strategy for Africa in the twenty-first century (Friedmann 2004: 135). It is veiled by concern with providing humanitarian assistance for the most needy, good governance for enhanced participation, and tenure reform to raise efficiency and participation in the market.

Table 6.2 (overleaf) indicates the checklist offered by agencies to explain African food insecurity.

At the heart of Africa's food crises for the FAO is poor food production in SSA. This is linked to the poor quality of natural assets owned or used by most African farmers, and a lack of access to information and technologies that provide remuneration (FAO 2004: np). The FAO calls for more resources to be directed to rural areas, as this is where 75 per cent of the world's hungry live. One of the reasons given for that hunger is the way in which resources for agriculture and rural development have declined by more than 50 per cent in the last 20 years (FAO 2005: 5). More investment is crucial to delivering the potential of African agriculture. Thus, reiterating the Africa Commission view of agriculture as the key to the continent's development, it applauds the African Union's commitment to increase the share of national budget allocation to agriculture (www.nepad.org/2005/files/caadp.php, accessed 4 March 2006). Increased investment is crucial to improve levels of agricultural production, to boost economic growth in agriculture and to develop rural infrastructure, roads, market access and education.

For the FAO, food insecurity is reproduced because it is passed from one generation to another by poor maternal nutrition and health; thus

Table 6.2 Determinants of hunger and the strategy to end starvation: a view from the donors

Causes of hunger	Solutions
Insufficient agricultural production	Increase investment
Poor governance	Improve governance; improve donor and host country relations
Poverty and poor nutritional status of the vulnerable	Reinforce poverty reduction; support women; limit population increases, increase spending on agriculture
Poor education	Increase government spending
Poor markets	Improve market access; improve land tenure and agricultural trade
Disease, esp. HIV/AIDS	Increase spending and education
Conflict	Improve governance
Resource degradation; drought and natural disaster	Improve environmental sustainability, empower the poor
Poor infrastructure	Green revolution
Poor safety nets	Increase spending

these areas are identified for a boost in investment. A strategy to reduce hunger requires a closure of the gender gap, an improvement in women's access to health and access to education (FAO 2005: 17).

The issue of vulnerability of Africa's rural producers is at the centre of the UN's Millennium Project (2005). In particular it is vulnerability centred in gender inequality, HIV/AIDS and climate change. But the UN is also exercised by the failure to convert public moral outrage against hunger and starvation into political action to prevent it recurring. To address this the UN focuses on the importance of advocacy, improving public awareness of hunger issues, strengthening data collection and building country organizations to deal with poverty reduction and hunger (UN Millennium Project 2005).

Table 6.3 shows the causes identified by the FAO as being at the heart of Africa's food crises at the end of 2005. The determinants of hunger for the FAO and other agencies are poverty, war, natural disasters, disease and epidemics, and political and economic shocks. The UN highlights the significance of household food security and vulnerability as 'underlying determinants' of hunger (UN Millennium Project 2005: 20). Strategy to ameliorate vulnerability must be 'multisectoral', and policy must target 'vulnerable populations'. It is important for all agencies to establish partnerships between donors and host governments, and host governments need to establish enabling environments for hunger to be reduced. That environment operates at three levels:

- the international, by improving partnerships with host states
- the national, with improved decision making and policy implementation
- the local, by improving food security for small-scale farmers.

These enabling environments have at their core the need to promote improved governance. The governance nexus includes improved institutions, promotion of sustainable peace and human rights. There are

Table 6.3 Countries requiring urgent external assistance (total: 27 countries)

Nature of food insecurity	Main reasons
Overall food shortages	
Burundi	Civil strife, IDPs and returnees
Eritrea	Drought, IDPs, returnees, high food prices
Ethiopia	Drought, IDPs, high food prices
Lesotho	Drought in parts
Malawi	Drought in parts, high food prices
Somalia	Civil strife, drought in parts
Swaziland	Drought in parts
Zimbabwe	Economic crisis
Generalized lack of access	
Liberia	Recent civil strife, IDPs
Mauritania	After-effects of 2004 drought and locusts
Niger	After-effects of 2004 drought and locusts
Sierra Leone	Returnees, refugees
Severe localized food insecurity	
Angola	Resettlement of returnees
Burkina Faso	After effects of 2004 drought and locusts
Chad	Refugees
Central African Rep.	Recent civil strife
D.R. Congo	Civil strife, IDPs and refugees
Congo Rep. of	IDPs, refugees
Côte d'Ivoire	Civil strife, IDPs
Guinea	IDPs, refugees
Kenya	Drought in parts
Mali	After-effects of 2004 drought and locusts
Mozambique	Drought in parts
Sudan	Civil strife, returnees, drought in parts
Tanzania, U.R.	Drought in parts
Uganda	Civil strife, IDPs
Zambia	Drought in parts

Source: FAO/GIEWS (2005: 2).

many similarities here with the Africa Commission findings that we explored in Chapter 2. Good governance is a 'key ingredient to fight hunger and promote economic development' (UN Millennium Project 2005: 74; see also Dreze and Sen 1989). The UN's argument is that corruption, excessive bureaucracy, inadequate planning and insufficient institutional capacity 'hold back the successful implementation of even the best conceived policies' (UN Millennium Project 2005: 74). Good governance is also important to avoid conflict, which is seen as a key element in blocking development and hunger alleviation. Thus the UN and the World Bank stress the importance of establishing effective government and improving accountability. And even where there is evidence of poor governance (or perhaps 'good enough governance'), it is important for donors to maintain engagement, for humanitarian reasons and 'investment in the promotion of political, economic, and social change' (UN Millennium Project 2005: 75).

The best opportunity for the promotion of a reduction in hunger, the UN and World Bank assert, is to embrace Poverty Reduction Strategy Papers, and for African governments to invest at least 10 per cent of national budgets in agriculture, in addition to investing further in rural energy, infrastructure, health, education and conservation. To deliver these improvements the UN stresses the importance of building local capacity; indeed this should be the focus of national and donor-funded activities (UN 2005a: 12). The local capacity is to be built by 'the creation of paraprofessional extension workers in agriculture, nutrition, and health, residing in villages identified as hunger hotspots' (UN 2005: 12).

It might seem strange that local capacity is built by external intervention but there is some sensitivity in the UN's comprehensive document. It recognizes, first, that poor people's access to productive resources needs to be increased for food security to be enhanced, and second, that local tenure arrangements 'such as community property rights can also be effective' (UN 2005: 12).

Understandably the UN is upbeat about meeting the MDGs. After all they originate with that international body. But there are several important issues that we need to be critical of, not least because they continue to embrace global partnerships, good governance and green revolution technology as panaceas for food insecurity. Quoting Secretary-General Kofi Annan speaking in Addis Ababa in July 2004, the UN stressed the importance of a 'uniquely African Green Revolution in the twenty-first century'. That revolution was to have a wider focus than hitherto has been the case. It was to include social and environmental sustainability that aimed simultaneously at biophysical, socioeconomic and political causes of hunger.

The new agenda for Kofi Annan required African governments to commit to the MDGs and to translate rhetoric into practical policy for improved food security. NEPAD is the vehicle for doing this in Africa to promote 'an agricultural-led development' fundamental for 'cutting hunger, reducing poverty, reducing the burden of food imports, opening the way to an expansion of exports and generating economic growth' (NEPAD 2005b: 1). The mechanism for doing that within NEPAD has become the Comprehensive Africa Agricultural Development Programme (CAADP).

The Comprehensive Africa Agriculture Development Programme

First adopted by African Ministers at the FAO Regional Conference for Africa in Cairo, February 2002, the CAADP was later agreed at the Africa Heads of State and Government in 2003. Inextricably linked to international donors, CAADP is a policy agenda to address the challenges African governments identify as being at the heart of the continent's agricultural crisis. It is a crisis of a sector that employs more than 60 per cent of people on the continent and accounts for more than 40 per cent of all foreign exchange earnings. The sector's crisis is most evident for NEPAD in persistent poverty, dwindling land and water resources, poor water management, droughts and floods, poor infrastructure, civil strife, and HIV/AIDS and other diseases. Although the 200 million Africans NEPAD identifies as suffering from under-nourishment are fewer than the figure used by the FAO, NEPAD mirrors the analysis of other agencies in its six targets to be achieved before 2015:

- improved agricultural productivity to attain 6 per cent average annual rate of growth, with particular attention for small-scale farmers and women
- creation of dynamic agricultural markets within countries and between regions
- integration of farmers into the market economy, improving market access to become net exporter of agricultural products
- achieving a more equitable distribution of wealth
- becoming a strategic player in agricultural science and technology development
- use of environmentally sound production methods with a culture of sustainable management of the natural resource base (NEPAD 2005b: 2).

The CAADP has a 'shopping list' to meet these targets. Four 'pillars' of the strategy include:

- increasing the area under sustainable land management
- improving rural infrastructure
- increasing food supply
- developing agricultural research.

Each pillar reflects other agency policies we have reviewed above, and while there is a driver in the NEPAD approach that implies the importance of Africans 'doing it for themselves', the opportunity for a continent-led strategy does little to counter the prescriptions of external agencies for Africa's ills. CAADP is first and foremost a strategy to boost trade in agricultural exports funded by donors. After the September 2003 meeting of NEPAD, the FAO, World Bank, IFAD and the Africa Development Bank, preparation began for the development of national medium-term investment programmes and bankable investment project profiles (NEPAD 2005b).

NEPAD is pledged to achieve a 6 per cent rate of economic growth per annum, yet this is nowhere near achievable and is more than twice the level achieved since 1973. Investment rates of 10 per cent of GDP are needed to attain 6 per cent growth rates, and they are not likely to be achieved either. It needs to be remembered that UNCTAD's list of 50 least-developed countries includes 34 from Africa, more than 70 per cent of all African countries.[1]

However, the profound optimism of NEPAD envisages improved Western aid and technology packages to enhance Africa's research and development apparatus through the US$1 billion combined grant and loan programme of the Multi-Country Agricultural Productivity Programme (MAPP). The innovation of MAPP is that it is intended to foster technical expertise within Africa, develop 'stakeholder' participation in the priorities for research, and to use a notion of 'subsidiarity' in the delivery of aid. Subsidiarity implies the importance of disseminating technology to the lowest possible level, although this is recognized to be mostly the national, rather than sub-national level, or it is used to refer to Africa's regions to help maximize market growth and economies of scale.

The overwhelming impetus of MAPP, and the CAADP more generally, is the need for Africa to expand trade. Half of MAPP's financial resources are to be sourced from the World Bank, and a key to promoting agricultural growth is the reform of the continent's markets and agricultural institutions. The driver for this will be agribusiness (a collective term for companies that are involved in the production, distribution and marketing of usually high-value and low-nutrition foodstuffs for European and US dinner tables).

There is a fundamental contradiction between NEPAD and CAADP's rhetoric of promoting food security for smallholders and the declared strategy that trade and agribusiness can become the catalyst for helping poor farmers. However, this is only a superficial contradiction because the reality of Africa's position, of its current inability to generate investment for agriculture from local savings and its acceptance of the steer from IFIs to open up economies for agribusiness, reflects the dominance of neoliberal formulae for Africa's 'renaissance'.

It is not surprising that the implementation strategy for CAADP formulated by NEPAD for East and Central Africa is to respond to high-value crop markets. To do this NEPAD sees the importance of African states in: providing an enabling environment to generate a positive investment climate; playing a facilitative role to bring different elements of the industry together; and assuming a pre-emptive role whereby African governments can intervene to provide a lead on issues that are 'beyond the narrow horizons of the business sector' (NEPAD 2005a: 6). This pre-emptive role implies a reservation about the efficacy of private capital especially to deliver growth and development in areas that might not seem to be as prof-itable as others. Concession is also made to the idea that large-scale agricultural plantations may no longer be universally suitable to boost food production. Thus companies (MNCs) will use out-growers for labour-intensive crops that need close supervision, where com-pany access to land is problematic, where it is important to spread risks from adverse climates and pests, and also where smallholders produce competitively.

Food, politics and power: the onward march of hunger

Donors have been preoccupied with addressing what they see to be causes of Africa's food gap: too little production in relation to popula-tion growth, weak governance and rural poverty. The remedy has been a desire to incorporate the continent into the world economy and to do so by encouraging cash crop production within the context of revamped and 'efficient markets', and export-led growth, and to do this by boosting investment in agriculture and in infrastructure more generally. This strategy is wrongheaded and will not lead to food secu-rity on the continent. And we can see why by exploring the silences of donor and government analyses. These are threefold:

- failure (or deliberate neglect) to understand and account for history and especially the context of international food regimes
- agrarian questions of class, rural transformation and accumulation
- politics and power, and especially the importance of rural violence.

International food regimes

Africa's uneven incorporation into the world capitalist system has involved its linkages with the international system of food production distribution and exchange (Friedmann 1993; Friedmann and McMichael 1989). The system of global regulation has been fashioned by MNCs that have sought to control the food chain from production to consumption and also to manage levels of investment, inputs into agriculture, cropping patterns and most recently of all, the genetic makeup of food.

There have been two major food regimes, governed by rules and regulations that have been less obvious and more implicit in the way they operate than similar rules for industrial trade. The first focused around 'Atlantic trade between England and the Americas' especially after 1870, and included settler regions in Europe and India. The 'second expanded after the Second World War to include all the former colonies of Europe', but excluded the Soviet Union until its collapse (Friedmann 2004: 125). This was governed by the United States.

The operation of these different regimes had impacts on food security in the Global South. Yet an understanding of this is absent from donor documents and concern with starvation and famine in Africa. Donor policies are intended precisely to further incorporate Africa into the contemporary food regime. For the policies we examined above are shaped by the view that the prevalence and recurrence of food insecurity is underpinned by Africa's exclusion from world markets in food and the production of high-value, low-nutrition foodstuffs to meet European and US demand.

There are two major reasons why an understanding of the world food regime is important to explain Africa's food insecurity. The first is that it helps explain the seeming anomaly of a world system where there are simultaneously food surpluses and deficits and widespread hunger, not only in the Global South but in the industrial North as well. While the abundance of food, notably grain in Europe and the United States, can be seen to be separate from the agrarian questions in the Global South that I explore below, they are also very much connected. Mountains of grain in Europe, for example, have given European countries the power of life and death over food-deficit countries and they have provided grain that is dumped on world markets. Grain mountains and the role of MNCs in the food system also offer the need for important critical appraisal of agribusiness in Africa as a vehicle for the promotion of agricultural trade.

Tony Blair's CFA called for the end to heavily subsidized European agriculture, and WTO talks in 2005/06 centred around attempts to get a deal that involved agricultural trade. Yet in January 2006 the EU's grain mountain, a product of protected EU agriculture, was the highest it had been for almost ten years. In early 2005 it was 15.8 Mt. The EU supports its farmers by agreeing to buy some crops at a minimum price. This system of 'intervention' takes place between November and May. The EU agrees to buy grain at a minimum price if farmers cannot sell it on commercial markets. Grain production has soared with bumper crops in 2004. The surplus was a result of the accession of Hungary, the Czech Republic and Slovakia, and the rationalization of the region's pig and poultry markets prior to EU entry, which limited the size of the feed market. Intervention stocks fell to about 4 Mt in 2004 because of high commercial prices that encouraged farmers to sell in the international market.

There has been much hand-wringing about the need for cuts to the EU agricultural budget, which accounts for 40 per cent of the Union's total budget. This was especially evident during the debates in the WTO, and especially the Doha and Hong Kong trade rounds. Brussels remains faced with a choice to subsidize exports or to reduce stocks released into the international market and incur the wrath of the United States and WTO. But a 12 Mt intervention in January 2005 cost the EU at least $1.65 billion, and competing export subsidies need to be very high to compete favourably with Argentine wheat, which can be delivered to North Africa grain purchasers at $15 to $20 a tonne cheaper (*Daily Times* 9 January 2005).

There is a long history to the dominance on international grain markets of the EU, United States and the Cairns group of major agri-cultural exporting countries, Argentina, Australia and Canada. Friedmann has reminded us how important is the historical under-standing of the ways in which food regimes have been established and transformed by the most powerful trade actors, dating back to the significance of the UK repeal of the Corn Laws in 1846. Thereafter the social contract that rulers were accountable for the reliable supply of food was breached. She notes that:

> The most important fact to note is that in the Settler-Colonial food regime power and wealth resided in the importing countries, which exported capital and labour to 'improve' (or as we would now say 'develop') lands taken by force from indigenous peoples.
>
> (Friedmann 2004: 126)

Thus the settler regimes in Kenya, South Africa and Namibia, the Lusophone colonies of Angola, Mozambique and Guinea Bissau, and French settlement in North Africa shaped the character of property rights, commoditization of land and labour, and the violent dispossession of Africans from local mechanisms of production and social reproduction.

[161]

The settler colonial food regime also established broad patterns of long-distance trade, diets in Europe and United States for wheat and beef and imports from the colonies, and – not just where there was the economic and political dominance of Europeans – of cash crops (coffee, tea, cocoa). The uneven demand for these products has continued. So too have the commercial farm models and control of most productive fertile land by often external capitalist interests.

After the Second World War a new food regime was generated by the new hegemon: the United States. Although championing free trade, it protected its agriculture and cut deals with European partners to exclude the Soviet Union from access to grain until *entente* in 1974. For the colonies, subsidized exports supported independence aspirations of providing cheap food for urban populations which were seen as drivers of industrialization. The new mercantile-industrial food regime in many ways marginalized local peasant producers as imports were cheaper and local production was geared more to export crops than self-provisioning. The industrialization of food production, the US farm model and commoditization were generated by and in turn fuelled the further growth of agribusiness.

The importance of agribusiness, the role of export agriculture and cash crops not consumed in Africa but in the United States and Europe are seen by donors as key to extricating much of Africa from its food crisis. But agribusiness historically has never delivered the promise of greater investment, and thus income and security, for African farmers. Indeed, the reverse has been the case. And there is little reason to believe that structures of commodity markets will deliver future food security. As a recent critic of global food markets has noted:

> African countries have extremely limited scope for diversifying into new markets or developing innovatory new crops, since they are beset by highly regulatory policies that restrict market access in Europe and North America. The cost of mediating food regulations and tariffs is considerable and involves a large expenditure on research, information systems and legal representation.
>
> (Amanor 2005: 58)

The new food regime has bestowed power on supermarket chains to control all aspects of the value chain of agriculture, and this is done with the rhetoric of flexible accumulation and flexible markets which bears little resemblance to the reality of inflexible poverty for African producers. Supermarkets access commodities across the globe, depending on the price and security of markets, the reliability of the workforce and the stability of local political regimes. Fair-trade is not exempt from this, for while it clearly offers greater returns to smallholders, certification and other bureaucratic procedures of registration deter many and ensure continued links with foreign capital.

Agribusiness cannot simply reduce poverty and hunger in Africa. For one thing agribusiness crowds out local producers because of its stronger market power and access to technology and inputs. This remains true even where agribusiness has relinquished concerns with controlling land ownership, long seen to be too politically risky in 'unstable' African countries. Where local food producers are hired as out-growers, forced to follow strictures for production and cropping set by companies, prices paid to farmers are often less than costs of production. The outcome in one reported case of palm oil plantation in Ghana's Eastern Region, where 7000 farmers were dispossessed of 9000 hectares of land, led to widespread unemployment and accelerated social differentiation (Amanor 2005: 61).

The argument given by donors for boosting Africa's food security by encouraging the emergence of new agricultural economies on the continent is based on false reasoning and false historical experience. Countries like Kenya, Mexico and Argentina have been cited as illustrations of new agricultural economies (Friedmann 1993) that have taken advantage of producing high-value foods. The assumption is that a new range of countries in Africa can join that club. Yet, first, the success of these countries is questionable, and second, where there has been growth it was conditional on a number of fortunate contingent factors. These were: good international market conditions and early booms because of the market failures of competitors (Watts and Goodman 1997: 11).

Critics of the international food system note the short-term favourable conditions of countries like Mexico, Brazil and others in Central America which were dependent on:

- usually, high domestic demand and rhetorical export-led growth
- dominance of foreign capital in all levels of export production
- processing and marketing
- strong state intervention to promote comparative advantages (Watts and Goodman 1997: 12).

In tracing Africa's economic crisis in Chapter 2, we noted the importance of a historical context, and we noted the way in which the fourfold price increase in petroleum 1974–79 was an immediate reason for the debt crisis. There were other underlying causes, not the least of which was the way in which post-war reconstruction around the United States and the payments system that was established by the IFIs built in a temporary respite to persistent and structural economic crisis. An additional factor was a food crisis in 1972–73. That resulted from a threefold increase in the price of grain and soya as the United States reached a *détente* with the Soviet Union and global grain surpluses quickly became deficits. As Friedmann has noted, 'the Third World was abandoned by the new food regime' as industrial strategies in Africa and elsewhere were quickly undermined by new international realities (2004: 133). These new realities included the inability to pay for increased food and energy bills and increased substitution by agribusiness of Southern raw materials like sugar and vegetable oils.

It is ironic that the international response to the food crisis in the Global South was the establishment of a world food summit by the FAO in 1974, where the laudable aims of rights to food and food security were proclaimed widely and have since been reiterated. Yet the assumption that the international community could reduce world hunger by simply making formal agreements to do so needs to be contested. Food insecurity has remained at the centre of Africa's development problems. And it remains so partly because of the international food regimes and movements of grain around the world that are a core feature of capitalist development.

Agrarian questions

The global context for food security is inadequate on its own to explain hunger and starvation in Africa. To understand that we need to do more than just explore the ways in which the global food system has managed movements of grain and cereals, and how Africa was especially penalized with hunger as a result of grain shortages in the 1970s. Alongside these factors we need to set a number of agrarian issues that link to the way in which agricultural production is organized by social classes that shape African strategies for accumulation. How do the international food system, the availability of food surpluses and high levels of value added in commodity chains impact on the ways in which agrarian structures are organized? To explore this we need to ask what is the extent to which global capitalism has penetrated African agrarian society, and with what kind of impact?

In returning to an exploration of what have been called agrarian questions, I am helping build a framework that is more appropriate than the one offered by donors and aid agencies. This is a framework that builds on the importance of identifying processes of the global food system with an understanding of household and commodity production in Africa. Agrarian questions were once popular in academic literature in the 1960s and 1970s. These questions were particularly focused on the relationship between peasants and capital. Historical studies of the development of capitalism show that the agrarian questions that continue to be crucial for understanding African food security relate to 'whether mechanisms within peasant households ensured the latter's survival in face of encroaching capital, or whether the polarisation of the peasantry into classes was inevitable' (Kayatekin 1998: 207).

Most debate among policy makers is silent on agrarian questions. Indeed these questions appear to be replaced with the ideologically 'neutral' 'food question' or debate about food security/insecurity. But the curious aspect of the popularization among agencies of starvation and hunger is the absence of reference to the producers of food: peasants and farmers who engage in economic and social relations with each other and with more powerful actors located in the countryside and the town, as well as global capitalist actors. Returning to theoretical questions of the ways in which peasant households promote livelihoods and the extent to which peasant societies are socially differentiated is crucial to understanding another irony of the famine debate and to turning one of the most popular concerns on its head. Why is it that so many survive food insecurity, famine and starvation? I shall return to this in the concluding section below. First let's see why agrarian questions help set up a way of exploring issues of food security in Africa.

The most recent and comprehensive examination of the dynamics of Africa's agrarian questions is given by Bernstein (2003, 2004). He draws on the work in India of T. J. Byres (1991). Important themes about the extent of commoditization of land and labour in Africa are raised in three questions:

- The first relates to what role rural classes, peasants and workers have in struggles for democracy and socialism.
- The second relates to the development of productive forces in the agricultural transition to capitalism.
- The third relates to how rural transformation contributes to capital accumulation necessary for industrialization.

These issues have been summarized as 'centred on the problematics of politics, production and accumulation' (Bernstein 2003: 203). They also raise a further set of issues. If the food crisis ushered in by the food system in the 1970s reflects a resolution of productivity issues for Western agrarian capitalism – where surpluses became regularized and have been unchallenged for 40 years – what chance is there that similar agrarian improvements in productivity and a parallel proletarianization of Africa's work force will mark Africa's food security in the contemporary period?

I look in a moment at the case of Sudan where issues of war, displacement and creation of opportunities for accumulation have regularly generated starvation and famine, a key feature of late capitalism's accumulation by dispossession. First, however, I want to establish the importance of understanding the specificity of agrarian transformation in particular country contexts as a method of exploring the ways in which food insecurity emerges. National and local cases need to be placed in a theoretical and historical context of international capitalist development. Explanations for agrarian transitions have usually used the transition to capitalist agriculture in Europe as the model against which to judge the proximity or success of rural development in the Global South. Yet we know that the 'original' transformation in Europe, 'characterized by its exceptionally early and comprehensive disappearance of the peasantry' (Bernstein 2004: 136), was also situated in its own historical complexity. Agrarian transformation, and viability, in Africa and the Global South more generally is thus also contingent on the specificity of class power and inherited strategies for accumulation that have shaped these processes and which in turn are shaped by them. But unlike the transition to agrarian capitalism in Europe (the original transition), transitions in the Global South take place in the context of inherited colonialism and contemporary imperialism. Is it possible to identify common themes in Africa's agricultural performance that have been shaped by those processes of incorporation and expulsion?

Debates on Africa's food crises have focused on a mix of issues that together ask the same questions:

- Why has capitalism in Africa's countryside been unsuccessful?
- Why has African agriculture not raised productivity in relation to population growth to ensure provision of abundant cheap food for a rapidly proletarianizing work force?
- Why has it not provided capital for primitive accumulation to drive industrial growth by an African bourgeoisie?
- Why has there been insufficient locally produced food to avoid starvation?

The answers most readily given by international donors, as we saw above, have focused on market imperfections. They chose to ignore the view that market *power* is asymmetrical and they focused on poor infrastructure provision and inadequate access to capital. They have carefully avoided investment that can be managed and directed by African producers themselves, and the donors' policy list has also included targeting poor governance rather than opportunity for an active and meaningful democracy to hold national and international leaders to account.

And where donors have focused on rural producers themselves, they have not addressed issues of class and power but of access to tenure to help boost incentives for entrepreneurial activity to flourish. Explanations for the widespread fable that Africans lack entrepreneurship, and need incentives to provide not only for the wellbeing of their family and kin but also for rural markets, have been a preoccupation of many academic commentators as well as donors.

In asking why Africa has failed to be food secure or to transform agriculture along European or US lines, issues of inadequate infrastructure or governance have been eschewed for the view that farmers in Africa are irrational in their economic behaviour and prefer to embed themselves in an 'economy of affection' (Hyden 1983; compare Hopkins 1987 and Mitchell 2002). In this world peasants do not comply with the economic rules of the market. Neither do they conform to state policy regarding plans or programmes for rural development. Instead farmers organize agricultural practice and decision making by adherence to the importance of primordial loyalties of kinship and family (Chabal and Daloz 1999), and use the specificity of a peasant mode of production to protect and insulate themselves from the vagaries of the market.

The debate about the rationality of African farmers is unhelpful. It often reflects the Eurocentrism and prejudice of the commentators who engage in it. Yet it permeates both advocacy of and dissent from the spread of neoliberal solutions to Africa's food crisis. The dominance of neoliberal discourse has captured most debate. It asserts axiomatically that what Africa most needs is a good dose of the market, with occasionally an enabling state to facilitate limited resource access for the most poor, providing a safety net in the transition to capitalist transformation. Thus what persists is a perspective that Africans are the problem: they are either economically irrational, favouring support for family and kin rather than engaging with the market, or as even some critics of neoliberalism argue, they are rational but in adjusting to local conditions of often harsh and forbidding environments tend to prioritize pressures of self-provisioning (compare Cleaver and Schreiber 1994 with Richards 1985; Watts 1991; Berry 1993).

The value of returning to the particular agrarian question of the transition from agriculture to capitalism is that it requires commentators to look at specific rural complexities and opportunities for rural transformation. When it is possible to set aside the essentialism and teleology of crude political sociology that insists on judging African agriculture by its proximity or not to European economic transformation, it is possible to also explore household and gender dynamics of agricultural production and social reproduction. Agrarian questions also direct attention towards the ways in which rural power is maintained and by which social classes, and how they interact with powerful classes beyond the village.

The original transitions to capitalism in European agriculture cannot be replicated in Asia and Africa. Colonial imperialism generated a multitude of agrarian transitions and uneven patterns of commodification. It has involved uneven increases in expansion of agricultural trade from Africa, demands for some of the continent's cash crops, and only limited proletarianization, with workers and peasants often straddling town and countryside as worker-peasants or a peasantariat. This has raised the issue for some commentators of whether it is possible to have the resolution of a number of agrarian questions but not all of them. That also raises the question of whether all of them have been resolved in Europe, where the persistence of smallholders continues as well as high levels of subsidy and feudal political remnants.

If there is evidence of industrial capitalism in Africa, without widespread agrarian capitalism, does that mean *the* agrarian question regarding the significance and possibility of universal agricultural transformation emerging is dead (Watts and Goodman 1997: 6)? Has capitalism and thus the prevalence of commodity production penetrated all aspects of economic life in Africa, and if so how is that evident?

For Bernstein this is evidenced because peasants, seen as petty commodity producers (producers who are simultaneously capitalists and workers, owning or accessing means of production using their own labour), 'are unable to reproduce themselves outside the relations and processes of capitalist commodity production, when the latter ... constitute the conditions of existence of peasant farming and are internalized in its organization and activity' (Bernstein 2004: 129). It follows in this analysis that if, in the contemporary period of globalization, the agrarian question for capital has been resolved, without resolution in the Global South, other issues of concern in the transition of agrarian capitalism in Africa need to be addressed. These other issues which now need attention, for Bernstein are centred on the importance of new agrarian questions promoted by 'struggles of labour for means of livelihood and reproduction' (2003: 203).

Thus issues of future agrarian growth in Africa are inextricably linked to the character of commodity production on the continent, to the way in which global capitalism has penetrated rural social formations and the struggles there that have emerged contesting that incorporation, and the uneven capitalist development that has resulted. But even if, and probably especially if, commodity production has not become generalized or has not touched the livelihoods of all or even the majority of rural producers, we need to look still more closely at issues of agrarian transformation to see why and how food insecurity persists in Africa. For if the encroachment of globalization has been far from universal, and if the poverty that has resulted from Africa's incorporation into it is the intended outcome of that incorporation, we need not only to examine the agrarian questions that we have now raised but to revisit issues of accumulation by dispossession.

Power and politics: violence and dispossession

A most important shift in the debate about famine and food security emerged with the work of Sen (1981). He challenged the idea that mass mortality resulting from hunger was the result of a decline in food availability. Sen argued instead that most important of all in situations of food insecurity was people's ability to access food. Thus food in capitalism is like any other commodity: what is important is ensuring people's market access to it. Writing with Jean Dreze he noted:

> What we can eat depends on what food we are able to acquire. The mere presence of food in the economy, or in the market, does not entitle a person to consume it. In each social structure, given the prevailing legal, political, and economic arrangements, a person can establish command over alternative commodity bundles, any one bundle of which he or she can choose to consume. These bundles could be extensive, or very limited, and what a person can consume will be directly dependent on what these bundles are.
>
> (Dreze and Sen 1989: 9)

Critics of Sen have looked at his failure to adequately trace the historical ways in which people's entitlements to food have been constructed and the rather passive ways in which famine 'victims' are characterized. They have also criticized his focus on assetless wage-labourers (not entirely relevant for Africa), and argued that he ignored the violence in famine and that his view of famine is too economistic. Moreover he has not realized that food producers might starve to preserve their assets, and mortality occurs from things other than starvation (de Waal 1989, 1990; Woldesmeskel 1990).

Sen's highlighting the importance of market access helped undermine the World Bank view of the efficacy of markets as vehicles for promoting agricultural growth. He showed that markets are built around relationships of power. Yet the World Bank and its advocates, not only in the literature that I reviewed above but elsewhere too (de Soto 2000; World Bank 2002), have reiterated the importance to Africa of embracing enforceable property laws that will stimulate market growth.

The introduction of market-based property regimes and the promotion of privatized land tenure have been at the heart of agricultural reform throughout Africa. The assumption of donors is that before their intervention there had been an absence of a systematic property regime conducive to economic growth. Thus investment in agriculture and other sectors is dependent upon the establishment of property rights. This flies in the face of detailed case study knowledge that privatization of tenure has generated processes of land concentration and dispossession, reduced access and increased landlessness (Toulmin and Quan 2000).

> The establishment of private property rights not only produces new rigidities in ownership and use that undermines a long history of popular access, it also does not necessarily guarantee private property title-holders access to investment funds.
>
> (Olukoshi 2005: 15)

There is an additional flaw in the donor arguments for the importance of privatization of tenure and why the sanctity of private property will not help boost production or reduce poverty. Donor concern with landlessness prompts security of tenure to improve efficiency, yet that security can only be given to a few under the currently dominant models of privatization (some exceptions recognize the significance of community tenure arrangements), and in any case '"efficient use" generally means the ability to maximize return on investment and generation of profit on any given piece of property (whether a product or a piece of land) rather than gearing the use of that property to those most in need' (Andreasson 2006: 10). The lopsided focus on privatization and the free market to secure rights intended to boost production and food security has undermined household security and livelihoods. It has increased vulnerability and the hierarchical appropriation of resources; differential access, generational access, conjunctural access and entitlement failures (Bohle et al 1993).

Vulnerability to food insecurity, to marginalization of self-provisioning and the possibility of triggering acute food shortages is also shaped by temporal fluctuations (perhaps relating to seasonality and all that may mean in terms of resource access including labour power), spatial differentiation (geographical locations); it is therefore necessary to have a sense of how choice has been shaped historically. Thus we are brought back to the importance of going beyond simple notions of 'the poor' towards the need to see how the poor are differentiated and are not equally vulnerable to different crises and do not respond uniformly to crisis. Crucially too, we need to remind agencies and policy makers of the need to see how the rich are generated and benefit from the poverty of others.

With understatement it has been recently noted, 'It is not at all evident that the priority of the local agricultural population in many parts of Africa is the achievement of individualization, titling, registration and privatization.' Multiple tenure regimes do not inhibit growth but they do need increased public and state support, not least in locally determined improvements in resource access and a context in which 'African economies respond more to domestic impulses, and less to externally imposed models and solutions' (Olukoshi 2005: 15).

Privatization of tenure is part of a process of dispossession of the powerless and reinforcement of wealth for the more powerful. In Africa it has run alongside peaceful transitions towards limited market liberalization, as we have seen in the case of Egypt's change in tenure with the 1992 Law 96, and in contexts of war in Sudan (Johnson 2003), fierce confrontation in Zimbabwe (Moyo and Yeros 2005) and heightened conflict on reconstruction and land reform in South Africa and Namibia (Ntsebeza and Hall 2006).

The case of Sudan is important because it graphically highlights the relationship between dispossession, conflict and accumulation. It also graphically highlights the ways in which famines are not consequences of conflict but are often the goal of war (Macrae and Zwi 1994: 11). A continuous theme in Sudanese politics since independence in January 1956 has been the inability of a single bloc of classes to exercise hegemony and break from the sectarian political struggles of the two religious sects, the *Khatmiyya* and *Mahdist Ansar*. The difficulty of any regime in Sudan's history to generate legitimate government has been underscored and promoted by persistently recurrent economic crisis, famine and political instability. The extensive famine in south-western Sudan that killed 250,000 in 1988 and jeopardized more than a million lives in 1998 was created by the Sudanese state. Famine was a mechanism used by the state both to retain power by providing spoils for clients and to promote a pattern of capital accumulation. Human Rights Watch noted in 1998 that the fault for the famine lay 'primarily with Sudanese government and militias and opposition forces that precipitated the famine and deliberately diverted or looted food from the starving or blocked relief deliveries' (HRW 1999a: 1) As Keen noted:

> Processes of famine involved the forced transfer of assets from victims to beneficiary groups in a context of acute political powerlessness on the part of the victims. ... The 1985–1989 famine was the creation of a diverse coalition of interests that were themselves under intense political and economic pressures in the context of a shrinking resource base and significant environmental crisis in the north.
>
> (Keen 1994: 13,14)

The important issue here is not to make the simple point that war and conflict undermine agriculture because armies destroy and consume crops, destabilize markets and establish regimes which are based on waging war as a goal in itself, what de Waal has called 'the rapid development of political economies based upon militarized asset-stripping' (1993: 33). It is instead to see the way in which famine results from a particular strategy of primitive accumulation.

The Sudanese regime, especially after 1989, armed ethnic militias to wage war in the south of Sudan and to divide southerners against each other. Thus Baggara militias, well armed and discontented to the extent that they may have challenged government, were used by the Islamist regime in Bahr el Ghazal to attack Dinka communities, and to seize grain, livestock, children and women. Dinka grazing land in northern Bahr el Ghazal was also seized. And this took place while a relief effort, Operation Lifeline Sudan, was in place and more than US$1 million a day in relief was used. Donors in this case were identified as part of the problem, rather than the solution: they let the Sudanese government define the relief problem, they failed to monitor properly the delivery of relief and ensure it reached the intended beneficiaries, and they did not address the underlying conflict (Keen 1994: 175).

The government of Sudan responded to a range of challenges to its authority that included international debt and local recession. It had also been prevented by the SPLM from exploiting oil resources located in the southern war zone or completing the Jonglei Canal in the south. But while successive Sudanese regimes tried to complete the canal, to help conserve water from evaporation and satisfy Egyptian partners that wanted improved Nile flows north to support Egyptian agriculture, 450,000 Dinka, Shilluk and Nuer feared the canal would destroy their agropastoral systems. As early as 1974, rumours that Egyptian farmers would be settled in the canal area promoted rioting in Juba. Local farmers and the SPLA understood very clearly that 'By drying out the swamps and taking away the "grass curtain", the canal would open up the entire Sudd area for mechanized farming, the domain of the Jallaba, and also allow the north to move military equipment and troops into the south with greater ease' (Suliman 1999: 10).

The government of Sudan repeatedly used the south as an opportunity to promote capital accumulation for northern elites, and in so doing create conditions of acute food insecurity and famine. The ethno-nationalist regime promoted the interests of northern Arab elites who displaced Dinka and Nuer pastoralists and supported the Baggara. The state strategy during the entire civil war period from 1983 until the signing of the Comprehensive Peace Agreement in January 2005 was to appropriate land, first for mechanized farming and the grazing rights of client militias, and also for mining concessions. That strategy exacerbated a history of

widespread abuse of human rights by the state, international oil companies and southern movements which had vied with each other for the
rights to the spoils of war and primitive capital accumulation.

Sudan's civil war took 2 million lives and displaced 4 million
people, mainly from the south. Famine and disease were widespread.
Probably the biggest driver of accumulation for the regime was the
production of 500,000 barrels of oil a day from estimated reserves of
563 million barrels; Khartoum estimated reserves to be as high as 700
million barrels. Commercial deposits of oil were first announced by
Chevron in April 1981 in the Unity field of south-western Sudan. Map
6.2 indicates the main oil-producing areas of Western Upper
Nile/Unity State and one of the main piped routes to the Red Sea
(Verney 1999). Potential reserves are located in North-west Sudan, the
Blue Nile Basin and the Red Sea area in eastern Sudan.

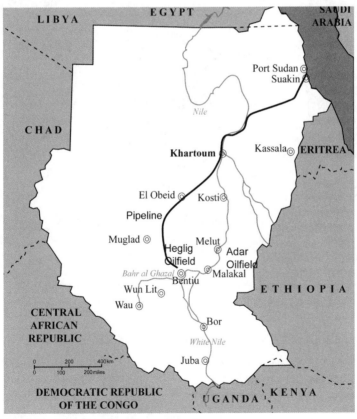

Map 6.2 Sudan: oil exploration and pipeline

Source: based on Sudan Country Analysis Brief,
www.eia.doe.gov/emeu/cabs/sudan.html

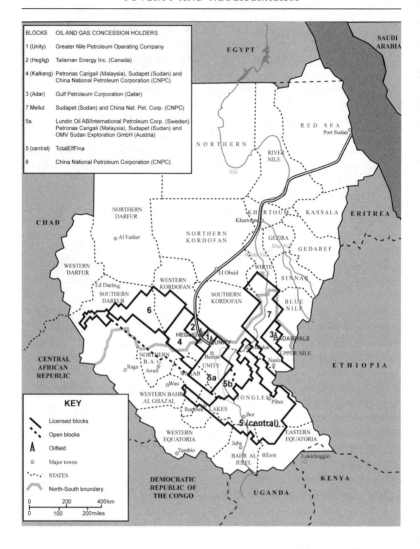

Map 6.3 Oil concessions in central and southern Sudan, ca 2002

Source: based on a map from USAID.

Between 1998 and 2001 more than 204,500 people were internally displaced from Western Upper Nile. The government of Sudan was directly responsible for forced displacement, and major oil exploration companies were also implicated. In 2005 a US$5 billion suit against Talisman Oil on behalf of the Nuer was presented by the Presbyterian Church. The government of Sudan argued that resident Nuer, Dinka and other southern Sudanese were security threats to the oil installations. Almost 200,000 people displaced from Bahr el Ghazal and Upper Nile oil-bearing areas went to neighbouring states. The Nuer and Dinka suffered the most, especially following Talisman's operation after 1999 subsequently sold in oil areas that had been demarcated as Blocks 1, 2 and 4. The total concessions area covers more than 212,000 square kilometres.

The war in southern Sudan impacted on the struggle over territory and also the capture of labour to work on the land. People were displaced along the so-called 'transitional zone' – Southern Kordofan, Southern Darfur, Blue Nile and the Sudan Ethiopian border – following the development of capitalized and mechanized agriculture from the 1970s. The Mechanized Farming Corporation, established in 1968 and funded by the World Bank in the mid-1970s, expanded production southwards and transformed the local ecology and societies. Conflicts were generated between local farmers and owners of big schemes. Farmers were forced to sell labour to the schemes, and pastoralists were driven from grazing lands. Agropastoralists were forced to make choices between either of their two activities and were thereby made more vulnerable to local hazards and impoverishment.

This social transformation promoted accumulation by ejecting indigenous farmers, and in so doing also generated conflicts between scheme owners and locals over access to land, and between locals and the state, as the government of Sudan was the ultimate guarantor of the process of dispossession (Suliman 1999: 10–13; Ahmed 1992). Northern capitalist mechanized-farming elites spread further south as they exhausted land for mechanized farming. The dispossession continued as smallholding farmers lost customary rights to land; there was erosion of land use by pastoralists and the creation of agricultural wage-labourers, whose numbers increased with drought and war in the 1980s and 1990s.

Before exploration for oil, therefore, successive Khartoum governments had promoted a process of disruption to local strategies for agricultural and pastoral production. As early as 1970, the Unregistered Land Act abolished customary rights of land use and restricted land access. The Act allowed leasing of land by the state to commercial large-scale farmers. And in 1974 a Law of Criminal Trespass improved leaseholder rights by further reducing pastoralist access to land and the access of smallholder farmers. The legislation increasingly concentrated political power in the central government in Khartoum, and also concentrated power over land in the hands of a northern Arab elite.

The longstanding civil war targeted civilians for their assets, not only their poverty. The conflict was driven by access to labour as well as land. Labour was required to work in the mechanized schemes around Wau, where in the 1990s government 'peace camps' kept Dinkas on low rations which made it necessary for them to work on neighbouring schemes as cheap labour. When the Dinka were resettled they were deposited on marginal land that was insufficient for their needs, ensuring they sought work on new agricultural schemes run by northern capitalists.

The signing of the Comprehensive Peace Agreement (CPA) in January 2005 was a major achievement in the struggle for peace and reconciliation in Sudan. It immediately led to the renewal of exploration rights by Total SA, Marathon Oil Corporation and the Kuwait Foreign Petroleum Company. Other major investors include the China National Petroleum Corporation, Gulf Oil Petroleum, Petronas and Malaysian Ranhill International. It is noteworthy, however, that major issues relating to access to land and mineral wealth were relegated to appendices or later discussion after the signing of the CPA. Moreover, there has not been any public access to agreements between the oil companies and Sudanese government relating to extraction rights, and no indication by early 2006 that procedures for land re-registration were under way.

The mining portfolio in government is retained by the northern government. Yet it has also been noticeable that the Sudan People's Liberation Army/Movement (SPLA/M), like the government and IFIs, has used a slogan 'peace through development' with little mention at all of a redistribution of revenue from oil and land resources between regions of the south to the most needy. The SPLA/M has not, for example, made any explicit commitment to defending local land tenure systems. The possibility remains that the liberation movements in the south and the new administration that emerges will use local resources of oil and the intervention of external mining companies to maximize revenue generation with scant regard of local needs and food security. Many such issues have been raised on the ground (Pantuliano 2005).

Famine and food insecurity in southern Sudan were the outcomes of a northern elite strategy of primitive accumulation. It has been a strategy that has transformed local productive systems and challenged the ways in which they have been reproduced. Accumulation by dispossession captures the violence of abjection confronting local populations in the face of agricultural 'modernization' and the weight of oil company investment. The oil sector is now seen as a saviour for the Sudanese, but little is discussed about the ways in which it transforms agricultural systems and the consequences of that transformation.

I have argued in this chapter that there needs to be a bringing together of the various explanations for food insecurity in Africa, that links the character of global food and the international capitalist system with local class formation and transformation. Donor policy and action fails to do this, and I have shown in detail that neoliberal bias is more likely to exacerbate than to relieve poverty in Africa. Famine is a direct consequence in Sudan of the way in which oil-led growth and dispossession of southern producers by mechanized schemes and semi-proletarianization of labour have deprived people of assets and means of production, thus increasing their vulnerability to acute food shortage. That dispossession has been violent and driven by conflict over the political sovereignty of people in the south, and southern political movements have also been complicit in famine promotion at different times in the conflict.

7 Resisting poverty and neoliberalism

This book has examined key themes in the way in which resources in the Global South have become mechanisms for sustaining poverty and global inequality. I have looked at the mechanism used by neoliberalism to everywhere seek to commoditize and control resources of labour, land, food, minerals and finance. The hierarchy of states, and especially Africa's position within it, has been sustained by policies of aid and trade and the neoliberal agenda to universalize the rule of capital and subordinate resistance to it.

I have noted how the representation of capitalist interests is depicted as universally positive for poor countries and that no alternative is deemed possible by G8 leaders. And if strategies for privatization, trade liberalization and market reform, where states take a less active role in the economy or governance, are resisted, then external assistance for those states is jeopardized. Donor-driven policies of neoliberalism have taken place alongside Western government declarations of concern with addressing world poverty. Witness the hype about the UN Millennium Development Goals, 2005 Year for Africa and repeated calls to reduce world poverty made at G8 and other international forums.

Notwithstanding the rhetoric by UK politicians like Tony Blair and Hilary Benn, and by rock stars and activists like Bono and Bob Geldof, to reduce global inequality, and particularly chronic poverty in Africa, it has been the policies of these politicians and the core capitalist economies whose interests they secure that have created and sustained international poverty. The falsehoods promulgated by world capitalist leaders that neoliberalism is the only answer to world poverty received impetus after the decline of East European communism in 1989. Victory for capitalism seemed secure. Yet as commentators and governments in the West demonstrated, the success of capitalism there has grown sustained popular opposition to it.

A core contradiction of capitalism is that it has always spawned resistance. It is important to remember the different strands of that opposition, which is brushed aside or ignored by world leaders who refuse to entertain alternatives to existing globalization. It is also important to see how Western governments have sought to capture opposition, restricting lawful protest to a static and placid notion of 'civil society', and to assess how the many different types of social movement that oppose capital offer hope and opportunity for an alternative to continued poverty and inequality.

A discussion of these themes is only introduced here for more detailed analysis and action in future. It is important to record some of them and to do so with optimism and confidence, as this develops the importance of understanding the limitations of capitalism and recognizing that it is not a permanent social system.

I have focused in most of this book on the impact that neoliberalism has had on the Global South, and particularly Africa and the Near East. I have assessed how the debates about poverty have been centred on neoliberal definitions and solutions, and how the optimism of the CFA and the hype around the year of Africa in 2005 failed to provide a radical analysis of the conditions that created crises in Africa. I have also highlighted how the political economy of resource-led growth has failed to provide a platform for growth, and how strategies for agricultural development have been insufficient to generate food security, how Western leaders failed to understand crucial issues of the way in which food became commodified and the consequences that has had for failures of agricultural modernization.

Throughout this book I have argued the importance of understanding the systemic way in which Africa has been subjugated by the economic and political internationalization of capital. For reasons of space I cannot in this chapter give a fully detailed analysis of the ways in which protest and opposition give grounds for optimism about the transformation of capitalism. It is, however, important to begin to trace resistance, to show how people in the Global South are not mere objects to the universal spread of capitalism. It is also important to show how struggles might in future focus on both immediate protest and longer-term opposition to power and accumulation by dispossession, which has often been at the centre of Africa's underdevelopment.

Resistance to capital and the way in which struggles form part of a real optimism for African futures need once again to be set alongside donor, and particularly UK government development, policy failings. This is important because of the declarations from Whitehall that the UK government drives, and remains at the centre of, international strategies to attack world poverty. Indeed, in 2006 the UK Labour government released its third White Paper (since it was first elected in 1997) on international development. It was called *Eliminating World Poverty: Making Governance Work for the Poor* (DfID 2006). That document prioritized democracy and governance reform as the condition for poverty reduction in Africa. Like the Africa Commission, the White Paper did not grasp the history of poverty and thus the contradiction that the policies the UK government promoted were more likely to sustain rather than eradicate poverty. It also failed to locate corruption in Africa within the sociohistorical context in which it appears.

I concluded Chapter 2 by showing just how democracy is rooted for policy makers and donors in passive divisions between formal politics, via the ballot box, elections, universal franchise and representative assemblies. And this is linked unproblematically to the arena outside the state and family called civil society. Challenges to authority by the dispossessed in Nigeria's oil-producing areas and their actions of sabotage and kidnap are dismissed by government officials and international policy makers as acts of lawlessness and criminality. Similarly, mass demonstrations and active protest against the WTO and heads of state meetings of the G8 are ridiculed by Western leaders as undemocratic and unrepresentative. Yet protests, attacks on oil installations and opposition to the institutions and organizations of late capitalism illustrated by mobilizations in Seattle, Prague, Genoa and Quebec but also Florence and Evian, Edinburgh and St Petersburg are equally legitimate. They are crucial in opposing the rule of capital and in seeking to promote alternative agendas to existing globalization. And we also need to note that these protests have not objected simply to the principles of globalization per se but to the kind of globalization that has emerged: a world where 20 per cent of the richest people account for more than 85 per cent of global consumption and where those consumption patterns attack the world's environment, challenge any autonomous activity and seek to universally spread commodity production.

Governance and the poor

Eliminating World Poverty: Making Governance Work for the Poor (DfID 2006) set out UK government policy for African governments to 'tackle poverty, and to work to end corruption, bad governance and conflict' (Blair's foreword: ii). The much-trumpeted document built on the fundamental mistakes of the CFA. These are the assumption that poor governance *causes* poverty and that good governance could be generated by external assistance. The document has also perpetuated the fallacy that state retrenchment is necessary in the South for economic growth to be a success. Yet while continuing to promote rhetorically the importance of state withdrawal from economic activity, although somewhat less crudely than the IMF zealots of the 1980s, contemporary donor policy has paradoxically served to enhance a development role for the state. The state role that donors advocate has, frustratingly for African leaders, been sporadic and unclear, laced with demands for greater space for intervention by private capital but, where this has inevitably been lacking in non-profitable areas of social welfare, the state and also civil society have been directed to intervene. While it was an essential plank of donor and IFI policy in the 1980s to cut back state activity and promote the spurious idea that economic growth would *ipso facto* ensue, the insistence by donors in the twenty-first century has been for extensive 'state reform' (Bernstein 2005: 116).

Successful economic reform is therefore inextricably linked and predicated upon aid-induced state reform and civil society intervention to reshape the entire edifice and culture of developing countries. Until such time as a reformed state can deliver the conditions for sound economic growth, civil society, NGOs and associational groups sympathetic to donor reform become the conduit for imperialist intervention.

This type of intervention is well laid out in the DfID 2006 White Paper. The intention was to deliver the 'contract' resulting from the Gleneagles Summit and CFA: the West would increase aid and deliver debt relief in return for African commitment to better governance (DfID 2006: ix). The White Paper confirmed again how donors set development agenda through the creation of 'false self-evidence'. And we noted in Chapter 2 that the contemporary period of economic and political reform, driven by the G8 and the IFIs, has focused on political control of Southern (governance) states, and this has been largely achieved by creating the development agendas that donors then choose to publicize and address.

The White Paper promoted the idea that 'Effective states and better governance are essential to combat poverty' (DfID 2006: 19). Good governance is marked by governments that have 'capability': the ability to perform their functions; 'responsiveness' where governments listen to their citizens and are 'accountable' for their actions to their people (DfID 2006: ix, 20). Where states are fragile and where capacity to reduce poverty is less good, DfID will continue to support governance reform and direct its assistance, if necessary, to units in civil society outside of government, and intensify monitoring and auditing.

Although each of these characteristics for good governance is laudable in itself, they are abstracted by DfID and other donors out of any historical or contemporary context. And they add confusion to an understanding of the state, civil society and resistance to neoliberalism. Governance is elevated as the most important plank for poverty alleviation. But the policies intended to provide for democracy are policies of market reform and administrative reform to ultimately enable a more efficient and smaller state to facilitate private investment: strategies which in effect require strong and vibrant, and also independent, sovereign states and not those weakened by external pressure to reform. Thus, apart from the much-heralded increase in aid for health and education, donor policy is primarily directed towards public financial management, police and civil service reform. These are all areas where privatization of provision has been at the heart of policy initiatives in Africa and where reform of state provision undermines autonomy. And while the policy rhetoric is to facilitate an improvement in opportunity for African entrepreneurs, the reforms will actually have the impact of opening African economies to external investment and investors – but only in areas of high return, profit and resource capture for international capital.

The White Paper betrays its ideological concern with support for compliant African states that are open for market reform when the document cites two contrasting experiences of Tanzania and Zimbabwe. The increasingly effective state in Tanzania is pitted against the failing state of Zimbabwe. Tanzania is hailed for improving public finances and reducing corruption, and as a result benefiting from economic growth of 6 per cent in 2000. In contrast Zimbabwe is illustrative of abuse of government power, destruction of the private sector in agriculture and low investor confidence. These examples are used to cite the importance of governance in reducing poverty, but they are used without reference to any political or economic context, discussion of the way in which Tanzania was brought reluctantly to the adjustment table or the difficulties it has experienced since 2000: economic growth had tumbled to 3.5 per cent in 2002–3 (World Bank 2004: 257). And Zimbabwe can only demonstrate for its ex-colonial power the pitfalls of seeking autonomy and independence (notwithstanding the draconian hold on power that Robert Mugabe has mustered) rather than closeness with London and settler farmer interest.

The paucity of DfID's analysis, the failure to explore real struggles on the continent for alternatives to the imposed agendas for state reform and existing globalization, and the inability to engage with them, together with the declarations regarding future conditionality, limit any prospect that the UK government can help deliver the elimination of world poverty. Two issues in particular reinforce this point: first, rapid growth is only seen as deliverable from the private sector 'working for international trade rules' and where 'natural resources are used sustainably' (DfID 2006: xii). Second, politics in Africa is limited and restricted to a moribund idea of civil society intended to placate the checklist of responsive government and used by donors to bypass reluctant reformers.

Trade rules – OK?

Trade growth is the medium through which donors argue Africa can deliver poverty reduction. I have stressed throughout this book that donors and the G8 have almost universally stressed that Africa's poverty is the result of the failure of the continent to be properly incorporated into the world economy. It is here, I have argued, that there is a disconnect between what Western governments and donors assert and what is actually happening in Africa.

As the G8 and IFIs comment on the parlous state of Africa, they create a development agenda that reinforces Western interests and perpetrates false characterizations of crisis. One example of this is the view that agreeing a new Doha trade round would reduce global poverty. The G8 in 2005 asserted that as many as 140 million people would be removed from poverty as a result of a further push to remove barriers to trade. This view was reinforced at the time of the collapse of the Doha round mid-2006 by the Commonwealth Secretary General. Writing in the *Independent* he noted that 'Trade coupled with fair and efficient government is the most effective route out of poverty that we know' (Letters, 27 July 2006). Yet a detailed analysis of the consequences of a completed Doha round noted that only 500,000 out of 340 million in Africa living on less than US$1 per day would benefit (Melamed 2006: 451–2). G8 and donors have repeatedly asserted that Africa's problem is that it is marginal in trade, that trade rules make it impossible for African producers to benefit equally with Northern partners.

Herein lies another falsehood, and one that provides justification for G8 calls to liberalize African trade regimes. Trade as a percentage of GDP for sub-Saharan Africa in 2004 was only a little less than it was for China. At 55 per cent of GDP it was more than twice the level of India's, although there were enormous country and regional variations. Chapter 5 stressed that a key problem for poverty reduction in Africa is that its incorporation into global trade remained too skewed as a primary resource exporter and importer of manufactured goods. I noted too how the price of raw materials has fallen repeatedly compared with the cost of imported manufactures. African exporters have also faced a fall in the price of labour-intensive commodities like textiles. That has been calamitous for Lesotho, whose terms of trade fell almost 10 per cent after 2000 (Melamed 2006: 453).

There are two further important issues that viewing Africa as marginally rather than unevenly incorporated in the world economy skip over. The first is that while trade justice campaigners have focused on high EU tariff barriers, African producers are as much limited in their export ability by European non-tariff obstacles. These include issues of quality control, reporting and documentation, correct packaging and labelling. Meeting these non-tariff barriers (NTBs) adds at least 10 per cent to African producer costs, and refusal of African goods to the EU on these grounds has risen dramatically: by six times in the period 1998–2002. It is also important to stress that new trade rules fundamentally jeopardize historic preferential trade agreements between the ACP and EU.

Second, before 2005 ACP countries could access EU markets

without giving the EU reciprocity. New WTO rules will ensure that ACP exporters must allow equal access to EU exporters. Although the Doha trade round has been repeatedly stalled and representations from the Global South have objected to opening of trade that will certainly intensify poverty in Africa, the EU and United States remain committed to opening developing country markets. African producers will definitely suffer if all countries have equal access to all markets.

Interpretation of the UK 2006 White Paper needs to be set against this discussion about the change in trade rules and the reality of just how uneven Africa's incorporation into the global trading system has been, and also where Africa's clear trading strengths lie. Donor insistence on political reform in Africa is linked with G8 strategies to promote economic globalization. Focusing on governance reform, targeting the ability of states in Africa to manage finances and streamline local civil service provision makes great sense to donors. It will help ensure the continued uneven incorporation of the continent into the world economy by reducing the power of the African state to control the movement of domestic goods and services. It opens national economies to international capital and investment, and reduces further any possibility of a strong and autonomous local class of entrepreneurs that could challenge international capital, and it does this while emphasizing the importance of African sovereignty to develop and enhance the authority of a local indigenous capitalist class. The contradiction of course is that for the 'African state' to deliver these reforms it needs to be first strengthened unless sovereignty is capitulated and legitimacy lost. Donors thus need to be careful just how actively they fund civil society rather than state capacity.

Uncivil society

Coupled with spurious talk about the ineffectiveness of African producers and the need for new trade rules to encourage African trade and imports into Europe is the G8 view that good governance is necessary for poverty eradication and that this is only possible with a strong civil society. Never well defined, and somewhat eschewed by the newly dominant term 'governance', the idea of civil society underpins the policy that rulers and politicians should be accountable for their actions. The virtues of civil society have long been taken for granted (DfID 2000; USAID 2006; World Bank 2000). In its broadest definition civil society refers to public space independent of the state where many different forms of associational life exist. Additionally, it has been used to refer to all activity outside the state, whether spontaneous or organized.

It was the protest movements that emerged to help transform the political regimes of Eastern Europe in the 1980s that many Western commentators saw capture the vibrancy of civil society. In that context and since, the notion of civil society became very much linked with 'opposition' to the state (Geremek 1996). Another view of civil society has also been adopted. This is pretty much a 'catch all' to refer to associations between firms, families and the state, and it has especially been used to refer to the presence of voluntary organizations that DfID sees as conduits for assistance if fragile states are deemed too corrupt to receive aid directly.

The idea of civil society is used un-problematically by donors: it is universally seen as a force for good, but seldom defined or understood in particular historical circumstances. If the term is used inclusively to refer to associations between people beyond the home and the state, donors should really examine what it is that the organization actually does to determine whether it can be called 'civil' or not. And of course the question of whether donors should be able to directly fund civil society organizations without discussion with nation states is often ignored.

For donors the issue of state sovereignty can be slurred over because of their belief in the righteousness of supporting civil society. Yet among other things if civil society is characterized by donors as always taking only an organized form, this concept will miss forms of protest and opposition that emerge in Africa that are not formal, well structured or prearranged. Those other struggles, what one writer has called the everyday struggles of the ordinary (Bayat 1997), are just as important and may well be as challenging to state power as advocacy groups that are established, registered and formal.

Donors have seldom been clear on what to include or exclude in the list of 'non-state' actors: those that operate outside the sphere of the state. For in many social formations it is clear that civic institutions like academic unions, public sector interest groups and those citizens who derive core income from the state are firmly embedded in the state system itself (Bangura 1999: 1). This raises issues related to the boundaries of civil society when associational groups are discussed. Are all groups and associations, irrespective of membership and the groups' aims and objectives, to be included as part of civil society? And are all to be encouraged? If civil society is to be linked with political liberalization, do all groups within it contribute to that process or is it more appropriate to discriminate in the assessment of the associations contributing to civil society?

Theoretical slippage when dealing with debates of contemporary civil society has meant that donors are careless in their understanding of what civil society means. Donors are simply in too much of a rush to fund associations that are perceived to be pro-reform or provide space for greater political representation. One of the difficulties with the term 'civil society', and a reason why donors are so confused by it, is that it emerged as part of the organic growth with European capitalist development and has not been adequately located in the Global South. This is not to minimize or fail to see the significance of activities outside the direct formal definition of the state, in Africa and elsewhere, but to ask why the term 'civil society' is used rather than a host of others like 'public space' or 'advocacy groups'. The difficulties with the term 'civil society' led one commentator to question its use and its simplistic linkage with democratization:

> the concept of civil society is difficult to pin down empirically, and the theoretical arguments with which it is involved are so closely associated with neo-liberal ideological campaigning, as to cast doubt on the value of the concept overall.
>
> (Allen 1997: 330)

The term carries the ideological assertions of its neoliberal origins. First, the preoccupation with associational life asserts that civil society is the source for liberal democratic values, namely openness, transparency, accountability and the rule of law. Second, civil society is seen as the motor for democracy, that is, a liberal democratic version. Third, civil society is posed in opposition to the state. Crucially, a flourishing civil society is seen to require a non-interventionist state: one that furthers the interests of market-oriented individual freedoms (Allen 1997: 335).

Donor investment in governance and civil society groups to hold governments to account and serve as vehicles for promoting efficient government that can reduce poverty has multiple failings. It is part of an ideological assault on African governments that ensures submission to external political reform and economic liberalization.

If the term 'civil society' is limited in the way in which donors have used it, for example with a preoccupation with NGOs and associational activity, it is useful to describe the processes by which states configure relations of consent and coercion.

Gramsci's concern in the spiralling Fascist Italy of the 1930s was to grapple with a topsy-turvy world where life outside or beyond the state at different times, and often in quick succession, became enmeshed with the state, separate from it or subordinate to it (Gramsci 1976; Showstack Sassoon 1978). This formulation of 'processes' is not meant to relegate any concrete 'spatial location' for civil society. Gramsci was clear, using the evocative language of trenches, ditches and fortifications around the state, that consent was manufactured and served to defuse any raw class relations of exploitation within and beyond the institutions of the state. Civil society thus becomes among other things the arena(s) in which culture, structures of power and creation of social order are reproduced and any possible class-based identity is undermined.

For Gramsci, the essential way in which dominant classes maintained authority was to present themselves as legitimate rulers. This was done, most of the time, by convincing subordinate classes of the hegemonic dominance and legitimacy of ruling (governing) class actions. The constant creation and re-creation of hegemony, rule by consent but when necessary by force, was for Gramsci the crucial factor characterizing the exercise of political power in the interests of the dominant economic classes. Civil society is only meaningful, then, as a political concept or to help explain political reality if it is seen as part of a relationship with the state. While contemporary donors and mainstream academic commentators have tended to talk about civil society in opposition to the state, or as a substitute for it, for Gramsci civil society could not exist without the state.

This leads to a paradox which donors fail to recognize: namely that 'strengthening civil society requires as a necessary indispensable condition the strengthening of the state: the state and civil society stand or fall together' (Chazan, quoted by Marcussen 1996: 421). It is thus mistaken to counterpose, as the UK government does, civil society to the state. This dichotomous view is guided by the ideological premise that states are necessarily bad and civil society, namely NGOs, are good. While this neoliberal concern was founded on the importance of securing individual rights, it has been harnessed since the 1980s in an ideological battle by donors against perceived corrupt and inefficient states. The resulting policy formula has been to downsize state activity and improve opportunities for individuals to organize collectively in civil society.

The need for much state reform in the South is beyond question in order to open up the arena of decision making, improve transparency and opportunities for political expression, and especially to promote and uphold the rule of law and human rights. However, donors have tended to insist on a crude formulation that has seen the state as a homogenous inefficient unit that is set against the need to empower individuals through NGOs or the market (Stewart 1997: 12). But in fact a vibrant civil society requires a strong state, and the imposition of NGOs will not of itself create democracy (among others see; Abdel Rahman 2004).

A strong civil society, a plethora of competing associational groups of different sizes with different foci, needs a strong state to help facilitate the arenas in which NGOs and other bodies can operate. States provide the rules of the game for participation and opportunities to express dissent. In short, states deliver the different political, social, economic and cultural processes whereby hegemonic classes remain dominant. States provide the framework, therefore, and are also subject to contradictions and oppositional forces that emerge from the myriad of conflicts that states can never fully contain. There is also another contradiction. Strong states are required for strong civil societies, and in being strong jeopardize the possibilities for NGOs to be independent and vigorous in their defence of their own agendas. Certainly it is possible to recall organizations that may have tried to pursue democratic reforms yet have had leaderships incorporated into government or the politics of clientelism (Allen 1997: 336). Talking more broadly, Allen has noted:

> there is no single pattern of relationships between regimes and elements of civil society. Not only are there some organizations close to authoritarian governments, but there is a general sense in which civil society as associational life depends on the state, while its growth may depend on material support from government.
>
> (Allen 1997: 336)

Instead of donors therefore seeking to undermine an often already fragmented state, they might more usefully seek to effectively enhance state capacity. Unfortunately, where this policy has been adopted it has tended to promote management reforms, including privatization, that have lessened rather than promoted state effectiveness and enabled spoils politics to continue (Bangura 1999: 5). In so doing, donors prioritize the political liberalization of the state that is intended to directly assist economic liberalization and globalization. State withdrawal from economic activity and social provision cannot be adequately compensated for by the new donor-funded entrants, and that intervention is divisive, fragmenting opposition political forces. In other words, while it is useful to view the relationship between the state and NGOs as one of a struggle for ideas, policy and active legitimacy, it would be wrong to invest in NGOs as the force for democratization simply because they are seen to perhaps emanate from beyond the state.

Struggling against capitalism

Resistance to existing globalization, to the uneven spread of capitalist relations of production and the transformation of people's livelihoods, has taken many forms and certainly goes beyond donor and agency-speak of governance and civil society. Although 'social movement' is used as an umbrella term to capture the multitude of resistance, this is not always helpful. It is instead necessary to try to capture the different ways in which commoditization impacts on local struggles in the Global South. It is important to explore how everyday struggles that are not always perceived to be acts of resistance are shaped by, as well as in turn shaping, the mechanisms for combined and uneven capitalist development. It is important therefore to look at local conditions of existence to see how they help frame an understanding of struggles against globalization. In trying to do this we can also put into perspective the large demonstrations that have received so much publicity since 1999 in the imperialist heartlands. Although protests against the G8 and IFIs have captured Western media reports, and responses by Western leaders have been often incredulous, we also need to understand how the struggles against privatization, the rule of the market and extension of private property are part of resistance to existing globalization in the Global South.

Power to the people?

A key feature of the twenty-first century is what one US anti-globalization activist has called 'a constitutional moment' (Danaher, *Observer* 29 April 2001). By that he meant that corporations have been writing a 'global constitution' that prioritizes profit making over rights to work and sustainable development. And the arena for that constitution writing has been the forum of the IFIs and the WTO. It is not surprising then that the biggest demonstrations against existing globalization have been against trade talks and heads of government meetings of industrialized countries.

Activists who have sabotaged those meetings and the public relations onslaught against them by the G8 have become a focus for further resistance. Resistance has usually emanated from national struggles in the industrial states and local struggles in the Global South. Thus the international demonstrations in Seattle and Prague for instance were 'crystallization points' of protest. They can be understood as emerging from struggles waged by the Zapatistas in Mexico that took off against the North American Free Trade agreement in 1994, and since have become very much more besides (Johnston and Laxer 2003). They also provided expression to industrial working-class strikes in France and South Korea in the 1990s (Brand and Wissen 2005: 10).

This does not mean that there has in any way been unanimity among protestors at international demonstrations about what it is that they have been seeking to achieve. That is not surprising. In many respects it has been key to the success of such a broad-based series of oppositions to globalization. Groups opposed to the WTO, for example, have objected to policies of privatization, environmental decay, trade rules that punish poor countries for their poverty and intensify it, attacks on worker and farmer rights and calls for the protection of human rights more generally. And demonstrators have wanted to promote everything from the destruction of capitalism and the democratization of IFIs to greater control over capitalist market power.

While the strength of a broad church of disparate warriors against capitalism has been important for the size of the opposition to globalization, that breadth has also been a weakness. It has been exploited by media and governments. Anarchist direct action has been deplored in the media as wanton destruction of private property, and government leaders have been quick to foster dissent for violent opposition among more passive elements of protest. And while strategies of opposition, although mainly peaceful, have been mixed, a major ambiguity among anti-globalization protestors has persisted. The difficulty in expressing a critique, not simply of existing globalization but how it has emerged and why its radical transformation is necessary, has meant it has not been well expressed.

The widely acclaimed Make Poverty History campaign seems to have repeatedly missed opportunities to explain why and how foreign debt emerged in Africa, because its single-issue campaign focused on reducing Africa's debt burden, not on the ways in which the debt emerged and not on the way in which the debt will recur unless there are radical changes to existing globalization. While that may have been important tactically, it did little to alert an increasingly aware public of the fundamental contradictions of capitalism as a social system that has been based on the creation of injustice, poverty and debt, and that continues to reproduce these processes while simultaneously providing for the greatest-ever expansion of the forces of production.

Against commoditization

Struggles against globalization centred in the capitalist heartland and targeting the institutions and politicians that further the cause of neoliberalism have received the most publicity and discussion in Europe and the United States. Focusing the struggle against neoliberalism at the heart of 'empire' is crucial in trying to shape agendas of action and transformation. Yet those struggles were predicated upon national and local struggles from below in the Global South, where people are daily confronted by the new colonization and accumulation by dispossession that I have documented, and by displacement, privatization, commoditization and the resulting transformation of class and gender relations.

Neoliberalism and globalization represent the contemporary pattern of commoditization on a world scale. And even where that process is partial and uneven, because of the resistance to it and because of the benefits to capital that might accrue from the preservation and only partial transformation of non-capitalist relations of production, the overriding impetus of capitalism is to commoditize all social as well as economic relationships. Indeed one of the hallmarks of capitalism, and not just its contemporary character, has been the ability to induce relations between people to take the form of relations between things; it is part of the way in which people have become alienated and divorced from being human (Marx 1974).

Resistance to that process has often been strongest among indigenous peoples, and there is much to be learnt from those struggles. For they help confirm one of the main targets for agents of capital: the transformation of households. Recognizing the importance of indigenous peoples does not detract from the significance of the broad-based anti-globalization movements, and neither does it reduce the importance of working-class opposition to globalization (Silver et al 2000; Munck 2002; Waterman 2001; cf. Löwy 2002). Nor does it encourage or defend projects for myriad new state building, nationalisms and chauvinism that might find a home in ethnic or regional identities in the Global South. It is instead to see clearly what the main consequence of globalization in different locations has been, and see where resistance to it has been important.

Indigenous people have been subjected to incorporation and fought against it across the world. They include, for instance, the Maya in Mexico, Sami in Norway, Native Americans in the United States and Kurds in the Near East. In Africa, colonial control of land, particularly in the settler colonies of East and southern Africa but also in Algeria in North Africa, became the focus for liberation struggles and spoils politics after independence.

Indigenous people have been at the centre of struggles to regain control of land seized by colonial authorities and retained by post-colonial states. I highlighted that process in Chapter 4 in relation to Zimbabwe, and many other illustrations exist in Africa. People, individually and in communities with others, have tried to take control of their own circumstances and sought to retrieve their land from occupiers or agents of the state or capital. In Kenya, for example, the Maasai continue to wage legal and other battles against barley farmers who have converted the Narok district for supply to the drinks industry, as they do in the Maasai Mara Game Reserve, which has reduced the grazing and hunting rights they once enjoyed. The Okiek have similarly been denied access to the Mau Forest (Macharia 2003: 196). Partly driven by publicity of the Zimbabwean case and partly by the persistent and mounting rural inequality, Kenya has experienced a mushrooming of struggles over land since 2000. Grassroots organizations have re-appropriated land from white settlers and African landholders, many of whom were government officials (Turner and Brownhill 2001: 117).

In Nigeria struggles over land in the oil-producing Niger Delta are inextricably tied to the exploitation of oil and government failure to promote regional development. Resistance there has been multifaceted, against oil companies, the government and local governors and traditional authorities. Early in 2006, the government of Nigeria was forced to address political and economic underdevelopment in the region, and there were initial signs that a new commitment to greater return from oil wealth would finally emerge. Yet local resistance from the Movement for the Survival of the Ogoni People (MOSOP) and Ijaw youth, and many other organizations, kept up the pressure to ensure delivery of the most basic services. Youth militias have taken to arms – contesting the authority of chiefs and addressing oil company failures to deliver on promises of work and development – and are at the forefront of struggles against existing globalization. Those struggles have often been driven by the desire to defend local opportunities for work and access to resources, including defence of land rights and access to clean water, employment and a toxin-free environment.

People and communities in the Global South have tried to safeguard their assets, local wealth and family relationships in struggles against land dispossessions, attempts to capture oil wealth and the promotion of commoditization of labour. They have also fought to retain a view of local community that in turn has historically structured different patterns of identity politics and resistance to commoditization. These are shifting terrains that confront capitalism, and the most important among them 'comes from communal ownership of resources in that it denies that private property rights are universal in human societies' (Hall and Fenelon 2003: 174). The recurrent attempt by the 'new world order' to promote commoditization has been likened to a *'fight for fertility'*. The focus in that fight:

> is for control over the processes and results of fertility: the capacity to reproduce and sustain life in all its forms, principally people, their labour power and their food. Land and labour, as well as the knowledge, bodies and time of women, are central to the process of enacting or realizing fertility.
>
> (Turner and Brownhill 2001: 107)

Local resistance to globalization has often been structured around rights to land, conflicts over food production and the integration into the market of basic household production and social reproduction. Social reproduction here refers to the ways in which families sustain themselves beyond economic production and physiological reproduction, by, for example, sustaining family health and education, customs and mores of marriage, and reciprocity with neighbours, kinship groups and others.

The important point here is that resistance to capital begins with the mechanisms used by households to preserve economic self-provisioning and social reproduction. A focus on the household, broadly defined, enables us to go beyond focusing solely on issues of the emergence of wage labour and commodity production as capitalism encroaches; two themes that this book has explored in detail.[1] A reminder of the importance of the household in the struggles with capitalist transformation also focuses attention on the role of women in the confrontation with globalization. And we can also trace the significance of the ways in which informal sectors, domestic petty commodity production, parallel trade, bartering and smuggling provide a link, and often an opposition to the internationalization of capital 'through small aspects of daily life'. As one commentator has noted, 'Households act as the fulcrum between world-systems penetration and local culture' (Pickering 2003: 202). And in exploring this fulcrum further we can understand more clearly the two-way interactive processes of incorporation and resistance.

Resistance at the grassroots to globalization begins in households that stand against pressures to commoditize self-provisioning. There are many accounts of the way in which women in particular have championed those struggles. They have ranged from active military service, to struggles against the British by Kenyan women in the Mau Mau uprising and for national liberation against fascism and racism in South Africa, Angola, Mozambique and Guinea Bissau. Grassroots resistance has also centred on women struggling to retain control of household assets, land and food production, as women across Africa have resisted commercialization of agriculture where that commercialization has involved one or both of two processes: greater financial reward to men as they seek to displace women from cash crop production, and attempts at commercialization of farming that undermine self-provisioning (Bryceson 2000; Berry 1994). Women have reacted strongly against threats to self-provisioning, and marginalization of their authority over household decision making that endangers domestic production and the social reproduction.

The resistance to pressures of commercialization has been strong across Africa. And it has been a resistance that has tried to find a place for constantly changing and revised cultural practices as communities are incorporated further into combined and uneven capitalist development.

It is very common for communities to try to maintain elements of indigenous and local culture while simultaneously being drawn into market transactions, wage labour and other activities driven by globalization. In seeking to preserve, but inevitably witnessing the transformation of local practices, the role of households as units of consumption remains important albeit sometimes limited in scope. Households have varying degrees of autonomy from the direct assault by corporations and the market:

> By determining which things will or must be purchased on the market, and by constructing social relations [that] work to avoid market consumption, households can play a significant role in shaping the economic potential and impact of markets within their local areas.

> (Pickering 2003: 206)

As the cash economy spreads, it is confronted by households that are never entirely in subjugation to national or international companies; they have priorities that are shaped by their own specificity as units of production and reproduction, and by shared community beliefs relating to the threats and opportunities given by the cash economy and commoditization. Under these circumstances, the principles of the market are confronted by, among other things, social cohesion and the threat to that cohesion posed by commercialization of self-provisioning activity. Social relationships within the family and the communities that interact with pressures for marketization provide a bulwark against globalization. They are often the fundamental premise upon which resistance to the internationalization of capital emerges.

Foremost among ideas within communities that make them resistant to capitalism are views on commoditization and wealth, and the challenges that these pose for the sustainability of (albeit constantly changing) indigenous or local communities. In a Lakota community in the United States, for example, 'Consumer demand is tempered by social attitudes against individual accumulation and greediness and toward generosity and responsibility for relatives, especially among children and elder people' (Pickering 2003: 207). A factor often distinguishing indigenous people from their dispossessors is the contrasting nature of views on wealth, accumulation and social support networks. There is evidence of this in the Egyptian countryside following the 1992 land tenure reform.

I dealt with the significance of Law 96 of 1992 in Chapter 4. One of the myths that the counter-revolution in Egypt's countryside promoted was the idea that it was passed peacefully and without opposition and resistance. But that is a false idea. I noted the extent of 'formal' violence, of the deaths, wounding and imprisonments. And alongside those protests and violent conflicts between tenants and the government of Egypt was another form of resistance. The change in the tenancy laws brought into stark relief some fundamental issues of community, 'tradition' and custom. While I would not seek to romanticize the Egyptian – or any other – village existence, there is evidence of a combination of household and village mobilization against powerful landowners that challenged government policy of accelerating commoditization of land and labour. Mobilization became centred over the challenge to village norms posed by the privatization of tenure. These village norms focused on values of rights and duties, *inter alia*, good neighbourliness, care of the land, financial obligation and consideration for neighbours which were threatened and undermined by the consequences of the 1992 legislation. Detailing a case study in the Delta Governorate of Daqahliya, one author has explored many types of conflict over land that emerged after 1992 (Tingay 2004). Her work supports other cases in the Delta and Upper Egypt (Bush 1999; Abdel Aal 2002).

Tingay (2004) discovered that small-scale farmers responded in particular ways to the changes in tenancy that led to dispossessions, particularly after October 1997 when the 1992 legislation became effective. The consequences of enormous hikes in rental values of land led villagers to be verbally critical of landowners who were identified as upsetting village norms of reciprocity, rights and duties. These obligations were universal but it was especially incumbent upon villagers who were relatively wealthy to safeguard village customs, rights and duties.

Village conflicts have often taken the form of struggles over land and water, but violent opposition in the circumstances of Egypt's repressive regime was never a realistic option for smallholders who were relatively powerless in relation to landlords. Smallholding tenants also had an additional problem when considering resistance to changes in tenure. The structure of landholdings meant that they might simultaneously own a tiny plot of land, rent land in and out, and also sharecrop; this made it extremely difficult to identify a single opponent or landowner against whom to fight over the new law.

While the government of Egypt stressed the peaceful transition to accelerated commoditization of land, farmers battled out a conflict which was at times violent, with terrible losses of life and persistent torture and arrest of tenants who challenged the law. And farmers also used the glue of community ethics to try to re-bind villagers together, albeit preserving in so doing patterns of inequality and power that structured lives prior to Law 96. Struggles were often therefore structured around farmers' attempts to preserve village norms that provided for levels of reciprocity between the wealthy and the less wealthy and were attacked by accelerated impoverishment of small tenants.

Villagers whose livelihoods were threatened by increases in rental values and other costs of production, which plunged many into debt and some into destitution, tried to hold larger landowners to account for what was seen as socially disruptive behaviour. At times village pressure was brought to bear on landowners not to raise rents as high as had sometimes been threatened. In these types of case the role of the market in determining prices and rents needed to be set alongside the logics of village life. Thus economic transactions did not always take place in 'the market' but through social networks of kinship and ties of affection. In these circumstances non-market relationships were not 'backward', failing to inhibit growth, but were being shaped by social relationships of production and reproduction that the protagonists of the market could not understand.

Because direct challenges to the coercion of the Egyptian state were likely to have been met by immense repression, tenants and small-holders found alternative and important forms of struggle. Those who were confronted by the new economic power of landlords opposed them through verbal criticism and whisper. They challenged village notables to hold landlords to account for the disrespect that they seemed to demonstrate in their failure to live up to the expectations of villagers in relation to established rights and duties. Villagers were angry that landlords did not respect the conventions of the village, whereby rights to land were safeguarded by custom and mores, and sought to impose a system of access only by cash for those who could afford the new high rents.

The absence of an open conflict by villagers against the consequences of Law 96 and against the actions of large landowners did not mean there was acceptance of the counter-revolution in Egypt's countryside. Instead resistance took place through informal and unstructured actions of farmers who were being dispossessed. Everyday struggles, the nego-tiation of life itself and struggles over access to resources within commu-nities, often reveal resistance and counter-hegemonic activity. Scott (1990: 200) has labelled this 'infrapolitics', and highlighted how strug-gles of everyday life from 'footdragging' and 'gossip' help to counter surveillance and authoritarianism. With peasant actions in parallel markets, households and communities, as we have seen (as well as the workplace and in the fields of landowners where contestation of access to resources persists), the nurturing and development of a counter-hegemonic resistance and worldview develops. That resistance can also quickly take the form of strikes and more violent and organized opposition if surveillance relaxes.

For Scott, infrapolitics is perhaps a 'foundational' form of politics upon which other institutionalized political action depends. In the context of repressive regimes where the watchful eye of the state limits opportunity for voicing grievances, it becomes the most important way in which the oppressed can act against their repression.

That form of resistance and struggle has been labelled the 'quiet encroachment of the ordinary':

> This refers to non-collective direct actions of individuals and families to acquire basic necessities (land, shelter, urban collective consumption, informal jobs, business opportunities) in a quiet, unassuming fashion.
>
> (Bayat 2000: iv)

Bayat formulated the idea of quiet encroachment (1997, 1998, 2002) while discussing essentially urban unrest. For him, it is:

> qualitatively different from defensive measures or coping mechanisms. ... It represents a silent, protracted, pervasive advancement of ordinary people – through open-ended and fleeting struggles without clear leaderships, ideology or structured organization – on the propertied and powerful in order to survive.
>
> (Bayat 1997: 5)

These types of struggles for Bayat were partly a product of social contracts where corporatist relations between the state and workers and peasants had existed. In those conditions, as for example in Nasser's Egypt in the 1950s and early 1960s, a social contract existed, one not without problems, where the state provided basic services and the subordinate classes agreed to political passivity. That legacy, within continuing repressive polities in the Middle East, has ensured that many struggles have taken the form of individualistic solutions to problems instead of class or group solidarities as the major vehicle for opposition.

Capitalism, power and social transformation

Struggles against contemporary capitalism, whether against the IFIs or against the incursion and partial transformation of non-capitalist relations of production, have a common unifying theme: the hope for an alternative to the universal spread of commoditization. I have indicated throughout this book that struggles over resources and the characterization of poverty and its causes by donors have shaped the uneven spread of commoditization. In turn struggles against globalization within the

capitalist heartlands and the Global South have contested the consequences of persistent inequality, and particularly the marginalization of
Africa.

This chapter has highlighted the different focuses of struggle
between broad-based international movements that attack existing
globalization, and rural-based struggles in Africa which have strug-
gled against social transformation and especially the commoditization
of land and labour. And I have highlighted how UK government and
other donor insistence upon the importance of governance, as a
concept abstracted from concrete historical and contemporary realities,
serves the imperial interest of insisting on the opening of economies for
international capitalism.

Indeed, I have argued that the use of governance and civil society as
potential mechanisms for advancing democracy in the Global South is
unhelpful. Those themes need to be rooted in an analysis of how states
seek to promote and sustain hegemony, by combining rule through
coercion and consent, and we need to understand how civil society is
mobilized as a concept and through political realities by dominant
classes to sustain and reproduce control.

In understanding how resistance emerges I have stressed the importance of changing the focus for future work and activism away from
macro-based analyses towards exploring the role of the household and
the way in which its organization shapes the relationship between self-
provisioning and commodity production. I have also suggested the
importance of the pivotal position of women within the household and
as actors struggling against the universal spread of commoditization.

Beginning with the household, even in the age of global movements
of capital and people, helps explain the persistence of parallel hybrid
capitalist and non-capitalist relations of production. That hybridity is
shaped by the vibrancy of indigenous communities to win struggles
over commoditization, or at least to shape them in a way in which they
can respond to existing and newly emerging patterns of inequality and
class formation. And that vibrancy cannot be 'read off' from any pre-
conceived schema that indicates that resistance to existing globalization
will automatically emerge from the working class, trade unionists and
organizations of labour. While the working class can and does protest
and organize for justice and equality, it is important to go behind what
might be the most discernible movements of opposition. For those
movements have themselves emerged from grassroot struggles and
patterns of resistance. What we observe as movements in action are
movements that have been generated from struggles elsewhere.

For example, the long marches of Commandante Marcos across
Mexico in 2006 were generated from struggles in rural Chiapas;
migrant worker demonstrations across the United States in the same

year had their roots not only in the cities of Los Angeles and New York but in towns and countryside in Mexico, Puerto Rico and countries in Central America. And mobilizations for land in Kenya and Zimbabwe, South Africa and Namibia may be most recognized when confronted by police and security forces in the capital cities or towns of those countries, yet they originate from struggles in households and villages where pressures of landlessness and thus for survival impact on households with women and children, the young and elderly.

Understanding why resistance takes the form that it does will help maximize the impact of struggles against capital. In the case of households, the patterns of resistance emerge in a general sense from reactions against the ways in which self-provisioning is challenged by commoditization. But the actual struggles that emerge will be shaped by specific and concrete relations of production and reproduction. In turn the social relations of globalization set constraints for opposition to it (Gruffydd Jones 2005: 56).

One major set of constraints is posed by the manner in which existing globalization seeks to deny opposition to it. But the contradictions of capitalism, most notably the immiseration that it generates and the failure to reduce global inequality, provide immense power to the oppressed to voice opposition to their poverty. In doing that, the poor also struggle to find a pattern or a model of resistance that maximizes opportunity for transformation of their livelihoods and over which they can retain control. That struggle is important, even where the outcomes may not be successful. The process of opposition itself helps generate and preserve 'dignity'.

> Dignity is the refusal to accept humiliation, oppression, exploitation, dehumanisation. It is a refusal which negates the negation of humanity. ... [It is] a politics dense with the dream of creating a world of mutual respect and dignity, filled with the knowledge that this dream involves the destruction of capitalism, of everything that dehumanises or de-subjectifies us.
>
> (Holloway 2005: 154)

People's dignity is challenged by their uneven incorporation into existing globalization. My accounts of the struggles over access to resources, labour, food, minerals and land, and the ways in which poverty and strategies intended to reduce it are shaped by the UK government and the IFIs, have concentrated on the persistence of global poverty, yet there is always the possibility for its genuine amelioration. I have stressed that this will not be delivered by the G8 and other dignitaries in the West or in Africa.

Although the horror of poverty and the ways in which it has been reproduced continue to shape the view of Africa, particularly in Western media and governments, struggles continue against the power of existing globalization, militarization and domination. The struggles that matter for the poor and the hungry are those that they shape and they control in promoting and recreating their humanity.

Notes

Chapter 1

1. This criticism in not reduced by the World Bank's attempt to take on board the importance of qualitative approaches to poverty, demonstrated by their 'voices of the poor' 'initiative'.
2. In reinforcing this point, Beinin notes how the title of one of the most widely used text books on the region, *A Political Economy of the Middle East*, by Richards and Waterbury (1996) dropped the subtitle *State, Class and Economic Development* from its second edition. Class was replaced by 'social actors'.
3. Gross investment in agriculture 1980–92 fell in Egypt from 31 per cent to 23 per cent, in Algeria from 37 per cent to 28 per cent, in Morocco from 23 per cent to 22 per cent, in Sudan from 12 per cent to 10 per cent and in Tunisia from 28 per cent to 26 per cent (El-Ghonemy 1999: 12).
4. Iran and Turkey, for instance, account for 34.4 per cent of the population and 38.6 per cent of the GDP of the region.
5. The Gini coefficient is a measure that shows how close a given distribution of income is to absolute equality or inequality. A figure closer to 0 represents absolute equality. As the coefficient approaches 1, the distribution of income approaches absolute inequality.
6. It seems the issue is not just one of employment *per se* but regular and sustained work that is crucial in sustaining an income flow. This is identified as one of the 'most important risk factors for poverty in Egypt' (Assaad et al 2001: 24; Datt et al 1998).
7. One area identified by the IFIs for improvement in the MENA is export agriculture. See *inter alia* Baroudi (1993) and, for a strong and interesting critique of the efficacy of globalization to ameliorate poverty, Milanovic (2003) and Chapter 2 below.
8. There is scope here for an interesting debate on the role of child labour and, linked to this, how child labour can be seen as a dynamic in the process of creating and reproducing poverty. Such a discussion falls outside the scope of this work, but see, among others, Amin and Lloyd (2002), Omar (nd) and Wahba (2001).

Chapter 2

1. The UN Millennium Development Goals are targets to be achieved by the world's poorest nations by 2015. They include halving the proportion of people living on less than US$1 a day between 1990 and 2015, halving the proportion of those suffering from hunger, ensuring by 2015 that all boys and girls complete primary education, reducing under-five mortality by two-thirds between 1990–2015 and reversing the spread of HIV/AIDS.
2. Trevor Manuel, South Africa's finance minister, for example, was the chair of the IMF/World Bank board of governors in 1999–2000, chair of the

IMF/World Bank Development Committee 2001–02 and co-chair of the March 2002 UN Financing for Development Conference in Monterrey.

3. Finland donated 0.76 per cent of GDP in 1991, but this has declined subsequently to 0.35.

4. The UK spent $16 billion on the war in Iraq and Afghanistan before the end of 2006. That paled to insignificance alongside the $350 billion in the United States for the Iraq war. This is equivalent to more than six times the US federal budget on K-12 education, and is an amount that would easily feed and provide basic healthcare, clean water and primary education to all the world's children. $100 billion would also meet the costs of all global anti-hunger efforts for five years. (See, for instance Julian Borger, 'Iraq War Will Cost Each US Family $3,415,' *Guardian* 25 June 2004; see also www.national priorities.org)

Chapter 3

1. International migrants are people who live in a country other than the one in which they were born (IOM 2005: 379).

2. This is particularly the view expressed by the tabloid press, but other media also fail to address a thoughtful view of asylum and labour migration issues. See *inter alia The Sun* 18 August 2003, and the way in which issues of foreign criminals were dealt with in May 2006.

3. It was not only British merchants in West Africa that organized the slave trade. For details of Dutch involvement, see van Dantzig (1978), and on the way in which local indigenous relations of production were transformed by the slave trade, see Fage (1969). There was also a major Arab slave movement of labour from the Slave Coast of West Africa to North Africa and the Middle East, and from East Africa to Reunion and the Gulf. Probably the most bestial occupation in Africa that relied on slave labour and an appallingly brutal labour regime to seize ivory and rubber was Belgiam control in Congo. For the most illuminating and also graphic and moving account of what has been called the first holocaust, see *King Leopold's Ghost* by Adam Hochschild (1998).

4. Although it should also be noted that migrant labour in South Africa was structured long before apartheid. In that earlier period, perhaps from 1910, supplies of labour were required in much greater quantities than could be handled through prison labour or wage pulls. It was a core element of 'Native Policy' under the system of segregation that dominated the Boer republics in the nineteenth century, and was enshrined in the 1910 Union of South Africa as official policy. What becomes central to the later apartheid system, however, is the way that the character of state administration and law underpinned it. I am grateful to Morris Szeftel for bringing this to my attention.

5. Popular press ranting about the fears of swamping of immigrants into the UK resulting from EU enlargement was unfounded. See Dustmann et al (2003) and for an example of the rant, *The Sun* 18 August 2003.

6. In December 2001 Tyson acquired IBP, the biggest beef processor in the United States, creating a $20 billion company, and was the biggest supplier of meat to McDonald's and Burger King. Tyson in fact was, as the *New York Times* put it, 'on probation' from 1997 for making illegal gifts to the then Agriculture Secretary. See *New York Times* 20 December 2001.

7. Much had been made of the claim that immigration policy in the United States did not radically alter after 9/11, but that assertion was inaccurate. We have already noted the reform of the immigration service and the failure to regularize 4 million undocumented Mexican workers in the United States. By mid-2003 it was also clear that figures for foreign students, 500,000 in 2002, were dramatically down. This was because from 1 August 2003, students applying for a first-time visa required a personal interview with a US official overseas before being granted a visa. Students contributed something like $12 billion to the US economy in 2002, but schools and colleges were now spending up to $500,000 each to help accelerate the interview and acceptance procedures and registration of applicants on a Department of Homeland Security database called SEVIS. Arab and Muslim students were hardest hit. Even US allies Saudi Arabia and Pakistan had a 65 per cent and 60 per cent drop in visas in fiscal 2002 (*Economist* 23 August 2003).

8. Increasingly dangerous methods of illegal traffickers to avoid detection led to the horrendous death by suffocation of 58 Chinese migrants in June 2000. They were found by immigration officials in Dover in the back of a Dutch-registered lorry. Estimated to have paid smugglers $20–30,000 each, the workers were thought to be heading to Chinese restaurants where they would be expected to pay off their debts.

Chapter 4

1. In Egypt, for example, in the years after the Nasser revolution and also since the mid-1980s agricultural liberalization, farmers who were required by law to produce quotas of cotton and other agricultural crops often refused to do so, bribing agricultural inspectors and deceiving ministry officials about the acreage planted with the stipulated crops.

2. Named after the alleged consequences for the Netherlands' economy after the discovery of North Sea oil and gas in the 1970s. The term refers to the undermining of agricultural development resulting from an overvalued exchange rate linked to oil-led growth, as food imports become cheaper than local development and as labour is sucked into the higher-wage sectors of resource extraction and finished products. See Chapter 5 for more on this.

3. This section draws on Bush (1999, 2000).

4. The land tax is revised every ten years and is based on the land's location and fertility.

5. The first anti-colonial *Chimurenga* was fought, and lost, in 1896–7 by the Ndebele against the seizure of land and occupation of South Western Zimbabwe by Cecil Rhodes' British South Africa Company and the Pioneer Column.

6. While it is difficult to get documented evidence of actual promises of finance for land sales, it seems the Labour government of James Callaghan had discussed providing £75 million to purchase land from the white farmers. The Lancaster House agreement was threatened with collapse when the Patriotic Front refused to budge on the absence of funding for land acquisition and the insistence by Margaret Thatcher and Lord Carrington on the willing-buyer willing-seller provisions. The UK government did make a grant of £20 million in 1980 and £10 million in 1981 with

an additional £17 million of aid loans from 1983–5. These loans required matching funding from the GoZ, but economic crisis and liquidity crises meant that a lot of the UK grant was never disbursed.

7. This is another parallel with Egypt, where Nasser's social contract with the *fellahin* ensured that they would in general not oppose the regime or be disruptive if they received the social and economic benefits of the revolution, at least in a moderate manner. See, among others Waterbury (1983) and Brown (1991).

8. The World Bank helped fund a pilot project with $5 million.

9. I am indebted to Sarah Bracking for sharing this information with me.

Chapter 5

1. Resource-poor countries such as Japan, the UK, Germany and Taiwan have performed much better with these resources than states with an abundance of minerals and oil, although their access to resources of any kind, of course, does not solely account for why they have been so economically dominant since 1945.

2. See Duffield 2000 for a discussion of the consequences of 'protracted internal and regionalized forms of conflict in the South'. This includes the argument that 'emerging political complexes', in Africa and elsewhere, are often linked to the phenomenon of war economies that have promoted the privatization of state services and the mushrooming of extralegal trans-border networks and trade.

3. See Shaw and Nyang'oro (2000) and compare this upbeat view of renaissance with Shaw and Inegbedion (1994). While Shaw and Nyang'oro recognize, it seems, the unevenness of Africa's recovery and the expression of the continent's renaissance promoted by Africa's post-insurgent states – Uganda, South Africa and Eritrea – they also note that it is a renaissance that is not immune from hijacking by the IFIs, nor does it preclude justification for intervention by African states in the internal affairs of others, namely in Rwanda and Congo. See also Cliffe (2002) and Saul (2003b).

4. Namibia's economy is heavily dependent upon mining, which contributed an annual average of 21.5 per cent of GDP between 1991 and 1995. In 1997 income from the export of metals was US$793 million, equivalent to 56.9 per cent of total export earnings; of this, diamonds represented $552 million, or 40.6 per cent. Namibia is the world's fifth largest producer of diamonds (*Africa Recovery* 1999).

5. See, inter alia, *Drillbits & Tailings*, 7 September 1998, and the attempts by a private tourmaline gem mine, Indigo Sky Gems, to evict 1000 'small' miners south of Karibib in Namibia in the summer of 1998. Indigo was a subsidiary of Branch Energy, owned by Tony Buckingham, a former British Special Air Services officer. Branch Energy shared offices and investments with Sandline, linked to the SA mercenary company Executive Outcomes. Indigo complained that local miners were smuggling tourmaline 'left, right and centre' and that the company was within its rights to expel the miners, despite the government of Namibia's support for the miners.

6. On the difficulties of mobilizing a cartel in the copper industry, namely the International Council of Copper Exporting Countries (CIPEC), founded in 1966, see Shafer (1994).

7. It is interesting that the success stories tend to be countries brought to heel either because of intense debt or because they are just about to enter into debt or financial crisis, perhaps as a result of a dramatic fall in the price of commodities. This point is well made by Gary and Lynn Karl (2003).

8. It is not only in Ghana that there has been an increased interest in African gold mining; it has extended to Tanzania and Mali (see *Engineering and Mining Journal* September 2000).

9. Botswana's GDP rate of growth 1980–90 was a staggering 10.3 per cent (and this despite a period of intense drought in the early 1980s). Growth had slowed to 4.4 per cent by 1990–94 but was 5.5 per cent in 1997–98 and 4.7 per cent 1998–99. Yet these growth figures, sustained by high levels of mineral extraction, notably diamonds, and high flows of aid seeking to maintain stability during the harshest years of apartheid and South Africa's regional destabilization, run alongside atrocious levels of poverty. In 1985–86, 33.3 per cent of the population eked out a living on less than US$1 a day and 61.4 per cent lived on less than US$2 a day (World Bank 2000, 1999, 1996).

10. The Movement for the Survival of the Ogoni People was founded in 1990 to confront the ravages of oil production in the Niger Delta, establish an Ogoni Bill of Rights and ensure greater representation of Ogoni interests in local and federal politics, including publicizing the environmental destruction by Shell and other oil companies of the Delta (see Saro-Wiwa 1992).

11. It is important to note though that the rhetoric of the government of Nigeria, and of Western interests, companies and UK parliamentary groups, has been to spin the idea that living conditions in the Delta region are not as bad as activists and advocacy groups assert. For instance, in the UK the All-Party Parliamentary Group on the Niger Delta (3–10 August 2005) suggested that according to 'most socioeconomic indicators, the Delta is performing better [sic] than most other parts of Nigeria'. They cite income poverty and primary school attendance, female literacy and child mortality among other things as evidence for this (p. 14), relying upon the Nigeria Demographic and Health Survey 1990 and 2003. Yet in October 2004 President Obasanjo noted, commenting on a peace deal with an Ijaw militia leader, that 'The obvious assessment so far is that not much impact has been made on the lives and living standards of most ordinary people of the Niger Delta' (quoted in Peel 2005: 7).

12. Clearly conditions are different for rich resource-dependent countries that can manage huge flows of rent without necessarily succumbing to 'Dutch disease'. An extreme example of this is Norway. The country with the world's highest GDP per head – £35,800 in 2005 – pumps 3.3 million barrels of oil a day but has had a very frugal management of the windfalls that have accrued because of oil wealth. Norway has a fund in excess of US$230 billion that is the direct result of oil revenue. But the Ministry of Finance requires that all this money is invested outside Norway. The intention, so far successful, is that governments in Oslo will not have to manage an overheated economy or the consequences of overvalued exchange rates and neglected agriculture. This draws much criticism within Norway, as many of the institutions of social welfare, schools, hospitals and housing are seen to be neglected; however, Norway has avoided what was seen to be the wasted expenditure of the UK Thatcher government years on financiers, unemployment and inflated exchange

rates (see, Patrick Collinson, 'Behind the world's biggest pension fund', *Guardian* 22 May 2006: 28).

13. This was certainly my experience when interviewing *Salamsey* gold miners in Ghana at the end of 2006 and in looking at the conflicts between these 'illegal' miners and the Ghanian state on the one hand and international mining companies on the other.

14. A US defence official implied senior members of the Nigerian Navy are involved in bunkering in what is described as a 'wild west atmosphere' in the Delta. Two Navy admirals were convicted of stealing an oil tanker in 2005 and Tafa Balogun, a former police inspector general, has been accused of stealing US$98 million, some of it from oil (see Donnelly 2005: 3).

Chapter 6

1. Least developed countries are defined by low per capita incomes of under $705; weak human assets based on nutrition, health, school enrolment and adult literacy; economic vulnerability based on indicators of instability of agricultural production; instability of goods and services; diversification from traditional economic activities; merchandise export concentration and economic smallness (UNCTAD 2006).

Chapter 7

1. I am aware that the term 'household' has many different interpretations, not the least based upon its family membership, but I use the term here to refer to those residing in one location, which when it comes to the social organization of production and social reproduction will involve more members than those in a single dwelling location.

Bibliography

Abdal Aal, Mohammed H. (2002) 'Agrarian Reform and Tenancy in Upper Egypt'. In Ray Bush (ed.) *Counter-Revolution in Egypt's Countryside*. London, Zed Books.

Abdel-Khalek, Gouda and Tignor, R. (1982) *The Political Economy of Income Distribution in Egypt*. New York and London: Holmes and Meier.

Abdelrahman, Maha M. (2004) *Civil Society Exposed: The Politics of NGOs in Egypt*. London: I.B. Tauris.

Abrahamson, Rita (2001) *Disciplining Democracy: Development Discourse and Good Governance in Africa*. New York: Zed Books.

—— (2004) 'A Breeding Ground for Terrorists? African and Britain's War on Terrorism', *Review of African Political Economy* 31(102), pp. 677–84

Abramovici, Pierre (2004) 'Precious Resources in Need of Protection: US and the New Scramble for Africa', *Le Monde Diplomatique*, July.

Adams, Martin (2000) *Breaking Ground: Development Aid for Land Reform*. London: Overseas Development Institute.

Adams, Richard H. Jnr and Page, John (2001) 'Holding the Line: Poverty Reduction in the Middle East and North Africa, 1970–2000'. Paper presented to the Annual Conference of the Economic Research Forum for the Arab Countries, Iran and Turkey, Bahrain (25–27 October).

Addy, Samuel N. (1998) 'Ghana: Revival of the Mineral Sector', *Resources Policy*, 24(4), pp. 229–39.

Adepoju, Aderanti (1995) 'Migration in Africa: An Overview'. In J. Baker and Tade Akin Aina (eds) *The Migration Experience in Africa*. Uppsala: Nordiska Afrikainstitutet.

African Development Bank (1997) *African Development Report 1997*. New York: Oxford University Press.

Ahmed, A.M. (1992) 'Rural Production Systems in the Sudan: A General Perspective'. In Martin Doornbos (ed.) *Beyond Conflict in the Horn: Prospects for Peace, Recovery and Development in Ethiopia, Somalia and the Sudan*. Trenton, N.J.: Red Sea Press.

Allen, Chris (1997) 'Who Needs Civil Society', *Review of African Political Economy*, 24(73), pp. 329–37.

—— (1999) 'Warfare, Endemic Violence and State Collapse in Africa', *Review of African Political Economy*, 26(81), pp. 367–84.

Ali, A. Ali and El Badawi, Ibrahim A. (2002) 'Poverty in the Arab World: The Role of Inequality and Growth'. In Ismail Sirageldin (ed.) *Human Capital: Population Economics in the Middle East*. Cairo: American University in Cairo Press.

Amann, Edmund and Baer, Werner (2002) 'Neoliberalism and its Consequences in Brazil', *Journal of Latin American Studies*, 34, pp. 945–59.

Amanor, Kojo Sebastian (2005) 'Agricultural Markets in West Africa: Frontiers, Agribusiness and Social Differentiation', *IDS Bulletin*, 36(2), June, pp. 58–62.

Amanor-Wilks, Dede (1995) *In Search of Hope for Zimbabwe's Farm Workers*. London: Panos and Dateline South Africa.

Amin, Sajeda and Lloyd, Cynthia B. (2002) 'Women's Lives and Rapid Fertility Decline: Some Lessons from Bangladesh and Egypt', *Population Research and Policy Review*, 21, pp. 275–317.

Amin, Samir (1995) 'Migrations in Contemporary Africa: A Retrospective View'. In J. Baker and Tade Akin Aina (eds) *The Migration Experience in Africa.* Uppsalla: Nordiska Afrikainstitutet.

Amuzegar, Jahangir (1999) *Managing the Oil Wealth: OPEC's Windfalls and Pitfalls.* London: IB Taurus.

Andreasson, Stefan (2006) 'Stand and Deliver: Private Property and the Politics of Global Dispossession', *Political Studies,* 54, pp. 3–22.

Ansari, Hamied (1986) *Egypt: The Stalled Society.* Albany, N.Y.: State University Press.

Appadurai, Arjun (2003) 'Disjuncture and Difference in the Global Cultural Economy'. In Jana Evans Braziel and Anit Mannur (eds) *Theorising Diaspora: A Reader.* Oxford: Blackwell.

Arendt, Hannah (1958) *The Human Condition.* Chicago: University of Chicago Press.

Arrighi, Giovanni (1967) *The Political Economy of Rhodesia.* The Hague: Mouton.

—— (2002) 'The African Crisis', *New Left Review II,* May/June, pp. 5–36.

Assaad, Ragui, Levison, Deborah and Zibani, Nadia (2001) 'The Effect of Child Work on School Enrollment in Egypt'. Paper presented to the ERF Conference 'The Analysis of Poverty and its Determinants in the Middle East and North Africa', Sana'a, Yemen (31 July–1 August).

Auty, Richard M. (1993) *Sustaining Development in the Mineral Economies: The Resource Curse Thesis.* London: Routledge.

—— (1995) *Patterns of Development: Resources, Policy and Economic Growth.* London: Edward Arnold.

Awudi, George B.K. (2002) 'The Role of Foreign Direct Investment in the Mining Sector of Ghana and the Environment'. Paper Presented to the Conference on Foreign Direct Investment and the Environment, OECD, Paris (7–8 February).

Bacha, Edmar L. and Klein, Herbert S. (eds) (1989) *Social Change in Brazil, 1945–1985.* Albuquerque: University of New Mexico Press.

Baker, Jonathan and Aina, Tade Aikin (eds) (1995) *The Migration Experience in Africa.* Uppsala: Nordiska Afrikainstitutet.

Baldwin-Edwards, Martin (2006) 'Between a Rock and a Hard Place: North Africa as a Region of Emigration, Immigration and Transit Migration', *Review of African Political Economy,* 33(108), pp. 311–24.

Bangura, Yusuf (1999) *New Direction in State Reform: Implications for Civil Society in Africa.* UNRISD Discussion Paper no. 113, September. Geneva: UNRISD.

Baroudi, Sami (1993) 'Egyptian Agricultural Exports since 1973', *Middle East Journal,* 47(1), winter, pp. 63–76.

Barraclough, S.L. (1994) 'The Legacy of Latin American Land Reform', *NACLA Report on the Americas,* Vol 28(3), Nov/Dec, pp. 16–21.

—— (1999) 'Land Reform in Developing Countries: The Role of the State and Other Actors', Discussion Paper no.1 01, June. Geneva: UNRISD.

—— (2001) 'The Role of the State and Other Actors in Land Reform'. In Krishna Ghimire (ed.) *Land Reform and Peasant Livelihoods: The Social Dynamics of Rural Poverty and Agrarian Reforms in Developing Countries.* London: I.T.

Barraclough Solon L. and Eguren, Fernando (2001) 'Agrarian Reform Issues and Initiatives in Three Andean Countries in South America'. In Krishna Ghimire (ed.) *Whose Land? Civil Society Perspectives on Land Reform and Rural Africa, Asia and Latin America.* Geneva: UNRISD.

Bates, Robert H. (1981) *Markets and States in Tropical Africa: The Political Basis of Agricultural Policies.* Berkeley: University of California Press.

Bayart, Jean-Francois, Eliss, Stephen and Hibou, Beatrice (1999) *The Criminalisation of the State in Africa*. Oxford: James Currey.

Bayat, Asef (1997) 'Cairo's Poor: Dilemmas of Survival and Solidarity', *Middle East Report*, 202, Spring.

—— (1998) *Street Politics: Poor People's Movements in Iran*. Cairo: American University Press.

—— (2000) *Social Movements, Activism and Social Development in the Middle East*. UNRISD Programme Paper on Civil Society and Social Movements. PP CSSM 3, Geneva: UNRISD.

—— (2002) 'Activism and Social Development in the Middle East', *International Journal of Middle East Studies*, 1, Winter, pp. 1–28.

—— (2003) 'The "Street" and the Politics of Dissent in the Arab World', *Middle East Report*, 226, Spring, pp. 10–17.

Bean, Richard Nelson (1975) *The British Trans-Atlantic Slave Trade 1650–1775*. New York: Arno.

Beinin, Joel (2001) *Workers and Peasants in the Modern Middle East*. Cambridge: Cambridge University Press.

Belkacem, Laabas (2001) 'Poverty Dynamics in Algeria'. Paper presented to the ERF Conference 'The Analysis of Poverty and its Determinants in the Middle East and North Africa', Sana'a, Yemen (31 July–1 August).

Berdal, Mats and Malone, David M. (eds) (2000) *Greed and Grievance: Economic Agendas in Civil Wars*. Boulder: Lynne Rienner.

Berthelemy, J-C., Kauffmann, C., Valfort, M-A. and Wegner, L. (2002) *Privatisation in Sub-Saharan Africa: Where do we Stand?* Paris: Organisation for Economic Co-operation and Development.

Bernstein, Henry (1994) 'Agrarian Classes in Capitalist Development'. In Leslie Sklair (ed.) *Capitalism and Development*. London: Routledge.

—— (1996) 'Agrarian Questions Then and Now', *Journal of Peasant Studies*, 24(1,2), Special Issue, pp. 22–59.

—— (2001) '"The Peasantry" in Global Capitalism and Development: Who, Where and Why?' In Leo Panitch and Colin Leys (eds) *Working Classes Global Realities*. Socialist Register. London: Merlin.

—— (2003) 'Land Reform in Southern Arica in World-Historical Perspective', *Review of African Political Economy*, 30(96), June, pp. 203–26.

—— (2004) 'Considering Africa's Agrarian Questions', *Historical Materialism*, 12(4), pp. 115–44.

—— (2005) 'Development Studies and the Marxists'. In Uma Kothari (ed.) *A Radical History of Development Studies: Individuals, Institutions and Ideologies*. Cape Town and London: David Philip and Zed Books.

Berry, Sara (1993) *No Condition is Permanent: Social Dynamics of Agrarian Change in Sub-Saharan Africa*. Wisconsin: University of Wisconsin Press.

Beynon, Huw and Ramalho, José (2001) 'Democracy and the Organization of Class Struggle in Brazil'. In Leo Panitch and Colin Leys (eds) *Working Classes Global Realities. Socialist Register 2001*. London: Merlin.

Bichler, Shimshon and Nitzan, Johnathan (2003) 'It's All About Oil', *News from Within*, 19(1), pp. 8–11.

Bijlmakers, Leon, A., Basset, Mary and Sanders, David (1998) 'Socioeconomic Stress, Health and Child Nutritional Status in Zimbabwe at a Time of Economic Structural Adjustment: A Three-Year Longitudinal Study'. *Nordiska Afrikainstitutet Research Report*, 105.

Binswanger, Hans P. (1991) 'Brazilian Policies that Encourage Deforestation in the Amazon', *World Development*, 19(7), pp. 821–9.

Boele, Richard, Fabig, Heike and Wheeler, David (2001) 'Shell, Nigeria and the Ogoni: A Study in Unsustainable Development. 1. The Story of Shell, Nigeria and the Ogoni People – Environment, Economy Relationships: Conflict and Prospects for Resolution', *Sustainable Development*, 9, pp. 74–86.

Bohle, H-G., Watts, M. and Downing, T.E. (1993) 'Who is Vulnerable: People and Places'. Paper presented to conference on Climate Change and World Food Security, University of Oxford (11–15 July), Mimeo.

Bond, Patrick (2006) *Looting Africa: The Economics of Exploitation*. London: Zed Books.

Bond, Patrick and Desai, Ashwin (2006) 'Explaining Uneven and Combined Development in South Africa'. In Bill Dunn (ed.) *Permanent Revolution: Results and Prospects 100 Years On*. London: Pluto.

Bond, Patrick and Dor, George (2003) 'Uneven Health Outcomes and Political Resistance Under Residual Neoliberalism in Africa', *International Journal of Health Services*, 33(3), pp. 607–30.

Booth, David (2005) *The Africa Commission Report: What About the Politics?* London: ODI.

Boseley, Sarah (2002) 'Aids Cuts Life Expectancy to 27', *Guardian*, 8 July.

Boserup, Ester (1965) *The Conditions of Agricultural Growth: The Economics of Agrarian Change Under Population Pressure*. London: Allen and Unwin.

Bowyer-Bower, T.A.S. (2000) 'Implications for Poverty of Land Reform in Zimbabwe: Insights from the Findings of the 1995 Poverty Assessment Survey Study'. In T.A.S. Bowyer-Bower and Colin Stoneman (eds) *Land Reform in Zimbabwe: Constraints and Prospects*. Aldershot: Ashgate.

Bowyer-Bower, T.A.S. and Stoneman, Colin (eds) (2000) *Land Reform in Zimbabwe: Constraints and Prospects*. Aldershot: Ashgate.

Bracking, Sarah (2003) 'The Political Economy of Chronic Poverty'. Working Paper for the Chronic Poverty Research Centre (February). Manchester: University of Manchester, Institute for Development Policy and Management.

—— (2005) 'Guided Miscreants: Liberalism, Myopias, and the Politics of Representation', *World Development*, 33(6), pp. 1011–24.

—— (2006) 'Accountability in Development Finance Projects: Between the Market and a Soft Place' (forthcoming).

Bracking, Sarah and Harrison, Graham (2003) 'Africa, Imperialism and New Forms of Accumulating', *Review of African Political Economy*, 30(95), pp. 5–10.

Brand, Ulrich and Wissen, Markus (2005) 'Neoliberal Globalization and the Internationalisation of Protest: A European Perspective', *Antipode*, 37, pp. 9–17.

Brandt, Willy (1980) *North–South: A Programme for Survival: A Report of the Independent Commission on International Deveopment*. London: Pan Books.

Branford, Sue and Rocha, Jan (2002) *Cutting the Wire*. London: Latin America Bureau.

Braziel, Jana Evans and Mannur, Anita (eds) (2003) *Theorizing Diaspora: A Reader*. Oxford: Blackwell.

Brittain, Victoria and Macalister, Terry (2001) 'Oil Firms Stoke up Sudan War', *Guardian*, 15 March.

Bromley, Simon (1994) *Rethinking Middle East Politics*. Oxford: Polity.

Brown, Nathan (1990) *Peasant Politics in Modern Egypt: The Struggle against the State*. New Haven and London: Yale University Press.

—— (1991) 'The Ignorance and Inscrutability of the Egyptian Peasantry'. In F. Kazemi and John Waterbury (eds) *Peasants and Politics in the Modern Middle East*. Miami: Florida International University Press.

Bryceson, Deborah (2000) 'Peasant Theories and Smallholder Policies: Past and Present'. In Deborah Bryceson, Cristobal Kay and Jos Mooij (eds) *Disappearing Peasantries? Rural Labour in Latin America, Asia and Africa*. London: Intermediate Technology Development Group.

—— (2002) 'The Scramble in Africa is Reorienting Rural Livelihoods', *World Development*, 30(5), pp735–39.

Bundy, Colin (1979) *The Rise and Fall of the South African Peasantry*. Berkeley: University of California Press.

Bunker, Stephen G. (1988) *Underdeveloping the Amazon: Extraction, Unequal Exchange, and the Failure of the Modern State*. Chicago and London: University of Chicago Press.

Burawoy, Michael (1976) 'The Functions and Reproduction of Migrant Labor: Comparative Material from Southern Africa and the United States', *American Journal of Sociology*, 82(5), pp. 1050–87.

Bush, Ray (1999) *Economic Crisis and the Politics of Reform in Egypt*. Boulder, Colo.: Westview.

—— (2000) 'An Agricultural Strategy without Farmers: Egypt's Countryside in the New Millenium', *Review of African Political Economy*, 84(27), June, pp. 235–49.

—— (ed.) (2002a) *Counter Revolution in Egypt's Countryside: Land and Farmers in the Era of Economic Reform*. London: Zed Books.

—— (2002b) 'More Losers than Winners in Egypt's Countryside: The Impact of Changes in Land Tenure'. In Ray Bush (ed.) *Counter Revolution in Egypt's Countryside*. pp.185–210. London: Zed Books.

—— (2003) 'The Impact of Globalisation on Food and Agriculture with special emphasis on the Middle East'. Paper presented to the Workshop on 'Globalization and Vulnerability of Middle Eastern Countries', University of California, Los Angeles (1–2 May).

Bush, Ray and Cliffe, Lionel (1984) 'Agrarian Policy in Migrant Labour Societies: Reform or Transformation in Zimbabwe?' *Review of African Political Economy*, 29, pp. 77–94.

Byres, Terence J. (1991) 'The Agrarian Question and Differing Forms of Capitalist Agrarian Transition: An Essay with Reference to Asia'. In Jan Breman and Sudipto Mundle (eds) *Rural Transformation in Asia*. Delhi: Oxford University Press.

—— (1996) *Capitalism From Above and Capitalism From Below: An Essay in Comparative Political Economy*. London: Macmillan.

—— (1998) 'Some Thoughts on a Heterodox View of the Causes of Low Agricultural Productivity', *Journal of Peasant Studies*, 26(1), October, pp. 159–69.

Cammack, Paul (2002) 'Neoliberalism, the World Bank and the New Politics of Development'. In U. Kothari and M. Minogue (eds) *Development Theory and Practice*. Basingstoke: Palgrave.

Campbell, Bonnie and Ericsson, M. (eds) (1996) *Restructuring of Global Aluminium*. London: Mining Journal Press.

Campling, Liam (2001) 'DRC: Rebels, Mines and Mercenaries', *West Africa*, 4275, pp. 24–6.

Carvalho, Georgia O. (2000) 'The Politics of Indigenous Land Rights in Brazil',

Bulletin of Latin American Research, 19, pp. 461–78.

Castles, Stephen (1999) 'International Migration and the Global Agenda: Reflections on the 1998 UN Technical Symposium', *International Migration*, 37(1), pp. 5–14.

Castles, Stephen and Davidson, A. (2000) *Citizenship and Migration*. Basingstoke: Palgrave.

Castles, Stephen and Miller, Mark J. (2003) *The Age of Migration: International Population Movements in the Modern World*. New York: Guilford.

Chabal, Patrick (2002) 'The Quest for Good Government and Development in Africa: Is NEPAD the Answer?' *International Affairs*, 78(3), pp. 447–62.

Chabal, Patrick and Daloz, Jean-Pascal (1999) *African Works: Disorder as Political Instrument*. Oxford: James Currey.

Cheru, Fantu (2002) *African Renaissance*. London: Zed Books.

Christian Aid (2005) *The Economics of Failure: The Real Cost of 'Free' Trade for Poor Countries*. Christian Aid Briefing Paper, June.

Christodoulou, D. (1990) *The Unpromised Land: Agrarian Reform and Conflict Worldwide*. London and New Jersey: Zed Books.

Clarke, J. (1997) 'Petro Politics in Congo', *Journal of Democracy*, 8(3), pp. 62–76.

Cleaver, Kevin A. and Schreiber, G.A. (1994) *Reversing the Spiral*. Washington: World Bank.

Cliffe, Lionel (1986) 'National Liberation Struggles and "Radicalisation" in Southern Africa'. Paper Presented to Review of African Political Economy Conference, Liverpool.

—— (1988) 'Zimbabwe's Agricultural "Success" and Food Security', *Review of African Political Economy*, 43, pp. 4–25.

—— (2000) 'The Politics of Land Reform in Zimbabwe'. In T.A.S. Bowyer-Bower and Colin Stoneman (eds) *Land Reform in Zimbabwe: Constraints and Prospects*, pp. 35–46. Aldershot: Ashgate.

—— (2002) 'African Renaissance?' In Tunde Zack-Williams, Diane Frost and Alex Thompson (eds) *Africa in Crisis*. London: Pluto.

Cliffe, Lionel and Luckham, Robin (1999) 'Complex Political Emergencies and the State: Failure and the Fate of the State', *Third World Quarterly*, 20(1), pp. 27–50.

—— (2000) 'What Happens to the State in Conflict?', *Political Disasters*, 24(4), pp. 291–313.

Coakley, George J. (1998) 'The Minerals Industry of Ghana'. http://minerals.usgs.gov/minerals/pubs/country/2003/ghmybo3.pdf.

Coakley, George J., Michalski, Bernadette and Mobbs, Philip M. (1998) 'The Minerals Industries of Africa'. http://minerals.usgs.gov/minerals/pubs/country/1999/africa99.pdf.

Cohen, Robin (1987) *The New Helots: Migrants in the International Division of Labour*. Aldershot: Gower.

Collicelli, Carla and Valerii, Massimiliano (2000) 'A New Methodology for Comparative Analysis of Poverty in the Mediterranean: A Model for Differential Analysis of Poverty at a Regional Level'. *Working Paper 2023*. Cairo: ERF.

Collier, Paul (2000a), 'Doing Well out of War: An Economic Perspective'. In M. Berdal and David M. Malone (eds) *Greed and Grievance*. Boulder: Lynne Rienner.

—— (2000b) 'Economic Causes of Civil Conflict and Their Implications for Policy', 15 June mimeo. Washington: World Bank.

Commission for Africa (CFA) (2005) *Our Common Interest: Report of the Commis-*

sion for Africa. March, London: CFA.

Craig, John (2000), 'Evaluating Privatisation in Zambia: A Tale of Two Processes', *Review of African Political Economy,* 27(85), pp. 357–66.

—— (2001), 'Putting Privatisation into Practice: The Case of Zambia Consolidated Copper Mines Limited', *Journal of Modern African Studies,* 39(3), pp. 389–410.

Curtis, Mark (2001) 'Boom Time for Few Signals Death for Many', *Guardian,* 15 March.

Cusworth, John (2000) 'A Review of the UK ODA Evaluation of the Land Resettlement Programme in 1988 and the Land Appraisal Mission of 1996'. In T.A.S. Bowyer-Bower and Colin Stoneman (eds) *Land Reform in Zimbabwe: Constraints and Prospects.* Aldershot: Ashgate.

Daily Times [Pakistan] (2005) 'EU Grain Mountain Rises Sets Policy Dilemma', 9 January.

Danaher, Kevin (2001) 'Power to the People', *Observer,* 29 April.

Danielson, Luke and Lagos, Gustavo (2001), 'The Role of the Minerals Sector in the Transition to Sustainable Development', May, IIED Opinion Paper, World Summit on Sustainable Development.

Datt, Gaurav, Jollife, Dean and Sharma, Manohar (1998) 'A Poverty Profile for Egypt: 1997', *Discussion Paper 49.* Washington, DC: International Food Policy Research Institute.

Davis, Mike (2001) *Late Victorian Holocausts: El Nino Famines and the Making of the Third World.* London: Verso.

Deigues, Carlos (1992) *The Social Dynamics of Deforestation in the Brazilian Amazon: An Overview.* Discussion Paper No. 36, July. Geneva: UNRISD.

Deininger, K. (1999) 'Making Negotiated Land Reform Work: Initial Experience from Colombia, Brazil and South Africa', *World Development,* 27(4), pp. 651–72.

Deininger, K. and Binswanger, H. (1999) 'The Evolution of the World Bank's Land Policy: Principles, Experience, and Future Challenges', *World Bank Research Observer,* 14(2), August, pp. 247–76.

Deininger, K., Hoogerveen, J.G.M. and Kinsey, B.H. (2000) 'Productivity and Equity Impacts of Land Reford: The Case of Zimbabwe'. Paper prepared for the IAAE meeting, Berlin, August.

Deininger, K. and Squires, L. (1996) 'A New Data Set Measuring Income Inequality', *World Bank Economic Review,* 10(3), pp. 565–91.

De Boeck, Filip (2001) 'Garimpeiro Worlds: Digging, Dying and "Hunting" for Diamonds in Angola', Review of African Political Economy', 28(90), pp. 549–62.

De Haas, Hein (2005) 'International Migration, Remittances and Development: Myths and Fact', *Global Migration Perspectives,* No. 3, www.goim.org/attachements/GMP%20No%2030pdf.

De Janvry, A. and Sadoulet, E. (1989) 'A Study in Resistance to Institutional Change: The Lost Game of Latin American Land Reform', *World Development,* 17(9), pp. 1397–1407.

—— (1993) 'Market, State, and Civil Organizations in Latin America Beyond the Debt Crisis: The Context for Rural Development', *World Development,* 21(4), pp. 659–74.

Department for International Development (DfID) (2000) *Eliminating World Poverty: Making Globalisation Work for the Poor.* London: HMSO.

—— (2005) *Why we Need to Work More Effectively in Fragile States.* London: DfID.

January.

—— (2006) *Eliminating World Poverty: Making Governance Work for the Poor.* London: HMSO.

De Soto, Hernando (2000) *The Mystery of Capital: Why Capitalism Triumphs in the West and Fails Everywhere Else.* US: Basic Books.

de Souza, Amaury (1997) 'Redressing Inequalities: Brazil's Social Agenda at Century's End'. In Susan Kaufman Purcell and Riordan Roett (eds) *Brazil Under Cardoso.* Boulder and London: Lynne Rienner.

de Soysa, Indra (2000) 'The Resource Curse: Are Civil Wars Driven by Rapacity or Paucity'. In M. Berdal and David M. Malone (eds) *Greed and Grievance.* Boulder: Lynne Rienner.

de Waal, Alex (1989) *Famine that Kills.* Oxford: Clarendon.

—— (1990) 'A Re-assessment of Entitlement Theory in the Light of the Recent Famines in Africa', *Development and Change,* 21, pp. 469–90.

—— (1993) 'War and Famine in Africa'. In Jeremy Swift (ed.) *New Approaches to Famine. IDS Bulletin,* 24(4), October, pp. 33–40.

—— (2002) 'What's new in the "New Partnership for Africa's Development"?' *International Affairs,* 78(3) pp. 463–75.

Donnan E. (1930) *Documents Illustrative of the History of the Slave Trade to America* (2 vols). Washington: Carnegie Institution of Washington.

Donnelly, John (2005) 'Burdens of Oil Weigh on Nigerians', www.globalpolicy. org/security/natres/oil/2005/1001burden.htm.

Dorner, Peter (1972) *Land Reform and Economic Development.* Harmondsworth: Penguin Modern Economic Texts.

DPR (2005) 'Exhilarating, Exhausting, Intriguing: The Report of the Africa Commission', *Development Policy Review,* 23(4), pp. 483–98.

Dreze, Jean and Sen, A. (1989) *Hunger and Public Action.* Oxford: Clarendon.

Duffield, Mark (1998) 'Post-modern Conflict, Warlords, Post-adjustment States and Private Protection', *Journal of Civil Wars,* 1(1), pp. 65–102.

—— (2000) 'Globalisation, Transborder Trade, and War Economies'. In M. Berdal and David M. Malone (eds) *Greed and Grievance.* Boulder: Lynne Rienner.

—— (2001) *Global Governance and the New Wars: The Merging of Development and Security.* London: Zed Books.

—— (2002) 'War as a Network Enterprise: The New Security Terrain and its Implications', *Journal of Cultural Values,* 6(1–2), spring, pp. 153–65.

—— (2005) 'Getting Savages to fight Barbarians: Development, Security and the Colonial Present', *Conflict, Security and Development,* 5(2) pp. 141–60.

Dustmann, Christian, Casanova, Maria, Fertig, Michael, Preston, Ian and Schmidt, Christoph M. (2003) *The Impact of EU Enlargement on Migration Flows.* Home Office Online Report 25/03 Research Development and Statistics Directorate, Home Office, www.homeoffice.gov.uk/rds/pdfs2/rdsolr2503.pdf.

Dustmann, Christian, Fabbri, Francesca, Preston, Ian and Wadsworth, Jonathan (2003) 'Labour Market Performance of Immigrants in the UK Labour Market'. Home Office Online Report 05/03, Research Development and Statistics Directorate, Home Office, www.homeoffice.gov.uk/rds/pdfs2/rdsolr0503.pdf.

Dyer, Geoff (1997) *State and Agricultural Productivity in Egypt.* London: Frank Cass.

Easterly, William (2003) 'The Cartel of Good Intentions: The Problem of Bureaucracy in Foreign Aid', *Policy Reform,* 16, pp. 1–28. http://www.nyu.edu/fas/institute/dri/Easterly/File/carteljan2003.pdf.

Economic Commission for Africa (ECA) (1989) *African Alternative Frameworks to*

Structural Adjustment Programmes for Socioeconomic Recovery and Transformation. Addis Ababa: ECA.

Economist (2002) 'How and When to Open the Door to Migrants', 2–8 November.

Economist Intelligence Unit (2001) *Zimbabwe Country Profile.* London: EIU.

Edkins, Jenny (2000) *Whose Hunger? Concepts of Famine, Practices of Aid.* Minneapolis: University of Minnesota Press.

El-Ghonemy, M.R. (1993) 'Food Security and Rural Development in North Africa', *Middle Eastern Studies,* 29(3), July, pp. 445–66.

—— (1998) *Affluence and Poverty in the Middle East.* London and New York: Routledge.

—— (1999) 'Recent Changes in Agrarian Reform and Rural Development Strategies in the Near East', *Land Reform,* 1(2), pp. 9–20.

El Khoury, Marianne (2001) 'Poverty and Social Mobility in Lebanon: A Few Wild Guesses'. Paper presented at the ERF Conference 'The Analysis of Poverty and its Determinants in the Middle East and North Africa', Sana'a, Yemen (31 July–1 August).

El Kogali, Saffaa E. and El Daw, Suliman (2001) 'Poverty, Human Capital and Gender: A Comparative Study of Yemen and Egypt'. Paper presented at the ERF Conference 'The Analysis of Poverty and its Determinants in the Middle East and North Africa', Sana'a, Yemen (31 July–1 August).

El Laithy, Heba (2001) 'The Gender Dimensions of Poverty in Egypt'. Paper presented at the ERF Conference 'The Analysis of Poverty and its Determinants in the Middle East and North Africa', Sana'a, Yemen (31 July–1 August).

El Said, Moataz and Löfgren, H. (2001) 'The Impact of Alternative Development Strategies on Growth and Distribution: Simulations with a Dynamic Model for Egypt'. Paper presented at the ERF Conference 'The Analysis of Poverty and its Determinants in the Middle East and North Africa', Sana'a, Yemen (31 July–1 August).

Elliot, Larry (2005) 'Rich Spend 25 Times More on Defence than Aid', *Guardian,* 6 July.

Ellis, Stephen (2003) 'Briefing: West Africa and its Oil', *African Affairs,* 102, pp. 135–8.

Engineering and Mining Journal (1998) 'Mining in Africa', 99(April), p.32.

Ericsson, Magnus and Tegen, Andreas (1999) 'African Mining in the Late 1990s: A Silver Lining?' *CDR Working Paper,* April, Copenhagen, Denmark.

EU Country Reports (2000) Economist Intelligence Unit Country Reports (2000), www.economist.com/countries.

European Commission (1999) 'Analysis and Forecasting of International Migration by Major Groups (Part 11)', *Eurostat Working Papers* (3/1999/E/no9).

Eurostat (2002) 'Migration Keeps the EU Population Growing', *Statistics in Focus.* Brussels: European Communities.

Evans, Peter (1979) *Dependent Development: The Alliance of Multinational, State and Local Capital in Brazil.* Princeton: Princeton University Press.

Fage, J.D. (1952) 'Some General Considerations Relevant to Historical Research in the Gold Coast', *Transactions of the Gold Coast and Togoland Historical Society,* 1(1).

—— (1969) 'Slavery and the Slave Trade in the Context of West African History', *Journal of African History,* 10(3), pp. 393–404.

Faist, Thomas (2000) *The Volume and Dynamics of International Migration and Transnational Social Spaces.* Oxford: Clarendon.

Fargues, Philippe (2003) 'Migration Across the Mediterranean: Looking

Upstream'. Paper Presented to the Workshop on the 'Political Economy of the Middle East and the Mediterranean: Assessing the State of the Field', European University Institute, Florence (23–24 May).

Faris, M.M. and Khan, M.H. (eds) (1993) *Sustainable Agriculture in Egypt*. Boulder and London: Lynne Rienner.

Fergany, Nader (1998) 'Unemployment and Poverty in Egypt'. In M.A. Kishk (ed.) *Poverty of Environment and Environment of Poverty*. Cairo: Dar El-Ahmadi lil Nasher.

—— (2002) 'Poverty and Unemployment in Rural Egypt'. In Ray Bush (ed.) *Counter Revolution in Egypt's Countryside*. London: Zed Books.

Ferguson, James (1999) *Expectations of Modernity: Myths and Meanings of Urban Life on the Zambian Copperbelt*. Berkeley: University of California Press.

First, Ruth (1982) *Black Gold: The Mozambican Miner, Proletarian and Peasant*. Brighton: Harvester Press.

Fishlow, Albert (1997) 'Is the Real Plan for Real?' In Susan Kaufman Purcell and Riordan Roett (eds) *Brazil Under Cardoso*. Boulder and London: Lynne Rienner.

Fisk, Robert (2003) 'A Million March in London, but Faced with Disaster the Arabs Are Like Mice', *Independent*, 18 February.

Fleshman, Michael (2002) 'The International Community and the Crisis in Nigeria's Oil Producing Communities', *Review of African Political Economy*, 29(91), pp. 153–163.

Fletcher, Lehman B. (ed.) (1996) *Egypt's Agriculture in a Reform Era*. Ames: Iowa State University Press.

Flint, Julie (2001) 'British Firms Fan Flames of War', *Observer*, 11 March.

Food and Agricultural Organisation of the UN (FAO) (2000) *Egypt: Common Country Assessment, Agriculture*. Cairo: Unpublished mimeo, October.

—— (2001) 'Mobilizing Resources to Fight Hunger'. Committee on World Food Security, 27th session, Rome (28 May–1 June).

—— (2003) 'The Elimination of Food Insecurity in the Horn of Africa', www.fao.org/docrep/003/x8406e/X8406e01.htm, accessed 28 February 2006.

—— (2004) *The State of Food Insecurity in the World 2004*. Rome: FAO.

—— (2005) *The State of Food Insecurity in the World 2005*. Rome: FAO.

FAO/GIEWS: Africa Report No.3, December 2005. Rome: FAO.

Forrest, Tom (1993) *Politics and Economic Development in Nigeria*. Oxford: Oxford University Press.

Foweraker, Joe (1981) *The Struggle for Land: A Political Economy of the Pioneer Frontier in Brazil From 1930 to the Present Day*. Cambridge: Cambridge University Press.

Francis, Elizabeth and Murray, Colin (2002) '"Introduction", in Special Issue on Changing Livelihoods', *Journal of Southern African Studies*, 28(3) pp. 485–7.

Friedmann, Harriet (1993) 'The Political Economy of Food: A Global Crisis', *New Left Review*, 197, Jan/Feb, pp. 29–57.

—— (2004) 'Feeding the Empire: The Pathologies of Globalized Agriculture'. In Leo Panitch and Colin Leys (eds) *The Empire Reloaded: Socialist Register 2005*. London: Merlin.

Friedmann, Harriet and McMichael, P. (1989) 'Agriculture and the State System, The Rise and Decline of National Agricultures, 1870 to the Present', *Sociologia Ruralis*, 14, pp. 93–118.

Frynas, J. G. (2001), 'Corporate and State Responses to Anti-Oil Protests in the Niger Delta', *African Affairs*, 100, pp. 27–54.

Gagnon, Georgette and Ryle, John (2001) 'Report of an Investigation into Oil Development, Conflict and Displacement in Western Upper Nile, Sudan'. October. Mimeo.

Gary, Ian and Karl, Terry Lynn (2003) *Bottom of the Barrel: Africa's Oil Boom and the Poor.* Baltimore, Md.: US Catholic Relief Services.

Gedicks, Al (2001) *Resource Rebels: Native Challenges to Mining and Oil Corporations.* Cambridge, Mass.: South End Press.

Geldof, Bob (2004) 'Why Africa?' Text of a speech delivered at the Bar Human Rights Commission bi-annual lecture at St Paul's Cathedral, 20 April.

Geremek, B. (1996) 'Civil Society Then and Now'. In Larry Diamond and Marc F. Plattner (eds) *The Global Resurgence of Democracy* (2nd edn). Baltimore and London: Johns Hopkins Press.

Ghazouani, Samir and Goaied, M. (2001) 'The Determinants of Urban and Rural Poverty in Tunisia'. Paper presented at the ERF Conference 'The Analysis of Poverty and its Determinants in the Middle East and North Africa', Sana'a, Yemen (31 July–1 August).

Ghimire, Krishna B. (ed.) (2001) *Whose Land? Civil Society Perspectives on Land Reform and Rural Africa, Asia and Latin America.* Geneva: UNRISD.

Global Witness (2002) *All the Presidents' Men*, Global Witness, March.

—— (1999) *A Crude Awakening*, Global Witness, December.

Glover, Stephen, Gott , Ceri, Loizillon, Anaïs, Portes, Jonathan, Price, Richard, Spencer, Sarah, Srinivasan, Vasanthi and Willis, Carole (2001) 'Migration: An Economic and Social Analysis'. Research Development and Statistics Directorate, Occasional Paper no. 67. London: Home Office.

Goodman, David (1989) 'Rural Economy and Society'. In Edmar L. Bacha and Herbert S. Klein (eds) *Social Change in Brazil, 1945–1985*. Albuquerque: University of New Mexico Press.

Gott, C. and Johnston, K. (2002) *The Migrant Population in the UK: Fiscal Effects.* Home Office, UK Government.

Government of Egypt (1990) *Agricultural Census*. Cairo: Ministry of Agriculture

—— (2000) *Agricultural Census*. Cairo: Ministry of Agriculture.

Gramsci, Antonio (1976) *Selections from the Prison Notebooks,* Quentin Hoare and Geoffrey Nowell-Smith (eds). London: Lawrence and Wishart.

Grany, Wyn (2006) 'Common Agricultural Policy', 30 January www.commonag policy.blogspot.com/2006/01/grain-mountain-growing.html, accessed 15 March 2006.

Grigg, David (1993) *The World Food Problem* (2nd edn). Oxford: Blackwell.

Grindle, Merilee, S. (2002) *Good Enough Governance: Poverty Reduction and Reform in Developing Countries.* London: DfID.

Gruffydd Jones, Branwen (2005) 'Globalisations, Violences and Resistances in Mozambique'. In Catherine Eschle and Bice Maiguashca (eds) *Critical Theories, International Relations, and 'The Anti-Globalisation Movement': The Politics of Global Resistance.* New York: Routledge.

Guanziroli, Carlos.E. (1998) 'La reforma agraria en el marco de una economía global: el caso de Brasil', *Land Reform*, 1, pp. 37–52.

Haddad, Laurence and Ahmed, A. (2003) 'Chronic and Transitory Poverty; Evidence from Egypt 1997–99', *World Development*, 31(1), pp. 71–85.

Hall, Anthony (ed.) (2000) *Amazonia at the Crossroads: The Challenge of Sustainable*

Development: London: Institute of Latin American Studies.

Hall, Thomas, D. and Fenelon, James (2003) 'Indigenous Resistance to Globalization: What does the Future Hold?' In Wilma A. Dunaway (ed.) *Emerging Issues in the 21st Century World-System: Crises and Resistance in the 21st Century World-System, Vol1.* Westport, Conn.: Praeger.

Halliday, Fred (1999) 'Millennial Middle East: Changing Orders, Shifting Borders'. Middle East Research and Information Project (MERIP) 213 (Winter). Available at www.merip.org/.

Hammar, Tomas and Tamas, Kristof (1997) 'Why Do People Go or Stay?' In Tomas Hammar, Grete Brochmann, Kristof Tamas and Thomas Faist (eds) *International Migration, Immobility and Development: Multidisciplinary Perspectives.* Oxford: Berg.

Hammond, John, L. (1999) 'Law and Disorder: The Brazilian Landless Farmworkers' Movement', *Bulletin of Latin American Research*, 18(4), pp. 469–89.

Harris, N. (2002) *Thinking the Unthinkable.* London: IB Tauris.

Harrison, Graham (2005) *Africa: The Construction of Governance States.* London: Routledge

Harts-Broekhuis, Annelet and Huisman, Henk (2001) 'Resettlement Revisited: Land Reform Results in Resource-Poor Regions in Zimbabwe', *Geoforum*, 32(3), August, pp. 285–98.

Harvey, David (2003) 'The "'New" Imperialism: Accumulation by Dispossession'. In Leo Panitch and Colin Leys (eds) *The New Imperial Challenge, Socialist Register 2004.* London: Merlin.

—— (2005) *The New Imperialism.* Oxford: Oxford University Press.

Hawthorne, Susan (2001) 'The Clash of Knowledge Systems: Local Diversity in the Wild versus Global Homogeneity in the Marketplace'. In Veronika Bennholdt-Thomsen and Claudia von Werlhof (eds) *There is an Alternative: Subsistence and Worldwide Resistance to Corporate Globalization.* London: Zed Books.

Hay, C. (1996) *Re-stating Social and Political Change.* Milton Keynes, Open University Press.

Hayter, Teresa (2004) *Open Borders: The Case Against Immigration Controls.* London: Pluto.

Hecht, Susanna and Cockburn, Alexander (1989) *The Fate of the Forest: Developers, Destroyers and Defenders of the Amazon.* London: Verso.

Hermele, Kenneth (1997) 'The Discourse on Migration and Development'. In Tomas Hammar, Grete Brochmann, Kristof Tamas and Thomas Faist (eds) *International Migration, Immobility and Development: Multidisciplinary Perspectives.* Oxford: Berg.

Hibou, Béatrice (2004) *Privatising the State.* London: Hurst.

—— (2006) 'Domination and Control in Tunisia: Economic Levers for the Exercise of Authoritarian Power', *Review of African Political Economy*, 33(108) pp. 185–206.

Hilson, Gavin (2004) 'Structural Adjustments in Ghana: Assessing the Impacts of Mining Sector Reform', *Africa Today*, 51(2), pp. 53–77.

HMG (Her Majesty's Government) (2000) *Eliminating World Poverty: Making Globalisation Work for the Poor.* White Paper on International Development. London: HMSO. Also www.dfid.gov.uk/pubs/files/whitepaper2000.pdf.

Hochschild, Adam (1998) *King Leopold's Ghost: A Story of Greed, Terror, and Heroism in Colonial Africa.* Boston: Houghton Mifflin.

Hodges, Tony (2001) *Angola: From Afro Stalinism to Petro-Diamond Capitalism.* Oxford: James Currey.

Hoefle, Scott, W. (2000) 'Patronage and Empowerment in the Central Amazon', *Bulletin of Latin American Research*, 19, pp. 479–99.

Hoffman, Helga (1989) 'Poverty and Prosperity: What is Changing?' In Edmar L. Bacha and Herbert S. Klein (eds) *Social Change in Brazil, 1945–1985.* Albuquerque: University of New Mexico Press.

Holloway, John (2005) *Change The World Without Taking Power: The Meaning of Revolution Today.* London: Pluto.

Hoogeveen, J.G.M. and Kinsey, Bill H. (2001) 'Land Reform, Growth and Equity: Emerging Evidence from Zimbabwe's Resettlement Programme: A Sequel', *Journal of Southern African Studies*, 27(1), pp. 127–36.

Hopkins, Nicholas (1987) *Agrarian Transformation in Egypt.* Boulder: Westview.

—— (1993) 'Small Farmer Households and Agricultural Sustainability in Egypt'. In Mohemad A. Faris and Mahmood Hasan Khan (eds) *Sustainable Agriculture in Egypt.* Boulder: Lynne Rienner.

Human Rights Watch (1999a) *Famine in Sudan 1998: The Human Rights Causes.* New York and London: Human Rights Watch.

—— (1999b) *Nigeria: The Price of Oil.* March, New York: Human Rights Watch.

—— (1999c) *Nigeria: Crackdown in the Niger Delta.* June, New York: Human Rights Watch.

Hyden, Goran (1980) *Beyond Ujamaa in Tanzania: Underdevelopment and the Uncaptured Peasantry.* London: Heinemann.

—— (1983) *No Shortcuts to Progress: African Development Management in Perspective.* Berkeley and Los Angeles: University of California Press.

Ibeanu, Okechukwu (2002) 'Janus Unbound: Petro-business and Petropolitics in the Niger Delta', *Review of African Political Economy*, 29(91), pp. 163–7.

International Food Policy Research Institute (2002) *Achieving Sustainable Food Security for All by 2020.* May, Washington: IFPRI.

International Fund for Agricultural Development (IFAD) (2001) *Rural Poverty Report 2001: The Challenge of Ending Rural Poverty.* Rome: IFAD.

International Institute for Environment and Development (IIED) (2002) *Breaking New Ground.* Mining, Minerals and Sustainable Development Group. London: IIED.

International Monetary Fund (IMF) (2005) *Regional Economic Outlook: Sub-Saharan Africa.* May. Washington: IMF.

International Organization for Migration (IOM) (2003) *World Migration 2003: Managing Migration, Challenges and Responses for People on the Move, Vol. 2.* Geneva: IOM.

—— (2005) *World Migration 2005.* Geneva: IOM.

Irz, Xavier, Lin, Lin, Thirtle, Colin and Wiggins, Steve (2001) 'Agricultural Productivity Growth and Poverty Alleviation', *Development Policy Review*, (19(4), December, pp. 449–66.

Johnson, Douglas H. (2003) *The Root Causes of Sudan's Civil Wars.* Oxford: James Currey.

Johnston, Josée and Laxer, Gordon (2003) 'Solidarity in the Age of Globalization: Lessons from the anti-MAI and Zapatista Struggles'. *Theory and Society*, 32, pp. 39–91.

Jordan, Bill (1996) *A Theory of Poverty and Social Exclusion.* Oxford: Polity.

Kandeel, Ayman and Nugent, Jeffrey B. (2000) 'Unravelling the Paradox in

Egypt's Trends in Income Inequality and Poverty'. In Ghassan Diba and Wassim Shahin (eds) *Earnings Inequality, Unemployment and Poverty in the Middle East and North Africa*. Westport, Conn.: Greenwood.

Kaplan, Robert D. (1997) *The Ends of the Earth: From Togo to Turkmenistan, from Iran to Cambodia, a Journey at the Dawn of the 21st Century*. New York: Vintage.

Karl, Terry Lynn (2001) *The Paradox of Plenty*. Berkeley: University of California Press.

Kay, C. (1998) 'Latin America's Agrarian Reform: Lights and Shadows', *Land Reform*, 2, pp. 9–29.

Kayatekin, Serap A. (1998) 'Observations on Some Theories of Current Agrarian Change', *Review of African Political Economy*, 25(76), pp. 207–19.

Keane, J (1988) *Civil Society and the State: New European Perspectives*. London: Verso.

Keen, David (1994) *The Benefits of Famine: A Political Economy of Famine and Relief in Southwestern Sudan, 1983–1989*. New Jersey: Princeton University Press.

—— (1998) *The Economic Functions of Violence in Civil Wars*. London: OUP for IISS.

—— (2000) 'Incentives and Disincentives for Violence'. In Mats Berdal and David M. Malone (eds) *Greed and Grievance: Economic Agendas in Civil Wars*. Boulder: Lynne Rienner.

Keenan, Jeremy. H. (2006) 'Security and Insecurity in North Africa', *Review of African Political Economy*, 33(108), 269–96.

Khasawneh, Mohamad (2001) 'Poverty Assessment Report: The Case of Jordan'. Paper presented at ERF Conference 'The Analysis of Poverty and its Determinants in the Middle East and North Africa', Sana'a, Yemen (31 July–1 August).

Kibble, Steve and Vanlerberghe, Paul (2000) *Land, Power and Poverty: Farm Workers and the Crisis in Zimbabwe*. London: CIIR.

King, R. (1977) *Land Reform: A World Survey*. London: G. Bell and Sons.

King, Russell (1995) 'Migrations, Globalisation and Place'. In Doreen Massey and Pat Jess (eds) *A Place in the World?* Oxford: Oxford University Press.

Kinsey, B. (1999) 'Land Reform, Growth and Equity: Emerging Evidence from Zimbabwe's Resettlement Programme', *Journal of Southern African Studies*, 25(2), pp. 173–96.

Kinsey, B., Burger, K. and Gunning, J.W. (1998) 'Coping with Drought in Zimbabwe: Survey Evidence on Responses of Rural Households to Risk', *World Development*, 26(1), pp. 39–110.

Koser, Khalid (2001) 'The Smuggling of Asylum Seekers into Western Europe: Contradictions, Conundrums, and Dilemmas'. In David Kyle and Rey Koslowski (eds) *Global Human Smuggling*. Baltimore and London: Johns Hopkins University Press.

Kothari, Uma (2002) 'Migration and Chronic Poverty'. Institute for Development Policy and Management, University of Manchester, Chronic Poverty Research Centre, Working Paper no. 16.

Kyle, David and Dale, John (2001) 'Smuggling the State Back In: Agents of Human Smuggling Reconsidered'. In David Kyle and Rey Koslowski (2001) *Global Human Smuggling*. Baltimore and London: Johns Hopkins University Press.

Kyle, David and Koslowski, Rey (2001) *Global Human Smuggling*. Baltimore and London: Johns Hopkins University Press.

Land Center for Human Rights (2002) 'Farmer Struggles Against Law 96 of 1992'. In Ray Bush (ed.) *Counter Revolution for Egypt's Countryside*. London: Zed.

Lanning, Greg (1979) *Africa Undermined*. Harmondsworth: Penguin.

Le Billion, Philippe (2000) 'The Political Economy of Resource Wars'. In J. Cilliers and C. Dietrich (eds) *Angola's War Economy: The Role of Oil and Diamonds*. South Africa: Institute for Security Studies.

Le Saout, D. and Rollinde, M. (1999) *Emeutes et Mouvements Sociaux au Maghreb*. Paris: Karthala.

Le Vine, Mark (2002) 'The UN Arab Human Development Report: A Critique'. Press Information Note 101, 26 July. Washington, DC: MERIP. Available online at: www.merip.org/mero/mero072602.html..

Lewis, W.A. (1955) *The Theory of Economic Growth*. London: Allen & Unwin.

Leys, Colin (1994) 'Confronting the African Tragedy', *New Left Review*, 1(204) March/April, pp. 33–47.

Lipton, Michael (1977) *Why Poor People Stay Poor: A Study of Urban Bias in World Development*. London: Temple Smith.

—— (1993) 'Land Reform as Commenced Business: The Evidence Against Stopping', *World Development*, 21(4), pp. 641–57.

—— (1997) 'Editorial: Poverty – Are There Holes in the Consensus?' *World Development*, 25(7), pp. 1003–7.

—— (2001) 'Challenges to Meet: Food and Nutrition Security in the New Millennium', *Proceedings of the Nutrition Society*, 60, pp. 203–14.

Lopez, Ramon (2003) 'The Policy Roots of Socioeconomic Stagnation and Environmental Implosion: Latin America 1950–2000', *World Development*, 31(2), pp. 259–80.

Löwy, Michael (2002) 'Towards an International Resistance Against Captialist Globalization', *Latin American Perspectives*, Issue 127, 29(6), pp. 127–31.

Loxley, John (2003) 'Imperialism and Economic Reform: NEPAD', *Review of African Political Economy*, 80(95), pp. 119–28.

Luxemburg, Rosa (1968) [1923] *The Accumulation of Capital*. New York: Monthly Review Press.

Macharia, Kinuthia (2003) 'Resistant Indigenous Identities in the 21st Century World-System: Selected African Cases'. In Wilma A. Dunaway (ed.) *Emerging Issues in the 21st Century World System: Crises and Resistance in the 21st Century World System, Vol 1*. Westport, Conn.: Praeger.

Macrae, Joanna and Anthony Zwi (eds) (1994) *War and Hunger: Rethinking International Responses to Complex Emergencies*. London: Zed Books and Save the Children Fund.

Magalhães, Mariano (1996) 'Taking by Force', *Brazzil*, available on www.brazzil.com accessed 13 February 2003.

Mahdavy, H. (1970) 'The Rentier State: The Case of Iran'. In M.A. Cook (ed.) *Studies in the Economic History of the Middle East from the Rise of Islam to the Present Day*. London: Oxford University Press.

Mamdani, Mahmood (1996) *Citizen and Subject: Contemporary Africa and the Legacy of Late Colonialism*. Princeton: Princeton University Press.

Marcussen, H.S. (1996) 'NGOs, the State and Civil Society', *Review of African Political Economy*, 23(69), pp. 405–23.

Martin, Philip (2003) 'Bordering on Control: Combatting Irregular Migration in North America and Europe', *International Organisation for Migration*, April.

Marx, Karl (1974) *Capital, Vol. 1*. Moscow: Progress Publishers.

—— (1977) *Grundrisse*. London: Penguin.

Massey, Doreen (1984) *Spatial Divisions of Labour*. London, Macmillan

Maxwell, Daniel and Wiebe, Keith (1999) 'Land Tenure and Food Security: Exploring Dynamic Linkages', *Development and Change*, 30, pp. 825–49.

Maxwell, Simon (2001) 'WDR 2000: Is There a New "New Poverty Agenda"?' *Development Policy Review*, 19(1), pp. 143–9.

—— (2005) 'Exhilarating. Exhausting. Intriquing. The report of the African Commission', *Development Policy Review*, 23(4), pp. 483–92.

Maxwell, Simon and Slater, Rachel (2003) 'Food Policy Old and New', *Development Policy Review*, 21(5–6), pp. 531–53.

McDowell, C. and deHaan, Arjan (1997) *Migration and Sustainable Livelihoods*, IDS Working Paper 65. Brighton: Institute of Development Studies.

McNamara, Robert S. (1973) *One Hundred Countries, Two Billion People: The Dimensions of Development*. New York: Praeger.

McPhail, Kathryn (2000) 'How Oil, Gas and Mining Projects Can Contribute to Development', *Finance and Development*, 37(4), December. www.imf.org/ external/pubs/ft/fandd/2000/ 12/mcphail.htm, accessed on 17 November 2006.

Melamed, Claire (2006) 'Briefing: Wrong Questions, Wrong Answers – Trade, Trade Talks and Africa', *African Affairs*, 420, pp. 451–60.

Milanovic, Branko (2003) 'The Two Faces of Globalization: Against Globalization as We Know It', *World Development*, 31(4), pp. 667–83.

Miles, Robert (1987) *Capitalism and Unfree Labour: Anomaly or necessity?* London: Tavistock.

Milieudefensie (2000) *Victims of their own Fortunes*. October, Netherlands: Friends of the Earth International. Available from www.milieudefensie.nl/globalising /publicaties/raporten/nigeria-rapport.pdf.

Ministry of Agriculture and Land Reclamation and USAID (1997) *Agricultural Policy Reform in Morocco: A Brief Overview*. Agricultural Policy Reform Program, Reform Design and Implementation Unit, Report No. 20 prepared by W. Tyner, December. Mimeo.

—— (1998) *Horticultural Sub-Sector Map*. Prepared by Ronald D. Krenz for APRP-RDI, Report no. 39, June. Cairo: Mimeo.

—— (1999a) Land Tenure Study Phase II by Mohemad Sharaf and Jane Gleeson, March. Cairo: USAID.

—— (1999b) *Study of New Land Allocation Policy in Egypt*, by Sayed Hussein et al. February. Cairo: USAID.

Mitchell, Simon (ed.) (1981) *The Logic of Poverty: The Case of the Brazilian Northeast*. London: Routledge and Kegan Paul.

Mitchell, Timothy(1998) 'The Market's Place'. In Nicholas S. Hopkins and Kirsten Westergaard (eds.) *Directions of Change in Rural Egypt*. Cairo: The American University Press in Cairo Press.

—— (1999) 'No Factories, No Problems: The Logic of Neo-Liberalism in Egypt', *Review of African Political Economy*, 26(82), pp. 455–468.

—— (2002) *Rule of Experts: Egypt, Techno-Politics*. Berkeley and London: Modernity University of California Press.

Mkandawire, Thandika (2005) 'The Global Economic Context'. In Ben Wisner, Camilla Toulmin and Rutendo Chitiga (eds) *Towards a New Map of Africa*. London: Earthscan.

Monbiot, G. (2003) 'Poor but Pedicured', *Guardian*, 6 May 2003

Moore, Bruce H. (2001) 'Empowering the Rural Poor Through Land Reform and Improved Access to Productive Assets'. In Krishna B. Ghimire (ed.) *Whose*

Land? Civil Society Perspectives on Land Reform and Rural Africa, Asia and Latin America. Geneva: UNRISD.

Moore, David (2004) 'Marxism and Marxist Intellectuals in Schizophrenic Zimbabwe: How Many Rights for Zimbabwe's Left? A Comment', *Historical Materialism*, 12(4), pp. 405–25.

Morris, Nigel (2004) 'Britain's Broken Pledges on Aid Cost Poorest Nations £9.5 Billion', *Independent*, 28 July.

Morrison, Christian (1991) 'Adjustment, Incomes and Poverty in Morocco', *World Development*, 19(11), pp. 1633–51.

Moyo, Sam (1995) *The Land Question in Zimbabwe.* Harare: SAPES.

—— (2000) *Land Reform under Structural Adjustment in Zimbabwe: Land Use Change in the Mashonaland Provinces.* Uppsala: Nordiska Afrikainstitutet.

Moyo, Sam, Rutherford, Blair and Amanor-Wilks, Dede (2000) 'Land Reform and Changing Social Relations for Farm Workers in Zimbabwe', *Review of African Political Economy*, 27(84), pp. 181–202.

Moyo, Sam and Yeros, Paris (eds) (2005) *Reclaiming the Land.* London: Zed.

Moyo, Sam and Yeros, Paris (2007) 'The Radicalised State: Zimbabwe's Interrupted Revolution', *Review of African Political Economy*, 34(111).

Munck, Ronaldo (2002) *Labour and Globalisation: A New Great Transformation?* London: Zed Books.

Myers, Keith (2005) *Petroleum, Poverty and Security.* Africa Programme, AFP BP 05/01. London: Chatham House.

Myers, Norman and Kent, Jennifer (2001) 'Food and Hunger in Sub-Saharan Africa', *The Environmentalist*, 21, pp. 41–69.

New Partnership for Africa's Development (NEPAD) (2005a) 'Implementing the CAADP Agenda', www.nepad.org.

—— (2005b) 'The Comprehensive Africa Development Programme' (CAADP),. NEPAD Secretariat Meeting Maputo, 15–18 February, available at www.nepad.org/2005/files/caadp.php, accessed 4 March 2006.

Nigeria Extractive Industries Transparency Initiative (2006) '1st Roundtable on the NEITI Audit Results'. www.neiti.org/Reports%20for%20first%20round%20table.htm, accessed 25 May 2006.

Ntzebeza, Lungisde and Hall, Ruth (eds) (2006) *The Land Question in South Africa: The Challenge of Transformation and Redistribution.* Cape Town: PHPRC Press.

Observer (2001), Julie Flint, 'British firms fan flames of war', 11 March.

Organisation for African Unity (OAU) (1985) *African Priority Programmes for African Recovery 1986–1990.* Addis Ababa: OAU.

Olukoshi, Adebayo (2005) 'Investing in Africa: The Political Economy of Agricultural Growth', *IDS Bulletin*, 36(2), June, pp. 13–16.

Omar, Amna (n.d.) 'Socio-Economic and Demographic Determinants of Child Labor in Northern Sudan'. Mimeo.

Owen, Roger (2000) *State, Power and Politics in the Making of the Modern Middle East*, 2nd edition. London: Routledge.

Owusu, Francis (2003) 'Pragmatism and the Gradual Shift from Dependency to Neo-liberalism: The World Bank, African Leaders and Development Policy in Africa', *World Development*, 31(10), pp. 1655–72.

Oxfam (2003) *The Trade Report: Rigged Rules and Double Standards.* Oxford: Oxfam.

Palmer, R. (1977) *Land and Racial Domination in Rhodesia.* London: Heinemann.

Pantuliano, S (2005) *Comprehensive Peace? Causes and Consequences of Underdevelopment and Instability in Eastern Sudan.* NGO Paper, International Rescue

Committee et al. Dar es Salaam, Tanzania. Available at http://www.tear-fund.org/webdocs/Website/Campaigning/Policy%20and%20research/East%20Sudan%20Analysis%202005.pdf, accessed on 17 November 2006,

Papapanagos, Harry and Vickerman, Roger (2003) 'Borders, Migration and Labour Market Dynamics in a Changing Europe'. Department of Economics, Kent, Mimeo.

Papastergiadis, Nikos (2000) *The Turbulence of Migration: Globalization, Deterritorialization and Hybridity*. Oxford: Polity.

Parnwell, Mike and Rigg, Jonathan (2001) 'Global Dissatisfactions: Globalisation, Resistance and Compliance in Southeast Asia', *Singapore Journal of Tropical Geography*, 22(3), pp. 205–11.

Peel, Michael (2005) 'Crisis in the Niger Delta: How Failures of Transparency and Accountability are Destroying the Region'. Africa Programme, Armed Non-state Actors Project AFP BP 05/02. London: Chatham House.

Perelman, Michael (2000) *The Invention of Capitalism*. Durham and London: Duke University Press.

Perz, Stephen, G. (2002) 'The Changing Social Contexts of Deforestation in the Brazilian Amazon', *Social Science Quarterly*, 83(1), pp. 35–52.

Petras, James (1998) 'The New Revolutionary Peasantry: The Growth of Peasant-led Opposition to Neoliberalism', available at www.mstbrazil.org/petras1098.html, accessed on 31 January 2002.

Phimister, Ian (1988) *A Social and Economic History of Zimbabwe, 1890–1948: Capital Accumulation and Class Struggle*. London: Longman.

Pickering, Kathleen (2003) 'The Dynamics of Everyday Incorporation and Anti-systemic Resistance: Lakota Culture in the 21st Century'. In Wilma A. Dunaway (ed.) *Emerging Issues in the 21st Century World-System: Crises and Resistance in the 21st Century World System*. Westport, Conn.: Praeger.

Poku, Nana (2002) 'Poverty, Debt and Africa's HIV/AIDS Crisis', in *International Affairs*, 78,(3) pp. 531–46.

Polzer, Tara (2001) 'Corruption: Deconstructing the World Bank Discourse'. DESTIN Working Paper Series, LSE No. 01–18, December.

Porteous, Tom (2005) 'British Government Policy in SubSaharan Africa Under New Labour', *International Affairs*, 81(2), pp. 281-97.

Pratt, Nicola (2002) 'Maintaining the Moral Economy: Egyptian State-Labour Relations in an Era of Economic Liberalization', *Arab Studies Journal*, 8(2/9), pp. 111–29.

Radice, Hugo (2006) 'Neo Liberal Globalisation: Imperialism without Empires?' In Alfredo Saad-Filho and D. Johnston (eds) *Neo Liberalism: A Critical Reader*. London: Pluto.

Raftopoulos, Brian and Phimister, Ian (2004) 'Zimbabwe Now: The Political Economy of Crisis and Coercion', *Historical Materialism*, 12(4), pp. 355–82.

Raikes, Philip (1988) *Modernising Hunger*. London: Catholic Institute for International Relations and James Currey.

Ranger, T. (1985) *Peasant Consciousness and Guerrilla War in Zimbabwe*. London: James Currey.

—— (1993) 'The Communal Areas of Zimbabwe'. In T. Bassett and D. Crummey (eds) *Land in African Agrarian Systems*. Madison: University of Wisconsin Press.

Reddy, Sanjay G. and Pogge, Thomas W. (2003) 'How Not To Count The Poor'. Mimeo, version 4.5 (26 March). Available online at www.columbia/edu/ca/economics/ReddyPageCuSem.pdf.

Reis, Jaime (1981) 'Hunger in the Northeast: Some Historical Aspects'. In Simon Mitchell (ed.) *The Logic of Poverty. The Case of the Brazilian Northeast*. London: Routledge and Kegan Paul.

Reno, William (2000), 'Shadow States and the Political Economy of Civil Wars'. In M. Berdal and David M. Malone (eds) *Greed and Grievance*. Boulder: Lynne Rienner.

Richards, Alan and Waterbury, John (1996) *A Political Economy of the Middle East*. Boulder, Colo.: Westview.

Richards, Paul (1985) *Indigenous Agricultural Revolution: Ecology and Food Production in West Africa*. London: Hutchinson.

Rigg, Jonathan (2006) 'Land, Farming, Livelihoods, and Poverty: Rethinking the Links in the Rural South', *World Development*, 34(1), pp. 180–202.

Rihan, M. and Nasr, M. (2001) 'Prospects for Land Reform and Civil Society Movements in the Near East and North Africa'. In Krishna B. Chimire (ed.) *Whose Land? Civil Society Perspectives on Land Reform and Rural Poverty Reduction*. Italy: IFAD.

Roberts, H. (2002) 'Moral Economy or Moral Polity? The Political Anthropology of Algerian Riots'. LSE Development Research Centre, Crisis States Programme Working Paper No 17 (October). London: London School of Economics.

Rocha, Geisa, M. (2002) 'Neo-Dependency in Brazil', *New Left Review*, 16, July–August, pp. 5–33.

Rocha, Jan (2000) *Brazil: A Guide to the People, Politics and Culture*. London: Latin America Bureau.

Roett, Riordan (1997) 'Brazilian Politics at Century's End'. In Susan Kaufman Purcell and Riordan Roett (eds) *Brazil Under Cardoso*. Boulder and London: Lynne Rienner.

Ross, Michael (1999) 'The Political Economy of the Resource Curse', *World Politics*, 51, January, pp. 297–322.

Rupert, Mark (2003) 'Globalising Common Sense: A Marxian-Gramscian (Re-Vision of the Politics of Governance/Resistance', *Review of International Studies*, 29, pp. 181–98.

Rutherford, Blair (2001a) 'Commercial Farm Workers and the Politics of (Dis)placement in Zimbabwe: Colonialism, Liberation and Democracy', *Journal of Agrarian Change*, 1(4), October, pp. 626–51.

—— (2001b) *Working on the Margins: Plantation Workers in Zimbabwe*. London: Zed Books.

Saad, Reem (1988) *Social History of an Agrarian Reform Village*. Cairo: Cairo Papers in Social Science, American University in Cairo.

—— (2002) 'Egyptian Politics and the Tenancy Law'. In Ray Bush (ed.) *Counter Revolution for Egypt's Countryside*. London: Zed.

Sachikonye, Lloyd, M (2003a) 'From "Growth with Equity" to "Fast-Track" Land Reform: The Debate on Zimbabwe's Land Question', *Review of African Political Economy*, 30(96), pp. 227–40..

—— (2003b) 'Land Reform for Poverty reduction? Social Exclusion and Farm Workers in Zimbabwe'. Paper presented to the Conference on 'Staying Poor: Chronic Poverty and Development Policy' organised by the IDPM, University of Manchester (April).

Saro-Wiwa, Ken (1992), *Genocide in Nigeria: The Ogoni Tragedy*. Port Harcourt: Saros International Publishers.

Sassen, Saskia (1999) *Guests and Aliens*. New York: New Press.

Saul, J. S. (2001) *Millennial Africa: Capitalism, Socialism, Democracy*. Trenton: Africa World Press.

—— (2003a) 'What is to be Learned? The Failure of African Socialisms and their Future'. In R. Albritton, J. Bell, S. Bell and R. Westra (eds) *Beyond Market and Plan: Toward New Socialisms*. London: Palgrave.

—— (2003b) 'Africa: The Next Liberation Struggle?' *Review of African Political Economy*, 30(96), pp. 187–202.

Schoef, Brooke G. (2003) 'Uganda: Lessons for AIDS Controls in Africa', *Review of African Political Economy*, 30(98), pp. 553–72.

Scott, James, C. (1976) *The Moral Economy of the Peasant: Rebellion and Subsistence in South East Asia*. New Haven and London: Yale University Press.

—— (1985) *Weapons of the Weak: Everyday Forms of Peasant Resistance*. New Haven and London: Yale University Press.

—— (1990) *Domination and the Arts of Resistance: Hidden Transcripts*. New Haven and London: Yale University Press.

—— (1998) *Seeing Like a State: How Certain Schemes to Improve the Human Condition Have Failed*. New Haven and London: Yale University Press.

Sen, A. (1981) *Poverty and Famine: An Essay on Entitlement and Deprivation*. Oxford: Clarendon.

Sfakianakis, John (2002) 'In Search of Bureaucrats and Entrepreneurs: The Political Economy of the Egyptian Agricultural Sector'. In Ray Bush (ed.) *Counter-Revolution in Egypt's Countryside*. London: Zed Books.

Shafer, Michael D. (1994) *Winners and Losers: How Sectors Shape the Development Prospects of States*. Ithaca and London: Cornell University Press.

Shanin, Teodor (ed.) (1976) *Peasants and Peasant Societies*. Harmondsworth: Penguin.

Shaw, Timothy M. and Inegbedion, John E. (1994), 'The Marginalization of Africa in the New World (Dis)Order'. In Richard Stubbs and Geoffrey R.D. Underhill (eds) *Political Economy and the Changing Global Order*. London: Macmillan.

Shaw, Timothy, M. and Nyang'oro, Julius E. (2000) 'African Renaissance in the New Millennium?' In Richard Stubbs and Geoffrey R.D. Underhill (eds) *Political Economy and the Changing Global Order*, 2nd edn. Oxford: Oxford University Press.

Shields, Michael A. and Price, Stephen Wheatley (2003) 'The Labour Market Outcomes and Psychological Well-being of Ethnic Minority Migrants in Britain'. Home Office Online Report 07/03. London: Research Development and Statistics Directorate.

Showstack Sassoon, Anne (1978) 'Hegemony and Political Intervention'. In Sally Hibbin (ed.) *Politics, Ideology and the State*. London: Lawrence and Wishart.

Silver, Beverley J. and Arrighi, Giovanni (2000) 'Workers North and South'. In Leo Panitch and Colin Leys (eds) *Socialist Register 2001*. London: Merlin.

Sirageldin, Ismail (2000) 'Elimination of Poverty: Challenges and Islamic Strategies'. ERF Working Paper 2018. Cairo: ERF.

Skeldon, Ronald (1997) *Migration and Development: A Global Perspective*. London: Longman.

Slack, Keith (2001) 'Social Impacts of Large Scale Mining in Developing Countries', http://www.bicusa.org/ptoc/htm/slack_social impacts.htm.

Smith, Jackie and Johnston, Hank (2002) 'Globalization and Resistance: An Introduction'. In Jackie Smith and Hank Johnston (eds) *Globalization and Resistance:*

Transnational Dimensions of Social Movements. Maryland: Rowman & Littlefield.

Sobhan, Rehman (1993) *Agrarian Reform and Social Transformation: Preconditions for Development.* London and New Jersey: Zed Books.

Soudi, Khalid (2001) 'Pauvreté et vulnérabilité sur le marché du travail: quelques dimensions de la fragilité de la position des pauvres'. Paper presented at ERF Conference 'The Analysis of Poverty and its Determinants in the Middle East and North Africa', Sana'a, Yemen (31 July–1 August).

Southern African Development Community. 'SADC-NEPAD Co-Operation in Agriculture, Extracted from Summary of NEPAD-related SADC Development Projects' (2001–4).

Soysa, Indra de (2000) 'The Resource Curse: Are Civil Wars Driven by Rapacity or Paucity?' In Mats Berdal and David M. Malone (eds) *Greed and Grievance: Economic Agendas in the Civil Wars.* Boulder: Lynne Rienner.

Stalker, Peter (2000) *Workers Without Frontiers: The Impact of Globalisation on International Migration.* Boulder: Lynne Rienner.

Stewart, Sheelagh (1997) 'Happy Ever After in the Marketplace: Non-Government Organizations and Uncivil Society', *Review of African Political Economy*, 24(71), pp. 11–34.

Stiglitz, Joseph (2002) *Globalization and its Discontents.* London: Penguin.

Stoneman, Colin (ed.) (1981) *Zimbabwe's Inheritance.* London: Macmillan.

Stoneman, Colin and Cliffe, Lionel (1989) *Zimbabwe: Politics, Economy and Society.* London and New York: Pinter.

Suliman, Mohamed (1999) *The Sudan: A Continent of Conflicts. A Report on the State of War and Peace in the Sudan.* Bern, Switzerland: Swiss Peace Foundation.

Sutcliffe, Bob (2003) 'Crossing Borders in the New Imperialism'. In Leo Panitch and Colin Leys (eds) *The New Imperial Challenge, Socialist Register 2004.* London: Merlin.

SW Radio (2005) 'Armed Police Stealing Farm Equipment in Mwenezi and Masvingo', Tereerai Karimakwenda, 14 November, available from http://www.swradioafrica.com/news141105/policestealing 141105.htm, accessed on 17 November 2006.

Szeftel, Morris (1998) 'Misunderstanding African Politics: Corruption and the Governance Agenda', *Review of African Political Economy*, 25(76), pp. 221–40.

—— (2000) 'Clientelism, Corruption and Catastrophe', *Review of African Political Economy*, 27(85), pp. 427–41.

Taleb, B.K. (1998) 'Vers la privatisation des terres: le role de l'etat dans la modernisation des régimes fonciers au Maroc', *Land Reform*, 1, pp. 55–68.

Taylor, J. Edward (1999) 'The New Economics of Labour Migration and the Role of Remittances in the Migration Process', *International Migration*, 37(1), pp. 63–88.

Thiesenhusen, William, C. (1995) 'Land Reform Lives!' *European Journal of Development Research*, 7(1), pp. 193–209.

Timmer, C. Peter (1995) 'Getting Agriculture Moving: Do Markets Provide the Right Signals?' *Food Policy*, 20(5), pp. 455–72.

Tingay, Caroline (2004) *Agrarian Transformation in Egypt: Conflict Dynamics and the Politics of Power from a Micro Perspective.* PhD dissertation submitted to Politik-und Sozialwissenschafter Prüfungsbüro, Freie Universität Berlin, Germany, November.

Todaro, Michael (1969) 'A Model of Labour Migration and Urban Unemployment in Less Developed Countries', *The American Economic Review*, 59(1). pp138–48

Torres, Magüi M. and Anderson, Michael (2004) *Fragile States: Defining Difficult Environments for Poverty Reduction, PRDE (Poverty Reduction in Difficult Environments)*. Working paper 7 August, Team Policy Division, UK, DfID.

Toulmin, C. and Quan, J. (eds) (2000) *Evolving Land Rights, Policy and Tenure in Africa*. London: IIED.

Turner, Terisa E. and Brownhill, Leigh S. (2001) '"Women Never Surrendered": The Mau Mau and Globalization from Below in Kenya 1980–2000'. In Veronika Bennholdt-Thomsen and Claudia von Werlhof (eds) *There is an Alternative: Subsistence and Worldwide Resistance to Corporate Globalization*. London: Zed Books.

UK Parliament All-Party Parliamentary Group on the Niger Delta (2005) *Delegation to the Niger Delta: 3–10th August*. December.

United Nations (2000) Replacement Migration: Is it a Solution to Declining and Ageing Populations?, www.un.org/esa/population/publications/migration/execsum.htm

—— (2005) *The Millennium Development Goals Report*. New York: UN.

UNAIDS (2004) *Report on the Global AIDS Epidemic*. Geneva:UNAIDS.

UNAIDS (2006) *Report on the Global AIDS Epidemic*. Geneva:UNAIDS.

UNCTAD (1999) *The Least Developed Countries 1999 Report*. New York: UN.

—— (2006) *The Least Developed Countries Report*. Geneva: UNCTAD.

United Nations Development Programme (UNDP) (1993) *Human Development Report*. Oxford and New York: Oxford University Press.

—— (1999) Zimbabwe Human Development Report 1999, Harare: UNDP with Poverty Reduction Forum and Institute of Development Studies.

—— (2000) *Zimbabwe Human Development Report 2000*. Harare: UNDP with Poverty Reduction Forum and Institute of Development Studies.

—— (2002a) *Arab Human Development Report 2002*. Jordan: UNDP.

—— (2002b) *Zimbabwe: Land Reform and Resettlement: Assessment and Suggested Framework For The Future Interim Mission Report*. January. Available at http://www.undp.org/rba/pubs/landreform.pdf, accessed on 17 November 2006.

—— (2002c) *Human Development Report*. Oxford and New York: Oxford University Press.

—— (2003) *Human Development Report 2003*. Oxford: Oxford University Press.

—— (2005) *Human Development Report 2005*. Oxford: Oxford University Press.

United Nations Millennium Project (2005) *Halving Hunger: It Can be Done*. UN Millennium Project Task Force on Hunger. London: Earthscan.

United States Agency for International Development (USAID) (1998a) 'USAID/Egypt Agriculture', www.info.usaid.gov/eg/econ.htm.

—— (1998b) 'USAID/Egypt Economic Growth Overview', www.info.usaid.gov/eg/econ-ovr.htm.

—— (2000) Egypt. http://www.usaid.gov/gov/country/ane/eg/.

—— (2000) Agriculture Sector. http://www.usaid.gov/eg/proj-agr.htm.

—— (2000) Egypt. Congressional Presentation. http://usaid.gov/ pubs/cp2000/ane/egypt.html.

—— (2006) Strategic Framework for Africa, February, www.usaid.gov/pdfdocs/PDACG573.pdf.

USAID and Government of Egypt (1995) 'The Egyptian Agricultural Policy Reforms: An Overview'. Paper presented at Agricultural Policy Conference, Taking Stock: Eight Years of Egyptian Agricultural Policy Reforms, 26–28

March. Cairo: mimeo.

Vallings, Clair and Moreno-Torres, Magüi (2005) 'Drivers of Fragility: What Makes States Fragile?' PRDE Working Paper 7, April, UK: DfID.

Van Dantzig, A. (1978) *The Dutch and the Guinea Coast 1674–1742*. Accra: Ghana Academy of Arts and Science.

Van Hear, N. (1998) *New Diasporas: The Mass Exodus, Dispersal and Re-grouping of Migrant Communities*. London: UCL Press.

Verney, Peter (1999) *Raising the Stakes: Oil and Conflcit in Sudan*. Hebden Bridge: Sudan Update.

Vickerman, Roger (2002) 'Migration Myths', *Guardian*, 10 December.

Vogelgesang, F. (1998) 'After Land Reform, the Market?' *Land Reform*, 1, pp. 21–34.

Wahba, Jackline (2001) 'Child Labour and Poverty Transmission: No Room for Dreams'. ERF Working Paper 0108. Cairo: ERF.

Walton, J. and Seddon, D. (1994) *Free Markets and Food Riots: The Politics of Global Adjustment*. Oxford: Blackwell.

Waterbury, John (1983) *The Egypt of Nasser and Sadat: The Political Economy of Two Regimes*. Princeton, NJ: Princeton University Press.

Waterman, Peter (2001) 'Emancipating Labor Internationalism' (From the C20th Working Class, Unions and Socialism) Global Solidarity Dialog www.antenna.nl/~waterman/, accessed 15 January 2006.

Watkins, Kevin (2002) *Rigged Rules and Double Standards*. Oxford: Oxfam.

Watts, Michael (1991) 'Entitlement or Empowerment? Famine and Starvation in Africa', *Review of African Political Economy*, 51, pp. 9–26.

Watts, Michael and Goodman, David (1997) 'Agrarian Questions: Global Appetite, Local Metabolism: Nature, Culture, and Industry in Fin-de-Siècle Agro-Food Systems'. In David Goodman and Michael J. Watts (eds) *Globalising Food: Agrarian Questions and Global Restructuring*. London: Routledge.

Weiner, Myron (1995) *The Global Migration Crisis: Challenge to States and to Human Rights*. New York: HarperCollins.

Weinrich, A. (1975) *African Farmers in Rhodesia*. London: Oxford University Press.

Weston, Fred (2004) 'Niger Delta, the Price of Oil and the Class Struggle', www.marxist.com/niger-delta-oil-class-struggle300904.htm, 30 September, accessed on 9 July 2006.

White, David and Peel, Michael (2004) 'A Crucial Year for Credibility', *Financial Times*, Nigeria, 24 February, pp. 1–2.

Whitehead, Anne (2002) 'Tracking Livelihood Change: Theoretical, Methodological and Empirical Perspectives from North East Ghana', *Journal of Southern African Studies*, 28(3), pp. 575–99.

Williams, E. (1981) *Capitalism and Slavery*. London: Andre Deutsch.

Woldesmeskel, G. (1990) 'Famine and the Two Faces of Entitlement: A Comment on Sen', *World Development*, 18(3), pp. 491–5.

Woodhouse, Philip (2002) 'Development Policies and Environmental Agendas'. In Uma Kothari and Martin Minogue (eds) *Development Theory and Practice: Critical Perspectives*. Basingstoke: Palgrave.

Worby, Eric (2001) 'A Redivided Land? New Agrarian Conflicts and Questions in Zimbabwe', *Journal of Agrarian Change*, 1(4), October, pp. 475–510.

World Bank (1981) *Accelerated Development in Sub-Saharan Africa: An Agenda for Action*. Washington: World Bank.

—— (1990) *World Development Report: Poverty*. New York: Oxford University

Press.

—— (1992) *World Bank World Development Report*. Oxford: Oxford University Press.

—— (1995) *Claiming the Future: Choosing Prosperity in the Middle East and North Africa*. Washington: World Bank.

___ (1996) *World Development Report 1996: From Iran to Market*. New York: Oxford University Press.

___ (1997) *World Development Report 1997: The State in a Changing World*. New York: Oxford University Press.

_____ (1999) *World Development Report 1999/2000: Entering the Twenty-first Century*. New York: Oxford University Press.

—— (2000) *World Development Report 2000/2001: Attacking Poverty*. New York: Oxford University Press.

—— (2000a) *Can Africa Claim the 21st Century?* Washington: World Bank.

—— (2000b) *World Development Indicators*. Washington: World Bank.

—— (2002) *World Development Report*. Washington: Oxford University Press.

—— (2003) *World Development Report 2003: Sustainable Development in a Dynamic World*. New York: World Bank and Oxford University Press.

—— (2004) *World Development Report 2005. A Better Investment Climate for Everyone*. New York: World Bank and Oxford University Press.

World Development Movement (2004) Media Briefing: UK Government's Commission for Africa (29 April).

Yates, Douglas A. (1996) *The Rentier State in Africa: Oil Rent Dependency and Neocolonialism in the Republic of Gabon*. Trenton, N.J.: Africa World Press.

Zack-Williams, T. and Mohan, G. (2002) 'Africa, the African Diaspora and Development', *Review of African Political Economy*, 29(92), pp. 205–10.

Zartman, I.W. (ed.) (1995) *Collapsed States*. Boulder: Lynne Rienner.

Zegers de Beijl, R. (ed.) (2000) *Documenting Discrimination against Migrant Workers in the Labour Market*. Geneva: ILO.

Zoomers, A. (ed.) (2001) *Land and Sustainable Development*. Amsterdam: Kit Publishers.

Zoomers, A. and Haar, V.D. (eds) (2000) *Current Land Policy in Latin America: Regulating Land Tenure under Neoliberalism*. Amsterdam: Kit Publishers.

Zouari-Bouattour, Salma and Jallouli, Kamel (2001) 'Inequality of Expenses: Tunisian Case'. Paper presented at ERF Conference 'The Analysis of Poverty and its Determinants in the Middle East and North Africa', Sana'a, Yemen (31 July–1 August).

Index